POISON IVY

A Social Psychological Typology of Deviant Professors and Administrators in American Higher Education

Julian B. Roebuck and Komanduri S. Murty

iUniverse, Inc.
Bloomington

Poison Ivy
A Social Psychological Typology of Deviant Professors and
Administrators in American Higher Education

iUniverse books may be ordered through booksellers or by contacting:

iUniverse
1663 Liberty Drive
Bloomington, IN 47403
www.iuniverse.com
1-800-Authors (1-800-288-4677)

ISBN: 978-1-4502-7129-5 (pbk)
ISBN: 978-1-4502-7130-1 (ebk)

Printed in the United States of America

iUniverse rev. date: 11/30/2010

To Dr Alvin Lee Bertrand, Professor Emeritus, Louisiana State University and Dr Louis Wise, former VP Mississippi State University in Gratitude and Friendship

Contents

Foreword

Focusing on one of the most hallowed institutions in western culture, higher education, Roebuck and Murty have undertaken an important exploration into the psychodynamics of the social roles of faculty members and administrators as it relates to deviant behavior. As experienced scholars in higher education and students of deviant behavior, the authors have had many years to hone their observational skills. This volume is the result.

Having spent over a half century in higher education as a student and professor I instantly recognize the forms of deviance the authors discuss as well as the deviant types that are part of their typology. As I read the manuscript I repeated over and over, "I know that guy", and "How many times have I witnessed that behavior in academe?" They certainly have captured the essence of misbehavior and the types of actors in academe that misbehave. While a narrower view of deviance might treat many of the behaviors chronicled here as quirky, weird, outlandish, petty, and childish, which they certainly are, it would overlook that the presence of these behaviors often threatens people's lives and livelihoods as well as the very mission of higher education.

The typology they develop is devised from the linkages that exist among sanctionable deviance patterns, social background characteristics, structural and situational stress problems, and the subjects' personality (self concept, attitudes, character traits, and the presence or absence of personality disorders). Their thesis is that their sample of deviant academics when analyzed along the four dimensions above allows them to categorize academics into different types. While the types are not mutually exclusive with regard to all variables, the types reflect the predominance and intensity of the variables within each grouping (category).

The authors accurately conjecture that academia provides a safer haven for highly educated people with significant personality problems than does many other social institutions because of its culture of tolerance for differences. This would seem particularly true in the post-World War II explosion of public higher education in the United States. Before the war higher education was largely private and served an elite audience in much the same fashion as European higher education after which it was modeled. Public education before the war was primarily vocational in nature focusing on agricultural improvements and teacher preparation.

This post-war explosive growth coupled with the pervasive egalitarian view that higher education is for everyone has led to a concomitant growth in the professorate and because of demand and the prestige assigned to graduate higher education a proliferation of new graduate programs and departments (the authors record numerous instances where new hires were made because of informal considerations or with the primary consideration being necessity rather than the excellent qualifications of the candidate). This perhaps coupled with the stereotype of the professor as someone who couldn't make it in the "real world" has also let to the potential of having more misfits with apparent personality disorders becoming members of the professoriate.

This volume makes a dual contribution: first, to the study of deviant behavior and second, to personnel management in higher education. To the study of deviant behavior we come to quickly realize that what might at first appear to be the manifestations of a quirky personality we must realize that under certain institutional stressors, it can evolve into a highly dangerous and destructive situation. Most, if not all, institutions of higher learning have personnel and faculty handbooks that explicitly spell out behaviors and circumstances that can lead to non-renewal of contracts and even termination for cause even for tenured members of the professoriate. Moreover, these handbooks often preclude evaluations of collegiality and instead focus exclusively on teaching, research and service. Even with these handbooks universities often act like adhocracies—improvising on a case by case basis. This is a dangerous strategy for many reasons. When followed it is done out of fear of the publicity associated with litigation. When followed it is also done out of compassion for the perpetrator and a powerful urge for normalcy to return. What this process overlooks though is that most of the offenders are irredeemable and will continue to erode the mission of the university and pose a threat to the institution and sometimes a physical danger to its students and personnel. For these reasons Roebuck and Murty counsel exceptional caution and care in the hiring of faculty members and vigilance throughout the promotion and tenure process.

Dee Wood Harper, Jr., Ph.D
Professor of Sociology and
Graduate Program Coordinator
Department of Criminal Justice
Loyola University, New Orleans

Preface

Members of societies everywhere formulate rules and social control measures governing behavior, and custom and unstated understandings dictate proper and expected conduct in everyday life. Minor violations of these norms are subject to informal sanctioning provisions, and wide latitudes of behavior exist for rule breakers (deviants) varying according to the seriousness of offense, audiences to the deviant acts, as well as age, sex, persona and social status of offenders. Violations of the mores and the law are concrete, officially proclaimed, and applicable to everyone designated by specified rules. Those charged with serious known about transgressions are subject to "trial" entailing formal proceedings conducted by group leaders, administrative boards or courts of law. Thus, deviance is triangular (three dimensional): (1) rule, (2) rule breaker, and (3) relevant sanction.

Wrongdoing (deviance) by wrongdoers (deviants) ranges in our society from rudeness, faux pas and unseemly behavior to rumor mongering, libel, spying, voyeurism, malingering, lying, stealing, addiction, prostitution, sexual harassment, assault, kidnapping, robbery, rape, treason, murder, etc. The more titillating, outrageous, or dastardly the behavior, the wider and keener is the audience. Deviants in the popular image range from social jerks to perverts, junkies, psychopaths, alcoholics, crazies, whores, pimps to sick, twisted, violent, murderers, pedophiles, dangerous scumbags—or at best decadent, evil, corrupt white-collar criminals (Goode 2008:1-30).

This monograph challenges this popular stereotype of deviance; that is, it does not deal with violators of social etiquette or nuts, sluts, and perverts (see Liazos 1972); but rather with a classification of highly educated, respectable, middle class college and university professors and administrators. To this end we constructed an empirical, behavioral typology in order to identify the different kinds of deviant (problematic, unadjusted and troublemaking) professors and administrators whom we have observed over the years, thereby permitting us to chart the specific deviant patterns of each. This typology is devised from the linkages of representative deviant subjects': (1) sanctionable deviance patterns with their (2) social background characteristics, (3a) structural and (3b) situational stress problems, and (4) personality (self concept, attitudes, character traits, and presence or absence of personality disorders). Our core assumption is that deviance and deviants are neither all alike, nor are the unique events or persons involved; and, that different types or groups of offenses and/or offenders exist and can be identified. Specifically, our thesis is that our known about deviant colleagues when analyzed along the four dimensions above enables us to group (categorize) them into different types. No type is mutually exclusive of others with regard to all variables, but is generated on the basis of the predominance and intensity of the variables within each grouping (Wolff 1950).

The rationale for the study extends beyond any theoretical need to construct another typology for the research literature. We found that our colleagues with certain negative social backgrounds, structural and/or situational stress problems, and inflexible maladaptive personality disorders were likely to be problematic cases in academia. Knowing these types could obviate their selection, or help with their social control, treatment, or dismissal proceedings should they be employed. Selection, social control, treatment, and dismissal procedures are addressed in Chapter 4.

We conjecture that academia provides a safer haven for highly educated people with significant personality problems than does many other social institutions. We found that our deviant colleagues with apparent personality disorders were not the popularly assumed eccentric, effete, nerdy types who seek academic positions because they cannot do anything else but teach; that is, those who bear the brunt of innocuous jokes about pointy-headed professors who do not know how to park their own bicycles. The deviancy of our subjects in the main comprises actors' routine wrongful acts devoid of "neither depth of thought nor any demonic dimension"—what Hannah Arendt called the *banality of evil*. Most were chronic problematic disrupters who did not belong in academia as professors or administrators without psychological treatment (and some even with treatment) especially when having committed serious violations.

The authors, as students and professors, have observed the academic *mis en scene* from the 1940s through 2009 and half of 2010, and have noted what we think is a move toward increased campus deviancy. Our content analysis of articles in *The Chronicle of Higher Education (2000-2010)* shows that this journal published three or four articles per issue on academic deviance within this time frame. The *Chronicle*, the premier publication of higher education in the United States, and a number of scholarly books and articles have reported various kinds of campus deviancy, however for the most part these general accounts are structural-functional studies written by professors for professors. None are concerned with an analytical, social psychological typology of deviant faculty members and administrators as is this study (see Hickson and Roebuck, 2009).

In Chapter 1 we: (1) comment on deviance as presented in the research literature, and state our approach; (2) render a brief description of the academic behavior setting in terms of its bureaucratic, hierarchical structure; (3) outline a few illustrative deviant typologies employed by sociologist criminologists, psychologists and psychiatrists; and, (4) detail the four study dimensions. Chapter 2 provides a theoretical operational base for the personality dimension of the typology, and explicates the methodology. In Chapter 3, the core section of the monograph, we describe and analyze twenty-seven deviant types we found among our colleagues in a personality profile format, and two non deviant types that engender envy and deviance among others (see *italicized types* below for quick reference). Nineteen of the 27 deviant types are professors; and, eight are administrators. Two of the 27 deviant types (Beecher, the Incompetent Teacher; and, Farmer, the Foreigner) did not exhibit any personality disorders. The complete list of the 29 types follows: (1) *Hamlin the Altruistic Guru*; (2) John the Bully Guru; (3) Karl the Archetype; (4) Fritz the Iceman; (5) Gyp the Lip, the Rumor Monger; (6) Ron the Con, the Dictator; (7) Eve the Vamp; (8) Todd the Stud, the Sexual Deviant; (9) Sky Pilot, Teacher the Preacher; (10) Peter the Rabbit; (11) Byrd the Nerd; (12) Farmer the Foreigner; (13) Glad the Inbreeder; (14) Ryder the Outsider; (15) Fred the ABD (all but the dissertation); (16) Luke the Kook; (17) *Sarai the Princess*; (18) Beecher the Incompetent Teacher; (19) Greene the Mean Assistant Dean; (20) Stuart the Career Student, (21) Bruiser the Successful Loser; (22) Don the Don Juan; (23) Pat the Dilettante; (24) Swindler the Liberal's Pet; (25) Judy the Greedy, (26) Taylor the Overreacher; (27) Brad the Unqualified Head; (28) Brown the Clown; and, (29) Bob the Ideologue. This typology is based on our study samples and we make no claim of universality; however, we postulate that our types exist (among others) throughout academia.

In Chapter 4, we: (1) comment on the common elements among all 27 deviant types; (2) assess the relative weight of three study dimensions (social background characteristics, the structural and/or situational stress problems, and personality characteristics) associated with subjects' deviancy patterns; and, emphasize that the personality factor is more significant than the other two dimensions; (3) present our typology as an aid in the screening, selection, monitoring, controlling, and treating of problematic personality types as a risk reduction strategy; (4) suggest a feasible personality typological inventory for future researchers; and, (5) provide general recommendations for institutional policy purposes. Additionally, this typology could aid the two specific groups dealt with herein, professors and administrators in identifying and better understanding campus deviancy in general. These two groups not only interact among and between themselves but with other campus groups (for example, staff members, students, and allied services) and off-campus groups (alumni, administrative boards, funding and compliance agencies, athletic associations, state legislators, state and federal officials, community support networks). All of the foregoing groups and entities are tied-in (in some ways) with deviant professors and administrators, as well as with campus deviancy in general.

As a caveat to the reader the deviant types profiled herein are not fictional for they reflect the characteristics of real people (along with the events surrounding them) in the academic community. We believe that a large number of those sampled would fit neatly into one or another of our constructed types; therefore, finding a particular person or persons in any one type as a perfect fit is impractical. In an attempt to maintain anonymity (as with any research study) we have avoided for the most part specific references to persons and institutions, though a few have been purposely designated for incisive reasons. We utilized modified *romans éclef* in designating the twenty-nine social psychological types. Colleges and universities must take specific events into consideration on a case-by-case basis for adopting suitable preventive and corrective measures suggested herein. Finally, this book is coauthored and represents coequal efforts in all respects. There is no junior or senior author.

CHAPTER 1
Overview: Approaches to Deviance, Typological Literature, and Study Dimensions

≡

Because this book is about different types of deviant professors and administrators, and the deviant acts they engage in, we: (1) define deviance as an area of study, and present the approach utilized herein; (2) describe briefly the academic setting of administrators and professors; (3) outline and discuss the typologies employed by some sociologist criminologists, psychologists, and psychiatrists in deviancy studies (usually alluded to by psychologists and psychiatrists as antisocial behavior); (4) summarize several illustrative deviant typologies in the research literature; and (5) define the four study dimensions.

1. Deviance: Definition and Approach

Deviance is generally described as the violation of customs, norms, rules of behavior, and laws in the place and culture where they occur; and, include acts of omission and commission, which may or may not be criminal. Conformity with the norms in one place and time may violate those in another. Deviancy studies examine the nature of the behavior itself and the reactions thereto as well as the deviant actors themselves. Sociologists study deviance as social forms of interaction and as part of an investigation of social structure and process: Why and how society and social relations work when violations of rules occur; deviance is a study of social control theory (Wolff 1950; Goode 2008).

Psychologists and psychiatrists view deviance in terms of the maladaptive characteristic ways of behaving and thinking of different personality types—

especially those with personality disorders and problems (see Barlow and Durand, 2009: 430-462). We examine deviancy in terms of: (1) the kinds of rule breaking by certain social-psychological types; (2) attendant rule makers and enforcers; (3) the nature of the deviant act; (4) behavior setting audiences to deviant acts; (5) reactions to deviant acts by enforcers and the deviant; and, (6) sanctions and/or labels applied to the deviant. (See also Dotter and Roebuck, 1988).

2. Academic Behavior Setting: Administrators and Faculty

Universities like their European ancestries are hierarchical in structure but wishy-washy in function as we shall see later on. However, they have increased in size, services and superfluous administrative personnel over the years. Usually somewhere near the campus center sits a large neogothic or neoclassical building commonly called the "power tower," and therein reside administrators (who are usually career administrators rather than scholars). According to many educators and scholars, the campus is no longer a protected zone for children of the privileged, wealthy elites (of the upper and upper middle classes) because of the changing composition of the student population (academically unprepared students, culturally deprived minority group students, and those from the lower classes); the increased freedom of students; for example, choice of courses and professors; permissive and uncontrolled exuberant conduct, and sexual life style; overall permissiveness (e.g., in class attendance and use of alcohol and drugs); commercialization of the campus; corrupting influence of intercollegiate sports; lowering of academic standards; and, loss of the liberal arts tradition—all this say some has turned the campus into a cheapened microcosm of the off-campus United States. Recent studies by Delbanco (2005); and, Hickson and Roebuck (2009) address this campus freedom, changes in the student body composition, and problematic situations purported to cause a drift toward deviancy; and, outline some campus deviancy patterns.

Presidents or chancellors are in charge of each campus and deal with the faculty and board of trustees; enforce rules; raise funds; bargain with foundations and federal agencies; consult with state legislators; and, engage in public relations (leaving most duties to professional bureaucrats).

The vice president for academic affairs or provost supervises deans. He deals with faculty affairs and makes the final decisions on collecting data and making decisions with regard to curriculum, faculty research, teaching competency, rule making and breaking; faculty hiring, tenure and promotions. The Vice President for Student Affairs has similar duties to the provost, though his/her responsibilities are directed towards students rather than faculty. Typically he delegates to his immediate subordinates, assistants or associate vice presidents. Major responsibilities in this position have to do with discipline and student academics. Other vice presidents perform similar administrative duties for their respective areas.

Deans at the college level are responsible for hiring procedures; developing curricula and academic programs; allocating funds within their schools; raising money; budget management; administrative procedures and settling disputes between separate schools within the university.

Heads or chairs in charge at the departmental level are selected by deans and hold office at deans' disposals. Chairs are chosen by faculty members and serve on a rotating basis. Heads and chairs oversee the hiring, firing, tenure; graduate school examinations; select graduate students and assign them to particular professors; help determine the curriculum; assign professors to particular classes; oversee the travel and library budget; hire and control the clerical staff; settle faculty disputes; recommend salaries. He/she manages the department with the support of a dean. Though universities claim to be democratic they are not. Major decisions flow from the top down; minor decisions are made by a variety of bureaucrats including research and grant administrators, alumni and foundation development staff, budgeting and accounting personnel, human resources management, and information technology operators, etc.

Among teaching faculty TAs (Teaching Assistants) are graduate students assigned to professors as assistants. They grade papers, help with research, monitor examinations, and sometimes teach freshman classes. Instructors hold MA degrees and usually teach freshman and sophomores while working on their PhDs. Assistant professors have PhDs and occupy the first rung of a professorial career ladder. Most are only a few years older than their students, and teach freshmen and sophomores. Associate professors have acceptable publication records (scholarly articles and books), are tenured, and enjoy some prestige at the departmental level, and in the profession. Full professors are those with the highest rank, prestige and power in academia, and have usually published more than colleagues.

3. The Typological Approach and Typologies from the Literature

Although most of our deviant subjects were not usually criminals in a legal sense, they were violators of sanctionable academic conduct norms (some of which were illegal). Typology studies have primarily dealt with delinquents, criminals, and those with personality disorders (primarily psychopaths). Some are person centered, some offense centered, and still others both. Our constructs and examples come from the typological research literature (see Bartol 2002, for further examples).

The core assumption of the typological approach is that conduct violations and offenders are neither all alike, nor are they unique events or persons. To the contrary a number of types or groups of offenses and/or offenders exist and can be identified and studied. The rationale for the construction of typologies is their usefulness in the selection, treating, and social control of various group memberships (personnel, patients, offenders, etc.). First, if groupings or types of norm violators exist explanations require that we develop separate theories for each form of rule breaking or kinds of rule breakers. Perhaps some offenders may be the products of psychological pressures of one kind or another, whereas others may engage in norm breaking because of social learning, situational pressures, associations with other norm breakers, etc. Second, if a number of distinct types exist, each may be a product of a different casual process. Therefore, it would be a mistake to apply a single form of correctional intervention, control, or treatment measure to these persons—perhaps, a manipulation of social environment for some; strict measures of social control for others; or, psychological treatment for still others.

In the sociological literature a distinction is made between *ideal types,* conjured up exaggerated types in the researcher's mind (opinion), in distinction from empirical types which one (presumably) extracts in the real world from research findings—that is, representations of real cases. Gibbons (1988, 1994) lists three criteria for evaluating criminological typologies: (1) They must be relatively clear and explicit in order that offenders can be assigned to the typology categories; (2) They should be made up of mutually exclusive types or categories, so that actual offenders or crime events fall into one of the types of the system (That is an impossible ideal in the authors' minds because rarely, if ever do all cases of any sort fall into mutually exclusive categories in any real-world typology.) The best we can do is to classify on the basis of the predominant offender type or predominant offense pattern as linked to a predominant social-psychological personality type; (3) The number of types should be relatively limited because an offender or offense pattern categorization consisting of large numbers would be immeasurable and useless to the researcher or practitioner. There must also be a closeness of fit between constructed types and actual offenders and offenses; but, there is usually a residual category of unclassified cases—and the problem of what to do with mixed cases.

Typologies in the literature are usually offense centered or person centered. Offense-centered typologies examine differences between various forms of conduct violations (for example, organized crime, street crime, property crime, violent crime) and their correlates, e.g., modus operandi, behavior setting, occurrence rate, arrest rates, sanctions of, society's reaction to recidivism, etc. Offender-centered construction systems identify deviant or criminal persons, offender types, offender careers, criminal roles, personality syndromes, etc. To reiterate, some attempt a combination approach of both of these.

Although terms like classification, taxonomy, and typology have not always been clearly delineated in the literature, a classification system or taxonomy usually refers to the full range of categories within a variable or set of variables—within which some phenomenon can be placed. Intelligence tests provide an example of a single-dimension classification, because it permits the placement of individuals into some groupings along intelligence levels. A multivariate classification is illustrated by a scheme for sorting out individuals by sex, educational attainment, income, etc. in which the classification system would include all of the logically-possible combinations of assignments along these dimensions. Some of the classes within the model might be *unpredicted* because no actual cases would be found to fall within them (See Gibbons 1977, 1988).

4. A Brief Overview of a Few Typological Constructions

(a). Roebuck (1967), constructed an empirical typology of adult convicted felons in 1954-55, based on 13 different arrest history patterns. The basic assumptions underlying this typology were: (1) that arrest patterns would indicate a particular type of criminal behavior or patterns of criminal careers; (2) that a considerable number of behavioral differences exist between the groups of offenders with different arrest patterns; and, (3) that offending types could be distinguished based on their social background and personality types. In brief, arrest history patterns are behavioral as well as legal categories of offenders. The 13 arrest history patterns included: (1) Mixed pattern (Jack-of-all-trades offender); (2) Double pattern of larceny and burglary; (3) Single pattern of narcotic drug laws; (4) Triple pattern of drunkenness, assault and larceny; (5) Double pattern of drunkenness and assault; (6) Single pattern of robbery; (7) No pattern; (8) Single pattern of gambling; (9) Single pattern of burglary; (10) Single pattern of sex offenders; (11) Single pattern of fraud; (12) Single pattern of auto theft; and, (13) Single pattern of forgery and counterfeiting. Social background correlates included orientation attributes (developmental history in family and developmental history in the community); and, personal characteristics such as occupation, employment records, marital history, age, I.Q., grade median test, military history, juvenile gang activity, and prison adjustment. Personality traits included self-concept and attitudes. Gleaned from intensive interviews; and test results of the Minnesota Multiphasic Personality Inventory (MMPI) and Eysenck Personality Questionnaire (EPQR) as interpreted by clinical psychologists and psychiatrists. He found that an overwhelming majority of the subjects were products of dysfunctional and economically deprived families; and that the most discriminating factor between the arrest patterns was the higher incidence of psychopathic personality for violent offenders when compared with others. However, 70 percent of all offenders' profiles were skewed toward the psychopathic personality type. Therefore he concluded that within this prison population under study, personality type was more significant (discriminating) than social background variables. This finding also confirmed his observations and analyses of incarcerated delinquents and felons over an eight-year period.

(b). Gibbons (1977, 1988) has developed the most detailed and comprehensive typologies in sociological criminology. His role career typologies of adult offenders and of juvenile delinquents are based on: (1) current offense behavior; (2) the interactional setting where offenses occurred; (3) criminal career of the offenders; (4) self-concept patterns; (5) role related attitudes; (6) social class and family background; (7) peer group associations; (8) contacts with defining agencies (police, courts, prisons, etc.). His adult offender typology consisted of 15 types: (1) Professional thief; (2) Professional "heavy" criminal; (3) Semi-professional property criminal; (4) Property offender "one-time loser"; (5) Automobile thief and joy Ryder; (6) Naive check forger; (7) White-collar criminal; (8) Professional fringe violator; (9) Embezzler; (10) Personal offender, one-time loser; (11) Psychopathic assaulter; (12) Violent sex offender; (13) Nonviolent sex offender (Rapo); (14) Nonviolent sex offender, statutory rape; and, (15) Narcotic addict, heroin. All types were accompanied by social control and treatment suggestions. Very little was mentioned about personality variables *per se*, but he did include a *psychopathic assaulter* as a type (very rare for a sociologist).

(c). **H. G. Eysenck's Theory of Personality and Crime**: Although there is no general consensus about what the basic personality dimensions are for the development of a personality inventory or typology, there are several contenders (see Barlow and Durand, 2009: 432; Eysenck and Eysenck, 1975). H. G. Eysenck is one of the few modern psychologists who has attempted to formulate a general universal theory of antisocial and/or criminal behavior (he prefers the term antisocial behavior). He proposes that antisocial behavior is the result of an intersection between certain environmental conditions and features of the nervous system; and, postulates that all behavior is either instrumentally conditioned involving the skeletal nervous system; or, Pavlovian conditioned (involving the autonomic nervous system). Learned behavior occurs because a stimulus and response are paired. Conditioned behavior involves contiguity with reinforcement. Moral behavior is conditioned rather than learned. His psychological-physiological system is based on the autonomic nervous system as underlying the behavioral traits of emotionality or neuroticism or antisocial personality type. This autonomic system consists of two antagonistic parts, the sympathetic and parasympathetic systems. The sympathetic system is devoted to fight or flight reactions. The parasympathetic system, when in action, inhibits the action of the sympathetic system by slowing down the heart, slowing down the rate of breathing, and aiding digestion. Eysenck equates emotionality and the autonomic system. He maintains that persons who are subject to strong emotions, even under conditions which would not call forth such strong emotions in normal persons, have been endowed by heredity with an autonomic system, the sympathetic branch of which is particularly strongly reactive to external stimuli. He points to the ascending reticular formation of the brain which is situated at the top of the spinal cord at the bottom of the brain as the most likely part of the nervous system serving as the locus of inhibition and excitation.

Eysenck utilized several studies (mostly his own) that employed a laboratory testing of subjects by conditioning rating devices, self-ratings, objective personality tests, and typological constructs (a syndrome of correlated traits). He reported the existence of three personality temperaments: extraversion, neuroticism, and psychoticism (extreme psychopathy). He found that several objective personality tests correlated highly with experimental evidence of a person's habitual behavior tendencies (as measured, for example, by motor suggestibility tests, sensory suggestibility tests, social suggestibility tests, and body-sway tests). The extreme extravert (psychoticism) model is sociable, craves excitement, takes chances and acts on the spur of the moment. He is impulsive, aggressive, temperamental, emotional and unreliable. The extreme introvert model is quit, retiring, introspective, serious, self-controlled and reliable. Unlike prior conceptualizations, Eysenck's view is that the extravert is low on excitation and high on inhibition; the introvert is high on excitation low on inhibition. The introvert conditions readily; the extravert conditions poorly. These three temperaments are derived from inherited differential nervous systems.

Eysenck generally recognizes the absence of pure discreet categories and would assign persons to particular positions on a continuum of extraversion-introversion. People suffering from mood disorders, psychasthenics or dysthymics, are generally found at the introverted extreme of the continuum; whereas the hysterics and psychopaths are found at the extraverted extreme.

By employing neuroticism and extraversion-introversion scores resulting from questionnaires of various *neurotic, criminal, and antisocial* groups (anxiety state patients, obsessional patients, psychosomatic patients, female prisoners, hysteric patients, male prisoners, psychopathic patients, and unmarried mothers), Eysenck found a high degree of introversion for the neurotic groups and a high degree of extraversion for the criminal, antisocial, and psychopathic groups. The psychopaths comprised the most extremely extraverted group, followed by the hysterics. Those suffering from anxiety states, the obsessive-compulsive groups, the phobics and the reactive depressants were extremely introverted.

Eysenck links inhibition and excitation to personality with the following postulates: Individuals differ in the rate of the buildup of inhibition, the strength of inhibition toleration, and the speed with which inhibition dissipates; extraverts build up inhibition quickly, demonstrate high degrees of inhibition and dissipate inhibition slowly; introverted people build up inhibition more slowly and to a lesser degree and dissipate it more quickly; introverts develop excitation more quickly and strongly; extraverts more slowly and weakly. In support of these propositions, high correlations are demonstrated between traits of introversion and extraversion (as determined from objective personality tests) and specific behavioral responses obtained in the laboratory (as tested by vigilance tests, tapping metal stylus tests, eye blink tests, puff of air tests, galvanic skin response tests, etc.) Conditioning produces a conscience through and by conditioned fear responses and autonomic *unpleasures* associated with antisocial activities. Stimulus generalization, the association of all those activities potentially dangerous, punishment producing, and fear and anxiety producing, contribute to the process. In short, antisocial, criminal or tabooed behavior engaged in by an individual represents a conditional stimulus; the unconditional stimulus is the immediate punishment of whatever kind that follows the prohibited, discovered behavior; and the response is the pain and fear produced in the individual. The normal individual, in the process of growing up, acquires a repertoire of conditioned fear response to various behaviors disapproved by various authority figures and peers. When childhood temptations are great, tabooed behavior may be given in to, but the resulting, autonomic fear-anxiety reactions are generally sufficient to deter further repetition of the disapproved act. Conversely those persons who have not made adequate connections, either because of poor conditionability (for example extraverts) or because the opportunity to do so was not presented (socialization), are more likely to display deviant and/or criminal behavior. These people do not anticipate averse events strongly enough to be deterred, because the association has not been sufficiently developed. Reprimanding one before or during a deviant act produces different affects than reprimanding one later on. Eysenck maintains that the growth in permissiveness at home, and in schools and courts has led to a significant reduction in the number of conditioning experiences to which children encounter. Conditioning within the home and school combined with certain nervous systems check or augment antisocial and deviant behavior.

The reactions of scholars to Eysenck's genetic, neurological and environmental conditioning thesis have been mixed and his conditioning emphasis has been questioned. Overall his descriptions of personality traits as found in the revision of the Eysenck Personality Questionnaire (EPQR) have been (arguably) accepted by many psychologists (Eysenck and Eysenck, 2008). His extraverts (psychopaths) do appear to be more prone to antisocial behavior than his introverts, and some other personality types. The authors do not necessarily agree with all of Eysenck's theory, however his work represents a broad, testable theory of personality and of criminality that continues to stimulate international research. Therefore we include his work outlined herein as one significant and plausible perspective on personality attributes and antisocial behavior; and, as findings opposed to deterministic sociological funk.

Other researchers have found that psychopaths have a variety of behavioral and neurophysiological characteristics differing from *normals*. For example, psychopaths have been found to be under aroused both autonomically and cortically to have abnormal brain waves, and to demonstrate cognitive perceptions similar to those of *social deviants* of different kinds (See Bartol 2002; Eysenck 1964, 1990, 1992; Eysenck and Gudjonsson, 1989).

(d). Steven Pinker (2002), a noted social psychologist, on the basis of an analysis of several studies in the fields of behavioral genetics, neuroscience, evolutionary psychology, human conditioning, sociobiology, endocrinology and personality and twin (study) investigations, postulates a genetic base for behavioral personality traits. He defines a behavioral trait, intelligence for example, as a stable property of a person that can be measured (he claims) by standard psychological and laboratory tests. Specific personality traits can, and have been, measured (for example, introversion or extroversion, neurotic, stable, etc.) that exist in five major ways in which personality can be summarized and measured (openness to experience, conscientiousness, extroversion-introversion, antagonism-agreeableness and neuroticism). Pinker further supports his and others' *heritable* findings (he claims) on specific character traits (honesty, dependability, etc.) from DNA and twin studies derived from the research literature. He claims that no matter what character traits or measures utilized to test them, identical twins reared apart are highly similar; identical twins reared together are more similar than fraternal twins reared together; biological siblings are far more similar than adoptive siblings, ... and so on (indicating he says a genetic base for personality traits).

Most of the traits he mentions were derived from one of the more widely accepted "normal personality dimensional models" constructed by several psychologists called the "Five-factor Model," or the "Big Five" : (1) extroversion (talkative, assertive, and active versus silent, passive and reserved; (2) agreeableness (kind, trusting, and warm versus hostile, selfish, and mistrustful); (3) conscientious (organized, thorough, and reliable versus careless, negligent, and unreliable); (4) neuroticism (even-tempered versus moody and temperamental); and (5) openness to experience (imaginative, curious, and creative versus shallow and imperceptive) . On each dimension people are rated high, low, or somewhere in between (see Golderg 1993).Cross-cultural research establishes the universal nature of these five dimensions, although there are individual differences across cultures (Barlow and Durand, 2009).

(e). The Diagnostic and Statistical Manual of Mental Disorder (DSM-IV), published by the American Psychiatric Association has become the world standard in the mental health field for the categorization, evaluation, and diagnosis of mental disorders. The stated purpose of DSM-IV is *to provide clear descriptions of diagnostic categories in order to enable clinicians and investigators to diagnose, communicate about, study, and treat people with various mental disorders* (American Psychiatric Association 2000). According to the fourth edition, text revision of the Diagnostic and Statistical Manual DSM-IV-TR (that we utilized), personality disorders are enduring patterns of perceptions and a collection of traits that have become rigid over time and maladaptive to an individual's functioning, or cause distress; and, are discernable in behavior that deviates from the norms of one's occupational milieu or culture. DSM-IV-TR personality disorders in brief are all patterns of thinking, feeling, and behaviors recognizable in one's conduct for a long time which cause significant stress and maladaptive behavior. They are not caused by a general medical condition or by the use of substances including medications; and, they are not products of mental illness (psychosis). These patterns are probably dimensional, not categorical; meaning that components (traits) are present in normal people, but are accentuated in those with the disorders in question. DSM-IV-TR personality disorder types have in common some negative characteristics; that is, there may be some overlapping in the exclusive categories (that subjects can be placed in). Where marked overlapping (co-morbidity) was found, we placed subjects in what we determined was his or her predominant personality disorder category. Only one of our personality profiles, no. 16, Luke the Kook, appeared to be a borderline psychotic. Ten personality disorders are divided into three clusters. Cluster A includes paranoid, schizoid, schizothpal types. Cluster B includes antisocial, borderline, histrionic, and narcissistic types. Cluster C includes avoidant, dependent, and obsessive compulsive types. (1) the paranoid personality disorder type is extremely mistrustful and suspicious of others without justification, reluctant to confide in others, bears grudges; (2) the schizoid type demonstrates a pattern of detachment from social relationships, and seems aloof, cold, and indifferent to others; and, has a restricted range of expression and emotion; (3) those with schizotypal personality disorder are usually socially isolated, and behave strangely; are suspicious and have odd beliefs; (4) the antisocial type has a long history of social norm violations and lying, a disregard for the rights and feelings of others; is extremely self-centered, cold, reckless, guiltless, recidivistic, deceitful, charming, cunning, impulsive, and manipulative; (5) those with a borderline personality disorder are unstable, impulsive, moody, suffer low self-esteem, and feel empty; express inappropriate anger; fear abandonment; (6) histrionics tend to be excessively emotional, suggestible, dramatic, shallow, seductive, and attention seeking; (7) narcissists are extremely conceited; overrate themselves; feel they are special and entitled to special treatment; are haughty, lack empathy, are social climbers and envious of others; (8) avoidants feel inadequate and are sensitive regarding the opinions of others and are hyper sensitive; anxious; avoid social relationships; fear rejection; (9) the dependent personality disorder type relies on others for direction, emotional support, and decision making; fear abandonment; want others to take care of them; (10) the obsessive-compulsive type insists that things be done their way; like to run things; are preoccupied with details and rules; over conscientious; rigid perfectionists (see Chapter 12 in Barlow and Durand, 2009 for our aid in preparing the foregoing outline of the DSM-IV-TR personality disorder summary). Barlow and Durand point out that treating people with personality disorders is often difficult because they do not see that their difficulties are a result of the way they relate to others. There is no real "cure" for them.

We choose the DSM-IV-TR classification as a model because we agree with its nomenclature, and because we thought our deviant subjects could be best classified within its taxonomy; that is, should they appear to have a personality disorder. Further this classification is based primarily on empirical behavioral descriptions rather than theory, and incorporates social and cultural factors in diagnostic analysis and personality descriptions.

5. The Four Study Dimensions

1. Subjects' deviant behavior patterns comprise sanctionable wrongdoing on and off campus milieus that violated academic and professional rules, and at times norms of the wider community as well, including the law. The behavior patterns involve interactions and relationships with campus residents

(students, colleagues, staff), family members, friends, and acquaintances; and, are detailed within the 27 deviant types of the typology.

2. Social background factors include: (a) family of orientation's socioeconomic class, organization, location, reputation, interpersonal relationships, community supports, disciplinary measures, and moral stance; (b) subjects' developmental family, school and community adjustments; (c) educational, conjugal and marital adjustments; (d) occupational and colleague (peer) adjustments.

3. (a) Structural and situational stress problems and (b) subjects' psychological and physiological responses to the specific stressors. There is a strong relationship between 'a' and 'b' (see Chapter 9 in Barlow and Durand, 2009). Psychological stress results from: (a) structural stress such as a maladjusted organization of the workplace, incompetent or vindictive supervisors or colleagues, dysfunctional family of orientation, etc.; (b) situational stress results from negative life events such as the death or betrayal of family members, friends, colleagues; losing jobs, divorce, accidents, disease or sickness, or personal defeats, personal attacks of others, etc. Psychological stress may lead to frustration that at times evokes antisocial behavior. For example, when individuals are prevented from responding in a way that produces rewards because of structural blockings, or blockages by other individuals (who seem to stand in their way) their behavioral responses become antagonistic, irritable, resentful, aggressive and antisocial in an effort to confront or resist the blockage and/or blockers. Such responses appear to result from an aversive internal state of arousal and stress—what subjects called frustration. Stressful frustration is at times brief, at others long lasting—depending on the individual's goals or rewards. Others around the frustrated one may confirm, reinforce, or deny the "victim's" definition of the situation. Psychological stress may cause unhealthy lifestyle behaviors, for example, faulty eating habits, smoking, drinking alcohol, and unnecessary risk-taking. A variety of studies suggest (strongly) that stress, anxiety, and anger when combined with poor coping skills and low social supports are implicated in physiological and psychological disorders (see Chapter 9 in Barlow and Durand, 2009).

4. Personality encompasses self concept, attitudes, character traits, and the presence or absence of personality disorders. (a) Self concept is how subjects view their physical and social identities (sex, age, physical appearance, health, social status, occupation, lifestyle), worldview, and self esteem (personal evaluation). (b) Attitudes are subjects' organismic states of readiness to respond in a characteristic way to a stimulus as an object, concept, or situation. (c) Character traits are the ingrained ways in which subjects experience, interact with, and think about everything that goes on around them (see the "Big Five

model" in Barlow and Durand, 2009). (d) Personality disorders are defined as in the DSM-IV-TR model.

The four social-psychological dimensional model used in the construction of this typology is based on a similar frame of reference and data collection model utilized by the authors over the years in several published, empirical deviancy studies of; for example, professional gamblers, confidence men, fences, thieves, prostitutes, organized criminals, wife beaters, armed robbers, rapists, assaulters, street whores, call girls, pimps, bootleggers, traffic offenders, drunk drivers, crooked police on the take, medical quacks, prison rioters, political criminals, embezzlers, drug addicts, medical quacks, alcoholics, Mexican prostitutes, rural offenders, Cuban felons, Saudi Arabian felons, Kuwaiti delinquents, incarcerated delinquents and felons, probation and parole violators, nightclub habitués, night people, college and university deviants among other deviants and criminals. Most of these types were analyzed in separate studies from the1950s through 2009. Our model comprises nine interrelated components: (1) rules and rule makers; (2) rule enforcers; (3) the actor's personality and social type; (4) the reported deviant acts and their nature; (5) apparent motivation of deviant acts; (6) specific behavior settings; (7) audiences to the acts; (8) societal or institutional reactions to the acts and actors; (9) the actor's reactions to the deviant label (see also Dotter and Roebuck, 1988). Rules are not necessarily applied uniformly to all persons, groups, or situations.

Situations and multiple outcomes are possible in the interaction process of the above nine components. Some persons who commit deviant acts may be discovered, apprehended, labeled and sanctioned, while other who do so may not be; some may be falsely accused of committing deviant acts; some labeled deviants may deny the stigma; and still others may actively seek the label. In this study we relied on what we observed and what we judged to be reliable information from other reports, including at times the deviant himself or herself; that is, the narrator's interpretation (see Howard Becker, 1963).

The rule makers and enforcers we were concerned with consisted of: state legislatures' rules, rule makers and enforcers pertaining to higher education; college and university boards of education; college and university administrators' rules and catalogues, handbooks and policy manuals; professional academic organizations' rules; state and federal law; and commonly accepted rules and behavior expected in academia. Our deviant actors, were on campus professors and administrators, and the deviants who were involved in their deviancies, were most often other campus residents (students, professors, administrators, staff, and colleagues). Secondary off-campus deviants were primarily other academicians, family members, friends, and acquaintances. Subjects' deviant behavior for the most part involved violations of academic rules and regulations. Behavior settings were located on campus or on other academic sites (for example, professional meetings). Audiences to deviancy acts were primarily campus residents. Reactions to subjects' deviancy varied and depended on many variables; for example, official academic knowledge of deviancy; seriousness of deviant conduct; audiences to deviant acts; status and power of the offender; conscientiousness, honesty, vigilance, and competence of academic administrators; academic policy and sanctioning procedures; deviant subjects' personality types and persona (presentation of self in everyday life); subjects' honesty, fortitude, and social supports (family, friends, legal representatives).

CHAPTER 2

Behavioral Settings, Theoretical Base, and Methodology

~~~

Though deviance persists throughout all social institutions in the United States, its form and nature varies in academe from that found elsewhere in the social system. A campus, is a relatively open and free place physically as well as socially; and, it manifestly functions to provide higher education, although it supports other competing interests and activities (for example, intercollegiate athletics). More so than in other formal social institutions, administrative roles are less clearly defined and at times conflicting. Further, campus groups tend to be less homogeneous than in other formal organizational settings; and, campuses are not self-contained systems like prisons (and security is not a major institutional goal). Therefore, one would expect to find there diverse patterns of deviancy, social controls, and sanctions, which render it difficult to determine the extent and magnitude of deviancy patterns. Scholars do not agree on the frequency of campus deviance though it is now more easily detected than in yester years (Robin 2005). The internet (the medium that has become the message) facilitates the incidence of deviance.

Academic deviance in the past was observed and monitored (if at all) by a passive academic audience in discrete surroundings of a well defined scholarly community. Now we have a broad range of participants, arbitrators, and rule makers. The increased number of practicing academicians, the tangled growth of professional societies, and self righteous citizens (in a republic of voyeurs) who enjoy seeking out and putting down deans and punishing other public figures with feet of clay, complicates the situation. Further, some scholars maintain that deviancy serves an important normative function; and is not a property inherent in any particular behavior (called deviance), but a property conferred upon that behavior for the functional purpose of inscribing or revising existing rules and regulations. Deviancy debates about the so-called increase in academic deviance comprise a necessary process of reflection rather than a symptom of moral decline, say some. Deviant behavior may be so in the eyes of the beholder; and, that it is only through "deviance" that we understand normalcy. We, the authors, take a more normative and conceptual approach to deviancy, and do not accept this esoteric and muddled postmodern position harkening back to the postulates of Michael Foucault and Jacques Derrida in the 1960's and 1970's, spurious copouts to doing nothing. We do not subscribe to an epidemic of academic deviancy, though we think it is increasing; and, that it might be reduced and/or controlled. In this work, we are concerned with *patterned, consequential, sanctionable and known about deviant behavior* that occurs among interacting persons, who occupy the *roles* of faculty, and administrators.

Theoretical Base

We reasoned that personality characteristics like honesty, for example, generate a consistent pattern of conduct across a range of serious problematic life situations; that is, an honest person tends to act and react in similar fashion when facing divergent problematic situations. In brief, character traits exhibit cross-situational stability. We theorized further that well integrated, stable personality types when facing real life, problematic situations and choices thereto would first think, talk about, and reflect upon said situations; as well as react to them in an expected, positive reasonable way—tasking into consideration any extenuating circumstances thereto (see Waldron 2009). Conversely, we expected those with apparent personality disorders (DPs) to react to such problem situations in a more erratic, spontaneous, and negative fashion. These assumptions along with the view that those with stable well integrated personalities adjust more readily in academia than those with personality disorders are validated by our social-psychological profiles in this work which follow in Chapter 3.

Contrariwise, we reject most of the findings in "experiments in ethics studies" conducted by psychologists who question (or negate) the validity of character-trait definitions, predictions, and crossover stability. Most of these studies are based on the answers to simple, constricted questions that can be easily coded: usually respondents' immediate, spontaneous, intuitive, unselected, and unqualified reactions (which are often revised by the respondents after further consideration, later on). Consequently, such studies are flawed and unreliable, just as are some other studies of this type that do not take into consideration additional variables erroneously deemed unimportant (see Appiah 2009). Some scholars suggest on the basis of extant data that psychologists give further study to character trait stability and predictability as measured in real life, serious problematic situations extending over-time-space periods; and that they utilize lengthy, essay questions which may be answered with reflective qualified answers (Waldron 2009). We agree, and this study is based on this principle.

For the operational purpose of the personality dimension in this study, we relied on a combination of both the Big Five and DSM-IV-TR models, explicated in Chapter 1. Such an approach was adopted earlier in a few studies, such as Westen and Shedler (1999) who identified 12 personality dimensions (as opposed to the Big Five in the Five-factor model previously alluded to) that not only overlapped with DSM-criteria, but also introduced new aspects of personality not previously tapped in the DSM model (Westen and Shedler, 1999a,1999b). In our case descriptions, we found all Big-Five and DSM personality characteristics with an exception of Schizotypical Personality Disorder type. Our professional backgrounds in working in prison settings as classification officers, social case workers, counselors and researchers; in half-way houses as well as in community crime prevention projects side-by-side with clinical psychologists and psychiatrists for a period of more than twenty years enabled us to identify those with obvious personality disorders. Moreover, for validity purposes, we presented our data to two board certified clinical psychologists and a psychiatrist and sought their professional opinions (and heeded them) in our personality identifications and descriptions.

Methodology

A two-member research team initiated a research project on deviance typology at a southeastern state university campus (where they were employed) in 1980. During the following year, it was clear that we needed data from additional university campuses in order to enhance the validity and representativeness of our data and sample; and, that a study on one campus would not suffice. Therefore, we decided to carry on the data collection from several campuses over a much longer period of time depending upon where we were located. Though we moved to different universities following the year 1984, we continued the data collection until 2009 on the succeeding campuses where we taught or had access to. We utilized the same observation/interview schedule and data collection techniques that we had initially employed in our first campus study on other university campuses. Thus the total sample consisted of 100 faculty members and administrators from nine university campus (see following section on sample for details). The study focused on faculty members and administrators within the scope of the following study dimensions: (1) sanctionable deviant interactional patterns from the norms of their professional milieu on and off campus involving students, colleagues, staff as well as relationships with family members and others; (2) social background factors: a. family of orientation's socioeconomic class, interpersonal relationships, and perceptions and world views; b. subject's developmental history—family, school, and community adjustments; and, c. education and conjugal adjustments; (3) (a) structural, and (b) situational stress problems; (4) personality including: self concept, attitudes, overall character descriptions, and the presence or absence of apparent personality disorder traits which varied from normal, and worked to an individual's disadvantage to the point they caused distress and impaired work, social, family, and/or interpersonal relationships. These patterns of behavior and thinking were treated as dimensional rather than categorical components which are present in normal people, but are accentuated in our deviant subjects who appeared to have personality disorders. We estimate that 10-16 percent in our study sample exhibit personality disorders, constituting a comparable size in the general population.

Study sample

For reasons of convenience and accessibility, we selected 100 cases of faculty and administrators from nine campuses: five southeast, two southwest, one west coast, and one mid Atlantic campuses, based on a judgmental sample. These campuses were convenient in the sense that one or both authors had had prior teaching experience there and/or personal contacts with several faculty and administrators at all of these schools. All the nine campuses are accredited by regional commissions, coeducational schools and award at the least a bachelor's degree (most award MAs and PhDs). The total sample consists of 100 respondents (southeast, 50 cases; southwest, 30 cases; west coast,12 cases; mid Atlantic, 8 cases) who were selected by a snowball sampling procedure. Further, we knew these 100 subjects as colleagues for various lengths of time over the years. Some were identified for deviant acts via campus disciplinary hearings, some through informal complaints from other colleagues; some through student oral and/written complaints to the department or individual instructors with whom they felt more comfortable; some through unspecified sources of rumors and scandals; and yet, some through personal knowledge and acquaintances. We interacted with most of them on and off campus in various formal and informal settings including visitations to their homes. The sampled respondents consisted of 70 faculty and 30 administrators; 85 white and 15 non-white; 92 males and 8 females; and, 98 PhDs and 2 ABDs. For all operational purposes, we shared our definition of 'deviance' with each respondent, even though some did not agree in part with our definition, or expressed some limitations or reservations with our definitions.

Data Collection Instrument

In our original model, we envisioned collecting information on every type of deviant act that study respondents knew about and/or engaged in. However, we realized such an attempt was impractical for the following reasons: it would be too inclusive and extensive, laborious, time consuming, and subject to considerable overlapping. Therefore we settled on a more concise and measurable *topical interview* schedule for data collection purposes that would enable us to delineate deviant behavior patterns as linked to personality types and social background characteristics and stressful situational problems. All respondents were informed in advance about our definition of deviance and methods to be used in the study. The interview schedule included the following items:

1. Social demographic characteristics: (a) Age, gender, marital status, education, religion, number of siblings; (b) present occupation, employment history, military history; (c) parental marital status at birth; parental interaction and supervision during childhood; (d) family structure and organization prior to adulthood; (e) socioeconomic status of the family; and, (f) moral tone of family of orientation.

2. Social psychological characteristics: (a) Mental health problems and history (if any); (b) diagnosis and treatment, history of personal and familial mental health illness; (c) alcohol and drug use; (d) physical condition; and, (e) personality assessment based on the Big Five and the DSM-IV-TR (personality disorder type) models.

3. Self concept and identities: Response to the following four topical questions during the personal interviews were utilized to measure these variables: (a) Who are you? (b) How would you describe yourself? (c) How would you think others see you? (d) How would you describe your emotional relationships and identification with parents and siblings?

4. Life history including personal relationship problems and structural and situational stress problems: Responses to the following questions were utilized to measure these background variables: (a) What kind of home did you come from? (b) Did you experience any childhood or adolescence problems at home? If so, explain. (c) How would you describe interpersonal relationships in your family of orientation? (d) Did you have any adjustment problems in school and/or college? If so, explain. (e) Did you ever have any community problems? If so explain. (f) Have you had any recent community problems? If so, explain. (g) Have you ever had any legal problems? If so, explain. (h) What kind of personal relationship problems have you had with others? (i) Have you ever had any courtship or marital problems? If so, explain. (j) Have you ever had any health problems? If so, explain.

5. Life-Style: (a) The behavioral and operational adaptations that you made while facing problems in your life history; and, (b) Your behavioral styles of interacting with others in central life activities (see Henslin, 1977:11-16). Responses to the following discussion topics: (i) language form, content and physical appearance; (ii) world of work; (iii) organizations, associations and recreation; (iv) sex and family life; and, (v) perceived social class membership.

6. World view: We define worldview from a nominalist perspective. The world is the universe to which people respond on the basis of their assigned meanings to this entity in everyday life; that is, a social construction of whatever one perceives it to be from one's own social experience, as opposed to the so-called objective world (see Lyman and Scott, 1970; Pfuhl 1986). Responses to the following topical questions were utilized for this perspective: (a) What type of area were you reared in? (b) What is your place in this world? (c) What are your life plans? (d) What do you think of the future? (e) What does the past mean to you? (f) How do you view the world and people in it? and, (g) What do you think about your country and the people in it?

7. Deviancy patterns and attitudes: Responses to the following question used during the personal interviews were utilized to measure this dimension: (a) What are your attitudes toward our basic social institutions? (b) How many times have you violated the law in the past knowing it was wrong? Explain. (c) Do you consider yourself a deviant? Explain. (d) Have you faced any extraordinary pressures or stress problems in your present position? In life? If so, explain. (e) How did you respond to these pressures or stress problems? If you had to do it over, would you respond differently? (f) How do you feel about people who commit deviant acts? (g) What kind of deviant acts have you engaged in during your professional career (i) on campus, (ii) off campus, (iii) individually; and (iv) in concert with others? (h) Have you ever been labeled a deviant? If so, how did you react to it? (i) How often do you see (i) faculty or (ii) administrators engaging in deviant acts? If so, what sort? How do you feel when you hear about these acts or see them? (j) Do you think stricter sanctioning procedures are warranted to prevent or minimize deviance in academia? (k) Have your ever been arrested? If yes, how many times? At what ages? What were the charges? (l) Did any of these arrests result in conviction or jail time? If so, for what charges and what were the sentences? (m) Do you consider yourself a deviant? If so, how do you feel about it? (n) What kind of problems do you currently have? (o) Have you ever thought you might have a personality disorder? If yes, explain.

Responses to these questions along with personal observations, institutional documents, the reports of others (i.e., friends, family members, administrators, colleagues) and media reports helped us compile 29 profile-types (of which 27 were deviant types and 2 were normal) which are described in the next chapter (see Chart 2.1). Though 100 respondents were classified under these 29 types (see Table 2.1), for description purposes, we selected representative subjects of each type; that is, those we were able to secure more detail and complete information on, thereby making each profile as comprehensive as possible. These 29 profiles include two normal, non-deviant types; two deviant adjusted personality types; and, five antisocial, five narcissistic, one avoidant, two histrionic, seven obsessive compulsive, two dependent, two borderline, and one paranoid personality disorder types. Four profiles were females, 25 were males; 19 were professors and 8 were administrators. All but two were middle class members with PhD degrees.

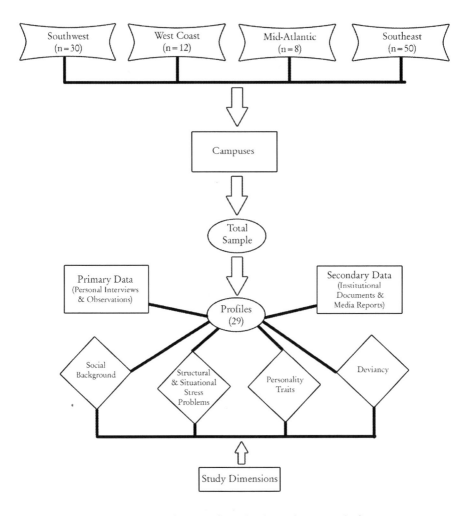

Chart 2.1: Schema of methods and materials for
typology of deviant faculty and administrators

Table 2.1: Distribution of Sample Respondents by Profile Type and Personality Type

Profile Type (P=Professor, A=Administrator)	Number of Sample Subjects	Personality Type
1. Hamlin, the Altruistic Guru (P)	2	Non-deviant, Normal
2. John, the Bully Guru (P)	5	Antisocial Personality Disorder
3. Karl, the Archetype (P)	3	Narcissistic Personality Disorder
4. Fritz, the Iceman (P)	3	Narcissistic Personality Disorder
5. Gyp, the Lip (P)	4	Avoidant Personality Disorder
6. Ron, the Con (A)	3	Antisocial Personality Disorder
7. Eve, the Vamp (P)	2	Histrionic Personality Disorder
8. Todd, the Stud (A)	3	Narcissistic Personality Disorder
9. Sky Pilot (P)	3	Obsessive Compulsive Personality Disorder
10. Peter, the Rabbit (A)	4	Dependent Personality Disorder
11. Byrd, the Nerd (P)	5	Obsessive Compulsive Personality Disorder
12. Farmer, the Foreigner (P)	4	Normal, Adjusted Personality
13. Glad, the In-breeder (P)	5	Obsessive Compulsive Personality Disorder
14. Ryder, the Outsider (P)	4	Borderline Personality Disorder

15. Fred the ABD (P)	2	Borderline Personality Disorder
16. Luke, the Kook (A)	4	Paranoid Personality Disorder
17.Sarai, the Princess (P)	2	Non-deviant, Normal
18. Beecher, the Incompetent Teacher (P)	3	Normal, Adjusted Personality
19. Greene, the Mean Assistant Dean (A)	3	Obsessive Compulsive Personality Disorder
20. Stuart, the Career Student (P)	4	Dependent Personality Disorder
21. Bruiser, the Successful Loser (P)	3	Antisocial Personality Disorder
22. Don, the Don Juan (P)	3	Narcissistic Personality Disorder
23. Pat, the Dilettante (P)	3	Narcissistic Personality Disorder
24. Swindler, the Liberal's Pet (A)	5	Antisocial Personality Disorder
25. Judy, the Greedy (A)	4	Antisocial Personality Disorder
26. Taylor, the Over-reacher (P)	3	Obsessive Compulsive Personality Disorder
27. Brad, the Unqualified Head (A)	4	Obsessive Compulsive Personality Disorder
28. Brown, the Clown (P)	4	Histrionic Personality Disorder
29. Bob, the Ideologue (P)	3	Obsessive Compulsive Personality Disorder

Methods of Inquiry

Utilizing a triangulation technique (see Denzin 1978), we combined data collected via personal observations; personal interviews; available institutional documentary sources; reports from acquaintances, friends, colleagues, and family members; and, media reports. Personal observation involved observing the subjects on the campus at institutional functions and celebrations, departmental and school-wide faculty meetings, school/university committees, off-campus functions and retreats, professional meetings and conventions; at athletic events; and in campus offices and classrooms. These observations supplemented personal interview data.

The topical interviews as described above were held at mutually agreed upon times and places. Initially each respondent was assured of anonymity and the confidentiality of their responses. Some few respondents were able to complete the interview in a single sitting, while others required multiple (up to a maximum of 5) sittings. All interviews were conducted at various locations on campus, most in our offices. Interview time varied from one and one-half hour to five hours. Over the entire study period we interviewed 100 faculty members (assistant, associate, full professors and instructors) and administrators (department heads/chairs, deans, assistant deans).

We also collected information from documentary sources, including university memoranda, policies and procedures, official reports, departmental agendas and records, disciplinary proceedings and reports, web sites of newspapers and universities, and available public school and college/university records of all sorts, public arrest and trial reports, and other published institutional reports. These data were utilized to add to and verify respondents' comments regarding specific rule violations and sanctions as well as responses to other questions.

In addition, we utilized ten key informants (including one each from the nine selected campuses under study) who were tenured faculty members in departments of the liberal arts and/or social and behavioral sciences— all with a minimum service of 10 years, who were actively involved on various departmental and university-wide committees (including grievance committees). Some were the chairs of faculty assembly and/or faculty representatives on the university senate. All were personally known to at least one of the members of the research team. Each was asked to provide oral histories relating to deviance on their respective campuses and data on any of our interviewees (should they have any).

All data collection methods were designed to examine patterned deviancy as disclosed in interactions between members of structured campus groups. It became clear earlier on in the research project that some people were caught while committing deviant acts; were apprehended, labeled as deviant, and sanctioned, while others were not. Some few were falsely accused of committing a deviant act, while some labeled deviant denied the stigma or deviant label. We centered on patterned deviant acts and actors that were known about, and the process that led to discovery, sanctioning, and labeling (and reactions thereto).

CHAPTER 3
The Deviant Types

‹———

(1) Hamlin, the Altruistic Guru (non-deviant)

Hamlin was born and reared in an upper middle class, stable, harmonious family in the upper-small-town south. His father, a medical doctor, was a pleasant, outgoing, stable extrovert (for body types and personality, see Sheldon 1940, 1942), and an affectionate provider, a respectable member of his community. His mother, a former public high school teacher, was an intelligent, modest, conforming, caring housewife, and book club president. Hamlin, like his father, was a mild mannered, agreeable, conscientious, well-adjusted extrovert in his family, public school, and neighborhood. Bookish, but not nerdy, he played sports in a minor fashion; dated some well-adjusted, modest girls; went to a party now and then; drank moderately; did not fish or hunt, or chase females; enjoyed congenial relations with his two siblings, and a few carefully chosen friends, who like himself were or would-be intellectuals. In high school he planned to be a professor, and to this end took an AB, MA and ABD (all-but- the dissertation) from a private, prestigious, southern university located in the upper south. An erudite idealist and somewhat of a humanitarian but not flaky, he passed up offers from several universities as an instructor, and accepted an assistant professorship at a small local liberal arts, denominational college noted as being very liberal in its position regarding politics, race, economics, religion and social values (for example, woman's choice, civil rights). He dropped out of graduate school before completing the PhD because of family financial reasons (an ill father, and two siblings in college). Married with two children, he continued to work on his dissertation while teaching. Mesomorphic in body build he presented a pleasing, gentle, informal and engaging front to all. Most students admired, and many loved him as an excellent and exciting history teacher; and, some looked upon him as a caring, kindly father figure. One student commented, "He made the past come alive." He got along well with most of his peers even though he was more of a Unitarian than a traditional Christian, and attended campus chapel services only now and then as a required formality. Though not a prolific publisher, he co-authored a few journal articles with his former professors. An assiduous student of history, he attended professional meetings regularly, taught a 12-semester-hour load; kept up with current events; and, was on the campus from 9:00 a.m. until 5:00 p.m. in his office or in the library, Monday through Friday. All hours were office hours, and students visited him at will, intermittently. Talk and conversation centered on United States history and current events. Although he appreciated military history, as a pacifist, he lectured frequently on the utter stupidity of war. An anglophile, he frequently alluded to the English: their lifestyle, government and place in history in his anecdotal examples, illustrations and historical points of view—all intertwined with events and way of life in Eastern North Carolina and tidewater, Virginia, his ancestral homeland. In many ways he was reminiscent of an intelligent, village type English clergyman minus any narrow-minded religious baggage. He had traveled in the United Kingdom and advised his students to do so. "Visit the Houses of Parliament," he would say, "And compare them with what we have in Washington, DC." He maintained that there were no substantial reasons for the Revolutionary War against England, other than that of New England's commercial interests and that of southern planters' greed.

His classrooms overflowed. Students sat on window sills and on the floor; ate an occasional sandwich; came in and out at will, chatting quietly; walked up to the blackboard to better read his diagrams, but always kept a respectable distance from his person. Students sometimes asked questions out of turn and forgot to raise their hands when asking questions. All of this, however, occurred quietly with subdued voices. Unperturbed, Hamlin lectured on in a firm soft voice modulated to the shifting sound volumes, and despite traffic and vocal noises there was never chaos. Students managed to show him respect by their differential physical approaches; expressed regrets when tardy; begged his pardon when speaking out of turn, or when stumbling upon entering or leaving the classroom. He always pardoned them and soldiered on with dignity. Students also deferred to his student assistant who called the role, handed out instructions and retrieved papers and homework. One of his students remarked once on a courtesy-call visit to his classroom several years following his graduation: *"I was more upset about the noise and all the informality now than I was back in his classroom years ago."* His students kept up with him throughout the years; visited him, and sent presents at Christmas on his birthday or teacher's day. After finally taking a PhD, Hamlin managed to publish at least two journal articles per year; and, wrote a book on his Tidewater community—his was a real altruistic guru's success story.

Hamlin maintained his students' attention, cooperation and courtesy without utilizing formal disciplinary measures or a long list of rules because they knew he accepted them as they were; taught but did not preach; extended equal privileges; and, treated all with kindness and respect. He never used class notes or electronic aids. Not an ideologue, revisionist, nationalist, or historical philosopher, he presented a balanced view of how things were then, and how they were interpreted, and how things were now and how they were being interpreted though exception to his balance were some elements of English history. In an uncanny fashion he imprinted on students' minds bits of significant historical knowledge; for example, one of his students remembered details of one of his lectures on Hinton R. Helper's, *The Impending Crisis of the South*, years after graduation.

> *He annunciated only a few rules: Come to class, listen, ask questions, take tests, and respect others. He always answered test questions one day after tests were given, used the library, and was always civil to all others. If his rules were broken he would gently chide the rule breaker and encourage him/her to comply in the future which usually worked. He avoided lengthy discussions, if he could, with students about their personal problems if not connected with school problems. If pushed, he would say to them something like, "I'm not a psychologist or spiritual guide. Perhaps you should take these problems to the counseling center, your family, or to your clergyman.*

At times he would intercede with a school problem and champion his students' cause to the administration (that is, if meritorious). There were exceptions regarding students' personal problems; for instance, should the matter have to do with career choice he would with pleasure give the student his insights and opinions without hesitation at great length—especially what to do about the choice of a career, preparation for it; and the selection of the proper graduate school to attend; and, his insights about careers and knowledge of graduate schools were amazing. For example, when one student asked him once about his problem of career choice between History and Sociology, he began his long answer with the following preliminary sentence: "History of course because it covers everything that is essential one finds in Sociology, and more." (Perhaps he was right.) He was good at matching students with proper careers and the proper graduate schools to attend. Further, should the problem have to do with the physical health of a student or one of his family members, he was more than willing to discuss it. He would have made an excellent personnel officer in any formal organization, or a professor of history in any prestigious research institution.

On one occasion a group of rightwing fundamentalist students took a packet of his classroom notes (that they had taken for over a year) to a small marginal, but vociferous, faculty cabal of fundamentalists (at their solicitation). To this group Hamlin was an anathema, an atheist, and a dangerous guru who was leading his students astray. They had attacked him for years to the administration for his "radical teaching" and "loosey goosey classrooms," but had failed to receive redress. In reality they were jealous of his popularity with students and his scholarship as compared with theirs, as well as his eminence on campus, and in the region. To them, Hamlin was playacting as a phony Mr. Chips, and only interested in self glorification. Armed with what it called new evidence this marginal bloc pressed the administration to get rid of him. After perusing its notes the president, who was not enamored of this group anyway, dismissed its charges. Later this same angry cabal hired an attorney who, after a probing study, noted the college catalogue contained a rule stipulating that all faculty at the full-professorship rank must have PhDs by a certain date. Failing this, they must take an immediate one year's leave of absence to complete the PhD off campus, be dismissed, or reduced in rank and salary. When faced with this rule and a threatened lawsuit, the president ruled that Hamlin must take a leave of absence, return to his university and complete the PhD (Hamlin had been working on his dissertation at home which was near completion.) Nonetheless, he was compelled to take the leave and return to his distant prestigious campus. With a wife and two children, and under financial and emotional stress, he complied; took the forced leave and completed the PhD; returned and taught until retirement. But the cabal had won a pyrrhic victory that cost him and his family dearly. Most colleagues supported him, but a significant few of his supposedly "dear friends" did not—these few so-called liberals were secret members of the cabal that had tried to oust him permanently. Hamlin interpreted their betrayal as professional jealousy but forgave them without obvious hostility at any time; and, then explained to a real friend: *"I am forgiving them like the real man Jesus would have."* This forgiveness was never appreciated. Envious and deviant professors of this cabal's ilk rarely forgive good deeds of any kind.

This character sketch discloses the problematic situation of one campus guru who was not a deviant but who triggered deviant behavior in others; the victim of a cabal and of an honest but weak administration. The behavior setting, social actors, plot and actions of this drama are not rare; and, like a morality play, or a tragic grand opera, they are ubiquitous in academia. Frequently, however, the ABD guru of this kind has to give up precious time and energy that could be spent otherwise; for example, completing a PhD. The ABD is usually a non-publisher (deviant) who must endure the malice, pity and/or attack of his colleagues; some are really playacting, and deserve no pity. Unfortunately professors are eternally forming one bloc or cabal, of another for one reason or another; and, administrators are frequently caught in the middle between different types of cabals and 400 pound esteemed professors like Hamlin. What to do? We think professors should reject the guru role, and if vainglorious seek a more spiritual or popular occupation—like say preaching, selling or acting for example. The guru of any kind risks the envy and deviancy of colleagues.

This profile illustrates only one of the perennial problematic situations of ABDs in academia. (Later we discuss the problems of ABDs who never take the PhD). No matter how competent the ABD, he or she always faces a precarious situation in academia, and the authors think universities should avoid hiring them in the best interests of a department or the ABD teacher by employing all non-PhDs as instructors and MAs on a strictly temporary basis. Had professor Hamlin held the PhD from the beginning the cabal that tried to oust him may have never existed.

Hamlin had no pattern of deviancy, nor did he exhibit any personality disorder; and, his social background was advantageous, but he was a victim of a cabal of envious, malicious professors, which became operational because of structural weaknesses in his department and college's administrative structures and rules. The cabal was known about from its incipience and should have been broken up. Nevertheless, the envy of excellence is rampant among college and university professors and administrators. As Henry James Jr., an eminent social-psychological novelist, put it in his consciousness and character analyses of several fictional characters: "The innocently unaware may themselves be the cause of evil in others." (See Benet 1996:519-521). And what to do about this endemic proclivity of envy remains a problem; even, among professors and administrators with equal education and credentials (all with PhDs for example). Perhaps the scarcity of rewards in academia fosters fierce competition and deviancy.

(2) John, the Bully Guru

John grew up in an intact, upper middle class family located in a medium sized city in the deep south where his father, a college graduate and a stable conforming, extrovert, owned and operated a general merchandize store servicing farmers' supply needs in a large surrounding tobacco-growing agricultural area. He, along with a doting mother, an extrovert and a former high school teacher, three younger siblings formed an emotionally adequate household, excepting John's sneaky delinquency pattern and habit of lording it over his younger siblings. When caught in misbehavior, he lied out of the situation, casting blame on others. Moderate punishment for this action appeared to work temporarily, though he demonstrated little remorse for his selfish and aggressive actions. His mother too protective, his father too lax, both tended to discount what they called his peccadilloes. John was crafty, sly, deceitful, cool, and always said he was sorry for whatever misconduct he engaged in (usually minor lying, stealing and disobedience) when caught. His parents wondered if he really meant his repentances and promises to desist from future misconduct when confronted with his misbehavior. However, they agreed, after consulting a number of amateur so-called therapists, that John was experiencing "growing-up pains" as an older teenager who felt he should have some dominance rights over his younger siblings, and, that he should be granted extra privileges in the household, because he was the older sibling. John's parents thought he would stop his "minor delinquencies," and mellow out with age. He did not, and remained in a masked way sneaky, selfish, guiltless, unrepentant, unsympathetic, and aggressive. However, he presented an open and agreeable persona and avoided serious misconduct that could get him arrested or expelled from school. From a teenager he evinced leadership dreams and high educational aspirations, drilled into him by his ambitious mother. Mesomorphic in physical structure and an aggressive extrovert, he excelled in public elementary and high school sports. Nice looking, sensual, and ostensibly charming, he moved from one sexually promiscuous "girlfriend" to another. When things went his way, all went well with classmates; however, when blocked in whatever goals for whatever reasons, he became agitated and displayed inappropriate, antagonistic displeasure. Some classmates feared him, especially those with slight body builds. Aware of his quick impulse to anger, he tried hard to control it, and did at times with moderate success. Occasionally, he pushed male classmates he could not con around when they tried to stand up for their rights. While working in the family store at off-school hours throughout high school, he was reported to be a fair, but loudmouthed, conceited and impatient clerk.

Following high school graduation with good grades and high SAT scores he enrolled in a denominational liberal arts college (locally prestigious) where he majored in History and Sociology; played first-string body-contact sports; made average grades; apparently adapted fairly well overall, but remained remiss in truth-telling in problematic situations. Though he insisted on being in charge in work and social relationships, he assisted classmates at times, but in turn expected them to agree with him and lend him unquestionable support and loyalty at all times. And when they did not he displayed inappropriate anger; scolded them; and, frequently dropped them as friends. Further he remained sexually promiscuous and minus stable relationships with females or males. Further he considered older males, male teachers and coaches, overbearing authority figures; and, when they disciplined him for any reason, he reluctantly complied, but resented any sanctions, and held grudges. Coaches temporized with him because as one said: "He is a star whom we must have on the team. We know he has a loud mouth and resents it when we call him down for what borders on disrespect; but, we think he will settle down. He never pushes us too far anyway. He is too slick for that." John did not and his slickness, rebelliousness, aggressiveness, feelings of entitlements, and dearth of remorse for misconduct continued in a controlled fashion. Smooth and cunning he presented a false pleasing persona that fooled many.

Upon graduation from college, unsure about a career choice, John enrolled in his state's public, first-tier university where he sought an MA in the History department upon his mother's counsel. When graduated with a so-so academic record, he decided to be a professor (again, upon the urging of his mother who had always babied him, discounted his delinquencies, and, expressed great pride in his intelligence). He continued in school and completed the PhD, with a mediocre record. John's graduate school classmates did not like his braggadocio mien and callous behavior with females, and avoided him. He only found dates among weak promiscuous, off-campus females. Very intelligent, yet lazy and undisciplined he did not study very hard, and enjoyed a reckless, social life—booze and girls. He was not really interested in either teaching or research, but reasoned with his mother's counsel that he could lead a pleasant, leisurely life as a college professor. With the help of his father's local political pull he secured an assistant professorship at his almamater.

Now feeling comparatively safe and secure, he gradually tried to run the department despite low rank and lack of tenure. His purpose for control was not to harm anyone, or disrupt, but to insure a pleasant and easy occupational situation for himself. To this end he recruited, and ganged up with one disgruntled associate professor and one other weak assistant professor, both academically more competent than he, but passive unstable, introverts—so-called "weak sisters." This voting bloc of three was powerful in a small, five-man department. John convinced his followers he would be department head eventually, and in the meantime their best interests lay with him. A weak and dependent department head and a lazy inept dean (though both were scholars) permitted John's cabal to develop and operate.

John no longer had to worry about research or a publication record. Utilizing his social skills he also played up to students; gave them good grades; and became mentor, friend, confidant, and "intellectual" leader. Those few who did not "buy in" were quickly discarded and alienated from the club. John maintained that he and his cabal members had to teach certain classes at certain times because: "That's what suited the best interests of their students." Should his simple manipulations of departmental functions not work, there was always the implied fear of student petition. Should the head not comply, the students and the guru could go to the dean. When he was promoted to an associate professorship with tenure and made department head later on John no longer had to pretend interest in research and scholarship because now he could (and did) pose as an efficient administrator. His bullying increased in intensity including further harassment and the coercion of fear among all department members (clerical staff, professors, undergraduate and graduate students). John's daring and clever bullying made him "successful" in a sense, but weakened the department he headed. His bullying comprised most of the following methods utilized by bullying professors and administrators whom the authors had observed over the years:

1. The bully establishes for operational reasons his/her privacy by nonverbal undetectable behavior. For example, keeping one's office door closed and locked when talking with visitors; rumor mongering; seeking out any negative information (especially of a sexual nature) about current or potential enemies.

2. The bully searches for weaknesses in individual targets, or in an administrative system, and during an early preparatory phase, tests either; for example, by making an outrageous unreasonable request for travel funding, or release time for inane reasons. A number of these tests could determine what it would take for the administration or individual to say "no," "vacillate," or "shut up." The weaker the system or more naive the individual target, the more promising the situation would become. Should the bully discover that the victim or no one else is going to call his bluff or squawk; and, accede to his outlandish requests or veiled demands, then he is on his way.

3. The bully targets weak and/or disgruntled persons as members of his team. Manipulative strategies might include starting rumors that the chair is a racist or a sexist. Any "politically correct" slam or conspiratorial story about the target benefits the bully in today's world, where the "popular left" tends to buy into vigorous flamboyant statements, and where an academic institution or individual might fear legal action. The bully may claim that the target (the department head, for example) has provided low salary increases; and, that he/she will raise the salaries of those who join his club if, and when he becomes department head. (The fact is that deans and other administrators have more to

do with determining salary increases than department heads.) This and other workplace promises may promote success. Bullies discount "weak-sister" onlookers who are reluctant to join him, those they reason will not resist but, "Just sit on the sideline, and leave his group alone."

4. The bully instigates legal actions sometimes on campus, or with the legal community; for example, the Equal Employment Opportunity Commission or Office of Civil Rights, because he thinks complaints to these agencies are not usually fully investigated. Additionally, the bully may become protected as a whistle blower himself. Thus, he may get away with his actions until a new administration takes office.

5. The bully and his cabal members gang up on professors whom they do not like, and either squash them or drive them out of the department by way of social and departmental isolation, reputation slurs, false rumors, and personal discrediting.

6. The bully discounts or denies his victim's accomplishments in research, publications, grantsmanship, or recognitions and rewards for excellent teaching, etc.; turns other people against his victim; subjects victim to continual departmental or public criticism; subjects victim to unwarranted regulations without justification; forces victim to comply with needless rules; demands that victim produce unnecessary documentation for his time and effort as basis for tenure, retention, promotion, and salary increase.

7. The bully bribes graduate students to testify against his victims; harasses them for not cooperating in his tactics; exploits their labor and refuses to list their names on publications they worked on; assigns them to professors without regard to their desire or relevance of their research interest.

The authors noted a usual power imbalance between targeted victims and the bully; and, that the most severe faculty bullying is perpetuated by tenured and senior faculty against vulnerable, position-insecure, untenured faculty. For example, some powerful tenured professors we knew (a) successfully pressured more competent but vulnerable colleagues (usually untenured) to attach their names as coauthors to publications (journal articles and books) written exclusively by the pressured colleagues, victims; (b) pressured them to secure so-called coauthored book contracts from publishing houses they could never have obtained on their own; (c) in book preparations as so-called senior authors, they manipulated data and shaded the meanings thereof to suit themselves--leaving the crucial theory construction, methodology, and writing to junior authors---those who really contracted and wrote the books.

Deans and vice-presidents have sometimes used bullying tactics against senior independent tenured faculty, who were likely to or actually challenged any of their questionable policies; or who tried in any way to outshine "the boss." As one administrator said, "You need to keep an eye on those clowns. They have been here for a long time and can cause a lot of trouble, if they get out of control. That's why I need to remind them, I'm the boss to set the record straight."

The authors have also noted that academic bullies are usually disgruntled or insecure persons with either apparent antisocial disorder or paranoid disorder personality types—ambitious but not competent for leadership or scholarship; jealous of competent colleagues; and, hungry for power and recognition. Bullies cannot tolerate their peers or juniors getting ahead of them. Bullies we encountered were more successful in academically weak undergraduate and graduate programs where there were no strong, competent, vigilant department heads, deans, and other upper level administrators, and where there was no real appreciation of scholarship. Competent administrators in research oriented schools and established liberal arts schools did not condone bullying and fired any staff or faculty (with or without tenure) for engaging in bullying behavior.

The authors suggest that faculty members should protect themselves from bullies by: (1) building strong academic records; (2) keeping up-to-date documentation on every episode or encounter one has with bullies; (3) having in reserve some friends who are credible witnesses from one's own and other departments to testify to facts, should a bullying situation arise; (4) never meeting with a bully privately; (5) retaining or having access to a competent attorney; (6) making friends if possible with congenial and competent administrators who appreciate scholarship; (7) should one find that a pattern of bullying is permitted in his or her department one may want to seek employment elsewhere before a bully has a shot at the victim. Bullies never change, and reporting them to a department head or to the administration of a school that permits bullying is useless because bullying that is permitted in an institution is systemic, as well as an issue between individuals. Mediation and recourse to legal action in most cases is useless in such settings because the school where the victim is employed has more competent attorneys than those the victim can employ. The bottom line is should you not have one or more powerful administrators on your side to protect you from the bully, you lose. The media is of no help because it will usually back the university and defame you. The best recourse where bullying is a permitted pattern is to find another position and leave quickly. Even at a school that does not encourage bullying, should you be bullied by a powerful and popular bully you will be at risk even with tenure. What is tenure if one can be pushed around by a bully; and perhaps be subject to all sorts of punishments, like no promotion or no (or pitiful) salary increases. You will need in this case, a powerful administrator as your good friend to protect you. Lacking this you will need an excellent attorney, and a friendly department head or chair who thrives on fair play, or who appreciates your scholarship and personality. The bully does not play bean ball, and backing down from him at any juncture is sure defeat. So be prepared. Bullies are bad leaders though, they often float themselves into authoritative positions wherein they make decisions that are counterproductive for an institution and its membership (see Schmidt 2010). Avoid them if possible.

In summary, John represents the case of an intelligent but lazy, haughty and bullying professor who playacted at being a professor, while simultaneously enjoying the falsified lifestyle of an intellectual. Intelligence, possessing social skills, along with an aggressive, deceptive, and friendly persona enabled him to con or push others around. He resembles an antisocial personality disorder type and suffered no ascertainable structural or situational stress problems, and led a pleasant and carefree life. Those like John do not experience the degree of stress and frustration experienced by others when facing problematic situations. They act out (or off) their problems; and become other people's problems. There are no known successful therapeutic methods for those with antisocial personality disorder.

John retired as a full professor and a department head. Unfortunately his hurly-burly, macho, but crafty tactics are admired by many in our culture within and without academia. However, his type finds it hard to operate in competent, research oriented academic departments with strong heads supported by strong deans. John's bullying deviancy pattern was enhanced by coddling parents and a weak academic structure which permitted him to operate successfully with an inherent selfish and bullish behavioral style. Such types are hard to uncover and sanction because of their intelligence and disarming conviviality and pseudo charm. Those with such personalities who are mistakenly hired, and who become problematic must be firmly challenged, supervised and sanctioned when committing deviant acts like bullying. Better still dismiss them as soon as feasible because they never really mellow out and change until middle age, if then (See Chapter 12 in Barlow and Durand, 2009).

(3) Karl, the Archetype

Karl epitomizes a kind of romanticized European type professor, infrequently found in the United States since the 1960s, outside of some prestigious universities in the Northeast and Midwest. Some semblance of his echo, style, hauteur, and presentation of self in everyday life remains with many, if not most eminent full professors teaching in top tier research universities. His father was a judge, and his mother, the daughter of a German General. Born in an upper-class European family as an only child he was first educated in private secondary schools of the strict German type, where the classics, languages, history and the hard sciences were emphasized. Following a law degree and a graduate degree in political science from prestigious European universities in Germany and France, he studied history and philosophy for three more years in yet another prestigious European university.

He grew up in a home with servants under the strict disciplinary, but loving care of a domineering extroverted father and a doting somewhat submissive, intelligent, introverted mother. Purposefully placed in the company of important guests where his brilliance and good looks could be observed, he was sort of a showpiece for the family; and, as a youth came to see himself as a very special person, somewhat different from most others, and one entitled to special attention. Moreover, his parents encouraged him to engage in conversation with their educated and cultured visitors, and friends who were professionals, intellectuals and/or artists—and to never forget his social class status that required noblesse oblige to lesser lights.

Mesomorphic in build, handsome (within the criteria of his culture) and extroverted, he was very much like his father, and made stable and lasting acquaintances with older males and females of his social class. He was devoted to and shared a strong, affectionate relationship with both parents who lived with him after his marriage, and throughout their lives. Karl was aware of his assets, and though accepted and admired by classmates, professors, and colleagues many viewed him as amusingly arrogant and somewhat full of himself. Females were attracted to him and he responded, as was natural and the custom before marriage, but he never took them too seriously. Though not a Casanova, he led a normal sex life in keeping with his social class, age, place, and time. However, he simply did not have much time for females in a romantic way because of his fulltime pursuits as a scholar. He was never interested in a military, business, or legal career and wanted to be a professor from age 14, which both parents accepted and supported. From the beginning of his educational career he gained the praise of his parents and friends, all of whom he was ever trying to please; and, in turn, he expected, and invoked their continual adulation. Though he liked to impress others and was obviously class conscious to a fault, he was never offensive or brutal. He believed that people (as he said), "Wind up in the class they belong in," and he remained on the conservative political right throughout life. He played a good game of tennis intermittently but without zest or perseverance, because from adulthood he was preoccupied with a scholarly academic career and was known to be a workaholic. As his career progressed he worked at cultivating the acquaintanceships of prominent scholars in his field, Criminology and Penology, whom he admired and envied. Not a very social person, he was not a partygoer or member of any social clique and the socials he attended were tied-in either with professional meetings, occasional visits with eminent colleagues, or professional command performances.

A renaissance man in the European tradition, he knew art history (painting, architecture, sculpture, literature, music and opera) and was conversant in several languages including German, English, French, Russian and Italian. Several years after World War II, he emigrated with his parents to Chicago with a prestigious University of Chicago fellowship in hand; and, graduated five years later with a PhD in Social Psychology (from a Sociology Department). At graduation he preferred a position in a prestigious private university in keeping with his background and ambition, but found that his specialties, Criminology and Penology were not emphasized (or even taught) in such places, so he reluctantly accepted a position in a respectable mid-Atlantic university. Two of his TAs, other students, colleagues, and peers gave us the following paraphrased account of his career, bearing, and lifestyle.

Karl with a strong physical and graceful stance presented a formidable, self-assured, charming, urbane and formal self to students, colleagues and other professionals in lecture halls and in public, although he never appeared exceedingly and overtly overbearing. His two TAs we knew, knew him for more than 30 years as students, teaching assistants and colleagues, but never called him Karl. No one did except his wife, and she did not do so in public. He was Doctor or "Herr Professor" to all, even in small party gatherings; and, always dressed in dark, conservative tailored suites, white shirts, dull-colored ties and hats, black shoes and socks; wore no jewelry excepting an expensive but inconspicuous gold wristwatch with a plain black leather band, and gold cufflinks. He lectured from carefully, well prepared, up-to-date notes, in a clear well modulated, authoritative, slightly oratorical voice, looking with unwavering eyes (from time to time) straight ahead, to each side and to the back; paused to answer a few questions when hands went up; reserved five minutes at the end of each lecture for further questions which he answered then or later on in class. His stage presence was commanding but not obnoxious. Punctilious he entered the classroom on time, prohibited student verbal exchanges, ignored show-offs and inane, and "got you" questions;

kept regular office hours; had no time for listening to personal problems or small talk; and, would say when pressed, "Go to the student counseling center with your personal problems, I'm not your social worker or a clinical psychologist. I am only a Criminology professor in this particular class." He never discussed grades; you got what you got, and should you have beefs or problems with any tests, assignments or essay questions, you discussed them with one of his teaching assistants in the assistant's office, and not in his presence. Problems and errors were rare and were redressed by him via a TA if necessary. If asked for, he granted occasional interviews in his office, should requests pertain to Criminology or Law as taught in his classes and would never help students with work in other classes. A hard grader, only good students took his courses.

Tough and formidable with a slightly haughty mien, he was fair, honest, and superbly prepared to teach his subject matter in a manner students said they "got the gist" in his lectures easily. He told one TA once, "I have no use for courses in Education because you cannot teach anybody how to teach others. First, know your material, then present it in a clear, concise way, and make it interesting and challenging. If they do not get it, flunk them; we have too many students in college anyway. Many should be in trade schools or at work." Many TAs and other students told the authors that he was the best classroom teacher they ever had because he made complicated material easy to understand. Routinely he filled the blackboard with explanatory symbols, schemas, diagrams and models. Many of his former students became successful professors, researchers, government employees, and scholars, throughout the United States and in foreign countries. To some, he became somewhat of an academic cultic figure, which he would probably have laughed at, but appreciated (secretly).

Once, at an "important" (so it was thought then) professional meeting in a small group session, where someone told the chair (one of his former students, a thirty-five year old female scholar), "Dr. Karl has unexpectedly arrived." She left immediately in search of her mentor, and never (neither then nor later) gave any excuse for what most felt was her rude sudden departure. She was quite attractive, but Karl was too busy and cagey for playboy distractions. Moreover he was happily married to a very attractive German wife, though no children.

Females marveled and ate up his "European charm," though his affinity with male and female students and colleagues existed exclusively on a professional basis. He was never seen to flirt, banter, joke or "shoot the breeze," though many paid him open and personal homage (which he expected). He did like and appreciate his competent students and colleagues, but had no time for (in or out of class) incompetents; and, at inappropriate times he made this clear. One of his enduring problems was his dearth of interest in, or empathy for average (in performance) students or colleagues. Further he had difficulty in showing his appreciation of others; for example, when he did things for you, like extend recommendations or compliments, they were understated (like the English way), and if possible hidden. He gave the impression of avoiding "getting close" to anyone as if he feared such action would show weakness; and/or, that someone might take undue advantage of his expressed affection. No one had ever seen him emote, show despair, or elated emotion, and he was always "on," (on stage), and wound up with energy. Stiff and formal, he never discussed personal matters with others, and rarely issued public praises or compliments, because to him, no matter what one did well, it was what one was supposed to have done anyway as part of his or her duty—especially if it involved him in any way.

Occasionally he hosted a beer party at his modest, comfortable, middle class home during holidays, or when one of his eminent professor acquaintances visited the campus. Even here, a seminar type exchange program and atmosphere prevailed; and, though formally pleasant, there was never any intoxicated ambiance. One nursed one, two or three beers, but chanced no more; and, though an ample beverage supply was on hand including strong drink ostensibly available to all, no student dared to drink the hard stuff. And he never drank more than two or three drinks at a sitting, and always ate when drinking. Some said he was afraid, if intoxicated, he would let his guard down. He told one TA, "Europeans usually eat along with drinking, and therefore obviate over intoxication."

Karl was a qualitative scholar, a member of the Chicago School of Sociology (a social psychologist) and never claimed that Sociology was a science. And he said, "Sociology is only one way to analyze society and social relations." Again he remarked once, "Should you wish to know the culture, social relations and economic conditions existing in late 19th century Russia, read law and Count Leo Tolstoy's *War and Peace,* rather than Karl Heinnich Marx or a carload of economists and sociologists." Touchy about his thin but respectable publication record, Karl frequently mentioned his other accomplishments as a cover-up. And he told some of his colleagues that he was underpaid, and not appreciated enough by his department or the administration. When jokingly chided about his many trips to conferences and professional meetings overseas, he would exclaim, something like: "They (the administration) should be proud they got me to make these trips. They make the university look good."

Karl was neither a prolific publisher nor an empirical researcher but rather a polymath, an excellent teacher and an organizational man. (He published four or five monographs on the Sociology of Law, and a respectable number of theoretical journal articles (for his time)—all about, "what had been found," and "what I think," rather than, "what I found."

Karl never engaged in hands-on empirical research, although he "directed" countless MA theses and PhD dissertations based on empirical, first-hand, statistical as well as qualitative data. And it is here where his limitations lie. At times he found it necessary to refer some of his MA and PhD students who were writing theses and dissertations (which required innovative research design and sophisticated quantitative analysis) to other professors in the department, or to outside methodologists proficient in all kinds of current statistical techniques, and survey research methods. Nearby Washington, D.C. was awash with such PhD types, but they charged high fees which some of his students could not afford, but thought they had to pay. Moreover, some of his colleagues who called him (to his back) a prima donna complained to the head about these outside services, and the time they spent tutoring his students in his absences from campus. Additionally, some claimed that when abroad he made too many uncalled for excursions to art museums and operas which were not officially on his itinerary. He officially directed many empirical dissertations, but these were self-directed or accomplished with outside paid help either because he was too busy at professional meetings and conferences all over the world, or because he could not help with statistical analysis. Complaints about his absences increased over time, therefore, the head was put in a continual problematic position existing between Karl, a powerhouse, and some of his envious colleagues, a problem never solved and eventually led to a messy, raucous departmental split, and the resignation or reassignment of some professors. Karl with the support of professional organizations, the university administration, and some colleagues established a separate School of Criminology (and took with him the best scholars in the department). The point here is not the efficacy of the split, but rather that a certain type of professor effected it, which still rankles many on and off a once troubled university department. Karl established a separate school within the university which he had envisioned for fifteen years, but at great cost to many. Some professors said, "He finally got the power he wanted, and the prestige he deserved as the director of his school." The crucial problem was that Karl was never a garden variety sociologist but a social psychologist astride four disciplines—Sociology, Criminology, Law, and Psychology.

Karl was one of the chief founders of the American Society of Criminology and a premier Criminology journal, and he was also prominent in the International Society of Criminology. And with a personal hands-on approach, he founded 21 schools of Criminology in 21 foreign countries including some in South America, Europe, and the Near East—where he developed curricula, stipulated the criteria requirements for future professor applicants and for student applicants; and, guest-lectured in all 21. At one time or another throughout forty years he read countless papers at professional meetings; chaired Criminology sessions; and played significant roles in the power structure of several professional Criminology organizations. He kept an index name-card covering biographical data on all eminent, world-wide Criminologists, and corresponded with all of them. Despite all this (plus being an excellent classroom teacher and an intellectual conceptualizer), he was inadequate as an empirical researcher (requiring sophisticated statistical analysis); and, some of his students paid the price for this fault. Though he had many close acquaintances among eminent criminologists, students, and colleagues, he had no intimate friends outside his family circle (a brilliant wife and his parents). Many colleagues envied him, some admired him, some others feared him, and still others hated him, and found him difficult to please (and not a team player). Department heads did not know what to do with him. A good reader of others, but opaque, he was impossible to read. Some questioned who he really was, and when asked about his enigmatic self once, he answered: "I have many selves. Perhaps Erving Goffman was right, when he told an audience once: '*We present many selves to many others in diverse encounters; therefore, we are somewhat like onions with no central core, no real you or anybody else.*'" If ever he experienced significant structural or situational stress problems (very doubtful) no one ever knew about them (see Goffman 1959, 1963, 1971).

In summary, Karl was an alpha male who attracted and helped many; awed, discomforted and confused others; was envied by many others, and disliked by still others. Though successful he was a self-controlled narcissist and a slightly histrionic enigma. Though his students admired him, they never knew his assessment of their careers or publications, because he never discussed such things. Conversely, when he met them at various places within and outside the United States during national or international Criminology meetings, he was eager to talk about his accomplishments. Yet, despite a preoccupation with himself as both a scholar and an organizational man, he was a leader and an unforgettable though flawed academic model for many. He told a TA once that one of his former TAs, who had just published a book, was at the least a good barroom social psychologist. When said TA learned about this remark he said, "Well, Dr. Karl could have employed a more euphemistic research-setting term, like say, *nightclub.*" Unfortunately neither TA ever met him at a bar, and perhaps when there, he was at the Scala Milan Opera or the Tate Britain in London, the Lovre in Paris or at the Prado in Madrid.

Karl's pattern of deviance inhered in his isolation of himself (as a professor) from some students and colleagues because he considered them inferior. All students and professors are not brilliant, but some of them have a legitimate place in academia, and deserve attention. Further, flawed himself in the research area, he failed to provide necessary statistical aid to some of his graduate students. Moreover, he was not a team player and contributed to faulty bickering and to a nasty department split—that resulted in the resignations, leavings, and even firings of some innocent persons. And perhaps he made too many unscheduled side trips abroad to art galleries, museums, and opera houses. Karl's upper class social background was in part responsible for his detrimental feelings of superiority and entitlements; and, he did face structural and situational departmental problems and cleavages between the disciplines of Sociology and Criminology. The crucial basis of his deviancy, however was a marked narcissistic personality, one not needed in a democratic society. Behavior modification of his type is extremely difficult—and such a type should not be selected for the academy. Such types need and should be required to seek psychological treatment should they become problematic in academia, and dismissed should they not improve their attitude and conduct toward others.

(4) Fritz, the Iceman

Fritz was born in Sweden into a middle-middle class, harmonious, stable family parented by a pleasant, outgoing, energetic, extroverted father and an intelligent, well-educated, mature, dependable, well-adapted mother, an ambivert. He along with his two younger siblings were normal conforming children. The father, a university trained electrical engineer, emigrated to New York state with his family when Fritz was 10 years old. He, like his father, was a well built, mesomorphic type, agreeable, conscientious, and somewhat aggressive within "normal" bounds. His parents instilled in the minds of all three children that they were special people who should succeed. He made friends easily and engaged in most playground activities but was not interested in major physical contact sports. Some considered him a little too egotistic and bossy, but not obnoxiously so. He said once to a friend: "I do not have much to be modest about." He made excellent grades in public elementary and high school; entered a New York Ivy League university, and graduated with honors; and went on to take an MA and PhD in Economics. He had decided at high school graduation with parental approval to become a professor, and had always been especially good in math and statistics classes. University classmates and professors defined him as an egotistic, intelligent, very competitive person with a strong desire to succeed. Bookish he was not concerned with big money or corporate success and only wished to live a quiet scholarly life like his professors. Not a lady's man he married his first girlfriend, a nurse, a well-integrated practical person in undergraduate school and sired two normal children.

At graduation with a PhD, Fritz failed to find a teaching position in the northeast, preferably New York state, where his parents, friends and classmates lived, because of a poor job market. Therefore, he lived at home with two families for one year without a job. Then he looked southward where openings requiring his quantitative skills were available, and applied for several positions. Initially, in the position where he was hired, the department head wondered if he were not a little too brash, cocksure, openly ambitious, cosmopolitan, and just too academically "perfect" to fit in (in the rural deep south). And Fritz himself felt some trepidation, as a "foreigner" among so many soft and slow-talking southerners and wondered if his future colleagues thought like they talked. Two scholarly economic professors persuaded the search committee, chaired by a "good ole boy," and the department head to seriously consider the Ice Man (a latter appellation) from New York. The department head had been searching four years for a professor who could teach advanced quantitative research methods utilizing sophisticated statistical techniques; and, although he did not say so, someone competent enough to pass on some expert knowledge to the department's mediocre professors who taught research methods and survey research. Such a gifted applicant was hard to find because professors of this type were already employed in universities as associate or full professors elsewhere. But then the "Ice Man cometh" and applied. A very competent associate professor squired the 28 year-old brand new Ivy League PhD around when he came for his campus interview; explained the departmental and campus scenes; and, suggested that he put on a modest and deferential front during his interviews, and at his upcoming department greeting party. Fritz impressed this campus guide who had him spend his last night on campus at his house, and urged him to accept an offer should one be made. He also tried to allay Fritz's mild verbalized concerns about some of the "upscale bubba" professors who had "interrogated" him (he said) during his interviews. When Fritz told the associate professor, campus guide, at the airport before leaving: "I really want the job," said guide almost fainted with surprise and elation. Fritz had made out astonishingly well with most interviewers. However, same problems were raised in the departmental meetings where his application, and he himself were thoroughly discussed and dissected. Most said he was too young and inexperienced; many did not like his AB, MA, and PhD from Ivy League schools; others called him an *elitist*, and some questioned his foreign birth in Sweden (though he was a US citizen); still some others wondered if students would accept such a conceited professor with such a "pronounced Yankee accent," and defined him (correctly) as not being "one of us."

All (some grudgingly) admired his academic credentials nonetheless. A minority of four, "egghead" professors, from without the region along with some independents pushed for his selection. Eggheads were the publishers, good ole boys were the established full professors, independents were a mixed group from within and without the region, (some of whom published, some who did not). The later claimed their forte was teaching, and some of these were good teachers. A fourth group known as "duds" got by, but certainly didn't publish. The head, a published scholar, pointed out that the department had to employ someone within a month or lose the position, and that there were no other acceptable applicants left to interview. Five former applicants had been judged unacceptable by the faculty previously, although all had been acceptable to the head and to the dean. All five were highly qualified but were from without the region, and had degrees from prestigious schools in the Northeast and Midwest. The good ole boy survey research bloc, consisting of those who had published very little before or since receiving tenure, was the most reluctant group to hire him; however their leader was out of town on medical leave. The head, although favorably impressed had some doubts about this young, somewhat arrogant applicant "fitting in." In dire need of someone to teach three high level research courses before the beginning of classes in September, he offered the position to Fritz via telephone three days after he left the campus; and explained later that he had to fill the position quickly with someone.

The Ice Man, so-called by the students because of his formality, preciseness, self control when facing any problem situation, and above all his chutzpah was on his way. He announced in one of his beginning classes that he hoped to become the director of a new research center within the department soon—quite an ambition for a young assistant professor without tenure. Within four years he published 12 journal articles, one coauthored book, and read 10 papers at national professional meetings. Further, he was very popular with the graduate students who needed and appreciated his expertise in formulating hypotheses, and in writing MA theses and PhD dissertations. Moreover, surprisingly he seemed to get along well with the other professors in all departmental factions—a real whiz kid, who on the negative side reveled in his success, but was "The real thing, a scholar," said some of his students. He proclaimed to some wary well wishers, "Nothing succeeds like success and I am already successful."

However, when he applied for early tenure consideration after only three years on campus things changed. Six faculty members, all his strong supporters, cautioned him to wait for at least another year before applying. They did so on his behalf, fearing that the good ole boy bloc, comprising a powerful group in the department, would think him an upstart and deny him tenure then, and later on. Despite good advice, he applied and was rejected by a wide margin of votes. Crestfallen and angry, he lost his cool for the first time, and searched about for the names of those who had voted against his tenure. The good ole boys reasoned that he had sat on the fence far too long, and now was the time to pull him into their fold. So, several convinced him that the eggheads, and some independents under the egghead influence, had voted against his tenure. Some had but stipulated that he should be tenured the following year. Such news delivered to the Ice Man was of no solace, and he never forgave the eggheads whom he thought (erroneously) had betrayed him. He held grudges against those who appeared to have impeded his quick success; moved over into the good ole boys' camp; and made himself their surrogate scholar, researcher and publisher. Never again did he team up with any egghead to do any research; and moreover, he dissuaded his graduate students from taking some of their courses; and, adamantly refused to serve on some research committees with eggheads. (At this point he should have been forced to do his official duty, or fired should he have objected). He, from the beginning, steered clear of duds, those he considered worthless so-so professors in the department, though he did not malign them openly or anyone else.

He was tenured one year latter, promoted two years afterwards, and granted many privileges withheld from most others. Additionally, he was appointed head of a new departmental research center affording a research laboratory with telephone booths, computers, internet, and all kinds of electronic equipment, plus secretaries, graduate students, a library, several electric typewriters, etc. He accepted these perks as deserved entitlements; and when given the keys to the laboratory, refused "work entrance" to some eggheads, and to some of their graduate students. Hence much departmental survey research was conducted under his unofficial auspices, in "his lab." When several of the eggheads' graduate students slipped in to use his computer services without his permission, he raised hell to the department head who saw to it that "his lab" and its services were restricted to those students that he, the Ice Man, permitted in. Obviously he, the head, and the dean should have been held accountable, and censured and sanctioned for these restrictions. Although the head called a meeting about this and other similar incidents, and tried to smooth things over, some entrance restrictions (though tempered) remained in force. The head's excuse to one full professor was: "What do you want me to do? The Ice Man is the best one we have who really knows how to do advanced survey research, and the best one at teaching advanced survey research methods; and, he can run the research lab best." One full professor responded: "Then fire the smartass and get some other number cruncher in here to help you run the show. This is a university and no student should be denied access to a research center. Take the keys away from your boy, and let all graduate students in." The head countered, "Then you smart SOB, go out and find me another Ice Man, and I'll let all the students in." The good ole boys, although outranking the Ice Man had, surrendered much of their power to him; made him their champion; and, then had been swallowed up. They really worked in his lab as his assistants in a sense. Five years following tenure, the Ice Man was a full professor and most lab restrictions were finally discontinued.

The Ice Man quickly adopted and improved on the strategy and tactics of those who had made him their champion. He did this for example, by catering to the egos of those above him (department heads, deans, vice presidents); and, always throwing a bone or two to loyal underlings (like adding their names as coauthors on his publications; placing them on his research projects; putting a good word in on their behalf here and there, etc.) In brief, he exploited some to get there and stay there. Surprisingly, he also fitted in, in the off-campus community, and even become a fair shade-tree mechanic; wore bib overalls when tinkering with his Mercedes or watering his lawn; subscribed to the local paper which he never read; kept the New York Times hidden in his office desk. Additionally, he ate grits, cornbread, hush puppies, salted pork, (side meat) molasses, chitlins, catfish, pork chops and gravy, sauce meat turnip greens, greasy fries, dirty rice, pork and beans, clabber biscuits, wild game; listened to country music; drank bourbon (rather than scotch which he had once favored); thereby simulating, in part, the lifestyle of an upscale bubba. He and his wife even attended some Baptist church services occasionally; and sent their children to Sunday school though he was secular to the bone. But, of course, he shipped his children to New York for summer vacations, and enrolled them in Ivy League schools when they came of age. He also announced that he liked to fish and hunt, but had a back injury from a lacrosse team inquiry—la-di-da; but it worked like a charm. His simulation of a bubba lifestyle was not a pure cunning ruse. Perhaps so at first, but eventually he became a partially converted outsider to an insider's lifestyle, who in the beginning may have tried to con the con, but in the end joined the club.

Despite all of this, he remained the premier researcher in the department, a treasured asset, but one, one should be wary of. Outwardly friendly, but inwardly suspicious of some southerners; and, if crossed never forgot. In reference to females, he was true blue to his wife. As one female professor remarked once, "Fritz is too "poochy cushy" for an intellectual, but too straitlaced to play." Though a superior person and teacher his interest range was too narrow for that of an intellectual, nor did he claim to be one. Females liked him and he lapped up their adulation, but he was no womanizer, and too career conscious to be a playboy. He remarked once to one of his loyalists: "I haven't the time to play with doll baby sex kittens." Congenial in an emotionally controlled manner even around close colleagues, he was a quiet sullen bear in the company of those he did not like (but never physically threatening).

In summary, the Ice Man was a brilliant, industrious, success driven, vain, somewhat rigid and demanding professional who had difficulty empathizing with lesser lights in work settings, who felt that he was fully deserving of his many entitlements. He expected much of others, perhaps too much; but he also gave much. He was a dedicated teacher, superb theorist, researcher and analyst, and a sharp reader of others. And amazingly, he had an uncanny ability to fit in with diverse people in all kinds of cultures, places and situations, which was quite remarkable for an ice man. Obviously he appeared to be a successful, intelligent, obsessive-compulsive, narcissistic, and cool personality type. He copied part of an existing pattern of departmental deviancy for self protection, and success; and he had no close friends, excepting his family of a wife and three children. Perhaps those like the ice man can do without real friends in academia. He remarked once, "Like they say in the District of Columbia, when you come here and want a friend, buy a dog." We, the authors, have worked with several colleagues of his type, and wish that we could have made more of them our friends, but such is not an easy task. One should never impede or seem to impede the success of those like Fritz. Empathy is not one of their finer qualities. Though not antisocial, deceptive, or coldblooded his type require strong and patient academic bosses. "He is too direct," said one colleague to another who suggested that Fritz should apply to the CIA for a spy job. Fritz was no phony and what you saw was what you got with him. The product of an advantaged social background imbued with a strong sense of personal worth and ambition, he adopted part of a preexisting pattern of deviancy in the name of self defense, and to get and stay ahead among those he saw as strangers. Fritz exhibited no outward signs of structural or situational stress problems though he took advantage of departmental structural problems. When he was faced with situational problems he should have sought psychological counseling and/or treatment. Those like him should not be hired, and if selected and become trouble makers they should be required to undergo psychological treatment. And should they not improve they should be fired.

(5) Gyp the Lip, the Rumor Monger

Gyp the Lip was born into a middle class family in the deep-south. His father, an ectomorph, was a nervous, jittery, shy, physically weak professor at a small denominational college located in a state capital, where he had some political pull. His mother was a strong willed domineering extroverted person who ruled her husband and three children. Gyp was neglected by his unstable, inner-directed, and emotionally remote father, and spoiled by an ambitious, doting mother. An ectomorph from the beginning he was an undersized, whining, nervous, irritable, demanding child. Weak physically and cranky by nature, he was unpopular among his peers who called him, a "mama's boy" (which he was). His father made himself very busy at work; therefore, his mother really reared and smothered him. Slightly above average intelligence, he made a passable public school adaptation where he made average grades; though, in a sense, he was homeschooled by his mother, who feared (correctly) he could not take the male joshing and competition on the school playground. He did attend public schools through the 12th grade, but went straight home each day after school, and avoided playground activities when possible—where he was laughed at by boys of his own age, who were larger, stronger, and more competitive than he. In brief he could not take the rough and tumble engaged in by his male classmates either physically or mentally. Gyp shied away from girls who found him shy, frail, strange and unattractive.

While attending college where his father taught, he majored in History and said, "I can't find anything interesting or easy enough about my other courses." After graduation with average grades, and not knowing what to do, he enrolled in what the locals called one of the state's "second-tier" universities (the major state university was a respectable institution). There he was known as a very rigid, moralistic, standoffish person with an apparent undeserved inflated ego—a person who tried to impose his rigid views on others. With the help of his mother, who paid tutors at times, he took an MA and a PhD in History and Education following a long tedious struggle. Then he secured a position in the History and Education Department at one of a sister state's second-tier universities. The fact that he had specialized in Colonial History, a subject no one else in the department where he applied, wanted to teach, helped him get a split position as an assistant professor in the History and the Education Departments. At this point he married an older plain, religiously devout woman who attended his parents' church, and who was far stabler, and far superior to him intellectually and character wise. A well adjusted extrovert, she helped him make shaky adjustments for the rest of his married life and lent him undeserved moral support.

As an assistant and later a middle-aged associate professor, with a nervous, irritable personality, he was known to his students as the weasel, or Gyp the Lip because he gossiped continually and compelled them to buy his "book," a printed manuscript by a local commercial printing shop, which he called a publication. He was unpopular among his colleagues who could not abide or understand him. As one remarked: "Only ninnies teach the history of the family, and he damn well looks and acts the part, anybody can teach that course." The faculty called him Gyp the Lip, because he preached to all who would listen to "Calvinist" positions on sex, courtship, and marriage. Moreover, he tried to make himself the overseerer and presumed guardian of all sexual conduct in his department; and, reported to the head any gossip or stories he heard about the sexual behavior of students and faculty on and off campus. These reports included: purported details on sexual activities among students, sexual contacts between students and faculty, rumored stories about faculty sexual relations (with each other's wives, husbands, boyfriends, girlfriends); the kissing, embracing, and all "making out" that supposedly went on within the physical space of the department (halls, offices, labs, libraries); and, any "untoward" sexual activity that occurred anywhere on and off campus. He snooped about making inquiries about who was dating whom, who had jilted whom, who was getting divorced, and who was engaged to whom. His chief concern dealt with gossip about male professors' presumed sexual contacts with female students, and with the physical sexual acts within the environs of the department. Once he asked a colleague if he knew that his female student assistant was having sex during the weekends in his office with one of her married professors. This colleague replied that he did not believe his story; and, that the accused student did not have a key to his office. The Lip still insisted that his reported sexual acts were ongoing and volunteered to join the office holder in a weekend sex watch to prove his accusations. The receiver of the tale refused, and never mentioned the "wild story" to anyone. But, he did become more wary of Gyp the Lip.

The head of the department, after a thorough investigation of several of the Gyp's reports which turned up nothing he considered significant, told the dean that his inquiries had resulted in nothing but inconvenience, and the demeaning embarrassment of some. Thereafter, he refused to take heed of Gyp's reports (most questionable, some partially true, most false and out of line, and none anyone's business). Few, if any, were significant. Not taking heed, however, was not enough; because, the head still listened to the Lip, who should have been dissuaded from further probing or fired. Eventually, when this rumor monger reported a false sex story about a male colleague and a coed, said accused lawyered up and shut the Lip down. However, the investigation entailed legal fees and cost the falsely accused stress, stigma, and wasted time, but cost the Lip nothing. Though not a macho, the victim said action like that described by W.J. Cash in the "Savage Ideal" as found in his book, *The Mind of the South* was appropriate in his situation. Married with a wife and four children, where was he to go in academia should the Gyp's false charges be believed and acted upon? Some of his alleged professor "friends" consoled him at the time, remarking, something like:"I would back you to the hilt if I knew you were not guilty." As the old adage goes: "With friends like that who needs enemies."

The above painful incident illustrates the harm that a professor like Gyp the Lip can cause via fabricated stories. (In the authors' opinion people in academia should take a tolerant, hands-off approach to private sexual encounters on campus; unless they break the law, as in the case of rape, date rape, sexual harassment, sexual assault, or break university rules pertaining to sexual conduct involving sexual relations between administrators or faculty with students. All relevant charges brought forward by sexual victims should be properly reported on campus to the administration and to off-campus police, investigated, and sanctioned on and off campus should such charges be validated.) Rumor mongers like Gyp the Lip should not be permitted to sniff around and spread dirt on others, and when detected they should be fired.

The problem or imminent challenge is that should the false accuser, like the Gyp the Lip in this case, have tenure and competent legal counsel, it is hard to get rid of him or her. A three ringed legal circus could ensue: the accusing lawyer, the university lawyer, and the lawyer of the one accused, for example, could be in the mix. Therefore, any clear-cut department, court or university board decision in these cases is problematic, and many times, unrewarding to any of the litigates. Moreover, during court or academic board proceeding, stigma may be applied to the accuser, the one accused, the witnesses, and perhaps the university administration itself, the overlord of all campus litigates. Frequently, the university is more concerned with its image in these cases than the facts of the case, the sanctioning of guilty perpetrators, or the sanctioning of those who falsely accuse others of serious sexual violations. Further, date rapes should never be hushed up.

In our experience false accusers like Gyp the Lip evade justice, if lawyered up. Like most of his kind, Gyp was a physically and mentally weak ninny, a pathetic character who aspired to social and professional heights he could never reach despite the help of his mother and others. Not overly intelligent, Gyp was socially and professionally a loser, but ambitious, he decided to change his image by cheating his way forward, and calling attention to himself as an important person regardless of his victims' pains. Gyp was spiteful, envious, disgruntled, anxious, edgy and malicious. Knowing he was a loser he suffered from earned low self esteem. Continually feeling rejection and humiliation by others, he utilized histrionic means to draw attention to himself, and also made feeble attempts to manipulate more successful others; demonstrated anger over minor annoyances; and placed the blame on others for his personal inadequacies. Additionally, Gyp was an alarmist, a liar, and an untrustworthy troublemaker who craved attention to the detriment of others. He resembled an avoidant personality disorder type—a wannabe who apparently suffered from sexual psychological fears and inadequacies. In our opinion, this type, other than those similar to the antisocial personality disorder type, comprises the most dangerous class of professors in academia.

Ironically, later on in his career Gyp (5'5" tall) was accused (many said with apparent validity) of having a sexual affair with a 5'9" homely, androgynous, female graduate student, who did not deny the accusation. The weak head of his department who used Gyp as a paper work editor and a gofer, refused to look into the matter. The Gyp weakly (and questionably) denied the report and explained to many of his colleagues later with explanations like, "Man, she is single, and a flirt, and after all I'm a normal man." Some colleagues reported that he was proud of sleeping with a "big ass broad" as he, the Gyp defined her. ("Broad," He was old fashioned to boot, as well as a hypocrite. He was really saying, *'I can take care of a real woman sexually.'*") Many wondered how he ever got his wife, who explained to some of her friends following marriage: "Well after all, he is a professor;" but she intimated to female friends later on that he was inadequate in bed.

Clearly, a personality disorder motivated Gyp the Lip's deviancy pattern. Nor did his fundamentalist social background including a doting mother, help this troubled and tormented weakling. Such types should not be selected in academia, and weeded out if they slip through the cracks and get hired. Regarding stress, his wife who finally divorced him, reported that he came home "stressed out" every week about some trivial happening in his department, though he denied any stress or structural problems. Gyp never should have been hired, and he should have been fired when his persistent snooping was found out about. His type is not prone to change even with therapy, though he needed psychological treatment, and he should have been required to seek such treatment when his snooping was first found out about. Those like him who continue snooping should be dismissed.

(6) Ron the Con: the Dictator

Ron, a mesomorphic extrovert, was born and reared into a lower middle class urban family of six, located in the upper south. He was the eldest child in a family, where both parents were factory workers. His father, a stable, aggressive extrovert was a high school graduate, an apparent honest, hard-working muscular, sober, religious, family man who was head of his household and respected in his community. His mother, also a high school graduate was a fairly adjusted, ambivert, who spoiled Ron from the jump. Things were economically tight in a family where all four siblings worked in factories during off-school hours; and, spent little time together while growing up or later on. All adapted to home, school, and community excepting Ron, who was "a rebel without a cause," and a disciplinary problem throughout his childhood and youth in all group situations (at home, school, and the community). He did not mind his mother; stole trivial goods belonging to family members and others; lied about trivial things; and played too rough with his sisters; beat-up some of his male companions; stayed out late at night; and, had difficulty with male authority figures early on. He seemed to have an underdeveloped super ego as evidenced by a lack of empathy for others, extreme selfishness, physical aggressiveness, and a dearth of guilt feelings. When caught for his delinquencies he resorted to conning tricks to escape punishment. He also failed to establish stable, affectionate relations with others; engaged in frequent risk-taking behavior (e.g. driving when intoxicated); and was unable to see himself as others did. Further, he had a demanding, belligerent, anti-authority attitude, and a perspective like he said: "What's mine is mine, and what's yours is also mine if I want it, heads I win, tails you lose." He assumed a blithe attitude and reasoned that he could bluff his way through any crisis situation because, he said, he had a "magical feeling" of being inviolate. For example, he was fearless and would take on two or three in a fist fight drunk or sober. His cardinal traits were: (1) extreme selfishness; (2) no sense of remorse or guilt; (3) the inability to relate in an affectionate way to others; (4) a lack of super ego controls; (5) the false notion that all others were really like him in personality type.

Ron's father tried to discipline him, but overlooked many of his shenanigans because he excelled in sports; and was a "real man" in his estimation, "a real macho." Many girls admired his muscular build, good looks, athletic prowess, sexuality, and his relaxed "devil-may-care" attitude. Promiscuous in high school he impregnated two girls who had abortions at his father's expense. Some male "friends" liked him because he was a show off and the life of every party, an athlete, and a real tattooed stud; but, they feared him physically, because of his quick vengeful, violent temper. He drank, smoked and gambled by age 15, but still remained his father's pet. This lax father protected him from arrest, and helped him become a star basketball player in high school and college. However, Ron did not turn out to be good enough for the pros. Intelligent, glib and very good at basic math, he was intellectually lazy and not motivated to sit still in class and listen to teachers, obey instructions and do tedious homework, or cooperate with others in group tasks. Obviously he never learned to take the role of the other, therefore, he was not concerned with others' welfare, and selfish to the core. He reasoned that all others who pretended to be unlike him were game playing. Nevertheless, despite his disciplinary problems he made overall average grades throughout grade and high school, and above average grades in math and science. Why and how did Ron apparently adapt enough to stay out of jail?

Several reasons why his delinquent acts did not preclude his graduation from high school were: (1) His father's protection. (2) A doting mother. (3) His star status as a basketball player. (4) His verbal alacrity, intelligence and superficial charm, enabling him to place blame on others for his acts, and feign innocence when guilty. (5) Lax school teachers and administrators. (6) Cool when caught red handed, he would utter such remarks as, "I'm so sorry. Forgive me because I'm not really like that. I just acted out of myself. I'm really a good person—just lost track of what I was doing. I promise you it will not happen again."

Following high school graduation, he sailed through a small respectable local college on athletic scholarships and the general perks and entitlements extended to jocks including: passing or better undeserved grades, special tutors, phony campus jobs, easy professors who adored jocks, and the aid of naïve girlfriends who wrote his essays and term papers. He also purchased classroom material like professors' tests, and class notes from frat-boy acquaintances. Finally his natural gifts in math and statistics, and his conning and bullying tactics helped.

In undergraduate school, he drank heavily; smoked pot; developed a habit of arguing angrily with professors about grades; cheated on tests, and stole test papers from professors' desks; brawled in the streets and bars; was arrested twice for assault (but was bailed out by campus cops and college administrative surrogates). Further, he impregnated two coeds, and told them when they asked for help: "You wanted it real bad, and I gave it to you real hard and good. Don't bother me about your baby. Maybe you will get lucky and the bastard will have beautiful blue eyes like mine." Promiscuity was not his core problem, but the shallow callous emotional relationships he effected with females along with his uncaring exploitation of them was a big problem. Moreover, he bullied his professors while arguing over grades; bullied male classmates; cut classes and verbally disrupted classrooms.

He bullied professors by occupying their office space in a threatening way; that is, by walking into their offices; standing very close to their desks; then towering over them; or by walking around to the side of professors' desks, kneeling down close beside them all while pleading one of his phony cases. These moves were made with calculated caution; that is, he never touched these professors and always allowed some arguable space between himself and them (his victims) should they make a formal charge, then he could proffer an arguable defense. (One of the authors has frequently observed this bullying tactic executed by students against professors, professors against professors, and administrators against professors. He had been a victim of one such demeaning and frightening tactics.) Academia, of all places, should not abide the physical bully or any other bully.

According to Ron's high school and college counseling office records he was not psychotic or neurotic, and was in touch with reality. He once said, "Suckers are born for real men like me to use. Some people are born to serve and real men like me are born to be served." During his senior year in college an Economics professor, who admired athletes, became his mentor. There had always been suckers around to overlook Ron's recklessness, and to help and encourage, "Such a good looking, and charming, intelligent athlete." This particular college mentor encouraged him to take an MA in Economics. Discouraged over not being selected to play basketball in the pros, and not keen about looking for a job (all he ever really wanted to do was play basketball and chase girls), Ron applied for admission, and was accepted in a Social Sciences Department housed in a regional, nearby university. He then told his mentor that Sociology was easier than Economics.

In graduate school, he drank less and eased up on pot, but did not stop conning, bullying, lying, cheating and chasing girls. He was not admired by other graduate students who tagged him as a conceited, untrustworthy bully and womanizer. With the help of senior coed English majors and that of two PhD professors from another university in the state (whom his father paid for services) he wrote an MA thesis, and later a marginal PhD dissertation. Many said he bullied and snowed his professors, some of whom, they said, were definitely afraid of him. The sad point is that Ron could have been a good student in graduate school without conning, and all the illicit aid he received; that is, had he not been encumbered with an apparent antisocial personality disorder. Certainly as evidenced by several test scores he possessed way above average intelligence, and he had special mathematical ability.

Following graduation, he quickly secured an assistant professorship in a bordering state's respectable university. How did this happen? Several reasons: (1) The enduring protection of his father and a doting mother. (2) Most of his high school and college delinquent, and criminal acts were not reported or recorded. (3) As a star athlete, he was overprotected by high school, college, and university coaches and administrators who covered up his shenanigans and antisocial acts to preserve institutional images. (4) As a cool, calculating, unscrupulous person and a consummate liar, he could talk himself out of trouble by shifting responsibility to others, or by contriving all sorts of plausible but spurious accounts. (5) A self proclaimed quantitative methods researcher (with some legitimacy) his type of service was in great demand. (Most Sociology departments in the southern region at the time were continually looking for professors with his quantitative credentials, in brief, a "numbers cruncher"—as they still are.)

Eventually he became a full professor because of his statistical, conning and bullying abilities, and later a department head for several synergetic reasons: (1) He was a compromise candidate; (2) He was supported by an administrator who adored star athletes; (3) A powerful numbers cruncher bloc's membership (though hesitant and wary) reasoned they could tame and corrupt "their boy"; (4) He promised to many that should he be appointed head, he would support more faculty promotions, tenure, and raises in the department (which he convinced them were long past due). In brief his colleagues underestimated him and made a Faustian bargain—and later on found they had been had. They rode a tiger's back and subsequently got emasculated and eaten up. (Perhaps they should have read more Rudyard Kipling.) However, some academics seem to get along well without "guts." These blind quantitative methodologists (or should we say technicians?) were preoccupied in Ron's case with statistical methodology *per se*, losing sight of what a researcher should be dealing with (theory, content, substance, triangulation, description, behavior settings, analysis, meaningfulness and significance of data, and results.) So busy with numbers and methods, they lost sight of the significance of their findings; published little other than conference proceedings, in-house working papers, and regional statistical reports—and lastly hired Ron.

Ron was one of these number crunchers who had been taught to concentrate on methods and so-called modals and experiments rather than theory, subject matter, the total research picture, or results. Eschewing scholarship and primarily interested in power, prestige, sex and money, he sized up the department quickly and targeted potential supporting cronies and enemies: (1) number-cruncher good ole boys who knew how to play academic games, (2) lazy upscale bubba type politicians who could be bought off (with bribes), (3) "weak sisters" and non-publishers—all potential supporters (4) scholars and publishers (usually but not necessarily the same) were irreversible enemies who must be run out of the department (or squelched) as soon as expeditiously possible.

Within five years Ron got rid of most of his enemies, and squashed and punished the remaining into submission. He dominated the department in all aspects through and by micromanagement, which he accomplished with: (1) the support of membership groups of 1, 2 and 3 above, that he cobbled into a cabal; and, (2) the acquiescence of a weak dean. Ron either chaired crucial committees or handpicked their chairs from a pool of his cronies; that is, the chairs of committees that made important decisions regarding: hiring, firing, tenure, promotions, salary, curriculum development (for both graduate and undergraduate programs); graduate school rules and regulations; and all disciplinary rules and decisions. Furthermore, he prepared and submitted the agendas for most departmental meetings and thereby controlled the time allowed for discussing each item on departmental meeting agenda. The committees chaired by his cronies were directed to contact him in person before and after departmental meetings to ascertain the outcomes he desired on agenda items. Sometimes these cronies were so obvious and direct in their preparatory remarks about agenda items, they would say to other committee members something like: "I think Dr. Ron expects us to make this decision ..." Ron's voting bloc also cowed and/or punished outsiders who dared to vote against his proposals.

He utilized the following tactics in broad outline form: conning, punishing, bullying, and mobbing (ganging up by several against one); game playing, rumor-mongering, spying, paper trailing, lying, character assassination, theft; and by violations of university rules whenever convenient and wherever he knew he could avoid getting caught or sanctioned for. Some of his idiosyncratic violations were falsifying recommendations; for example, those of PhD students seeking positions; violating the academic freedom and rights of professors; and a nepotism rule. He hired his wife (in a sub unit in the department) as one of his administrative assistants at a very comfortable salary, though she was not qualified for the position, and had no college degree.

The following additional examples (and sometime repetitions) of Ron's deviancy and sometime criminal acts are not (in all cases) listed in exclusive categories, because of overlapping. Therefore we submit a somewhat random list of some of these acts by way of illustration:

(1) <u>Conning</u>: Ron, despite his anathema, toward scholarship, put on countless bogus research and scholarship shows for the administration. For example, he set up a special survey research unit in the department he headed and staffed it with his favorite professors, along with the usual financial, clerical and technical support. After some administrative confusion, (who was responsible for doing what) this expensive pipedream project was terminated soon thereafter, when a duplication of services became obvious. He also touted and supported with released-time professors' aid, a five-year enology experiment whereby research and experiments were conducted ostensibly to produce a European-type grapevine which could equal that of California wine vines. This foolish project failed for obvious reasons. The very humid climate of the southeastern United States does not permit the growth of such vines. Eventually, this very expensive operation was eventually closed down (after five years of bluff).

(2) <u>Punishing</u>: Ron ran undesired professors out of the department or silenced

them by: restricting their salary raises, travel, and book order money; isolating them into ill equipped and distant office locations; withholding tenure or promotions; assigning them heavy teaching loads; denying them preferred courses to teach, denying them summer school teaching, sufficient clerical office help, and graduate student assistants; assigning them many 8:00 a.m. and evening classes; running them down verbally to all others, especially to graduate students and administrators (primarily face-to-face but not on paper which could be more easily challenged by a victim), and denigrating them in private meetings with cronies and administrators.

(3) <u>Bullying and Mobbing</u>: Ron at times invaded the personal physical space of these others in a threatening but somewhat veiled way; mobbed up with his favorite professors in the department he headed to malign or denigrate others; engaged in rumor mongering by spreading negative stories about those he did not like to some department members, colleagues and students in the department, and at professional meetings. Should any victim come to know that Ron was the source of these rumors and dare to confront him, Ron would caution said victim sardonically with threats like: "Don't mess with me, you know what happened to John who is no longer here. Stay away from me."

(4) <u>Spying</u> was Ron's forte. He used his secretary, clerical staff members, favorite graduate students and cronies in the observation and tracking of those he disliked, or felt threatened by because of their superior teaching/research or publication skills, or because of their disobedience. These operations targeted conversations and actions in classrooms, private offices, bars, parks, restaurants, apartments, hotels, professional meeting places, as well as the examination of written materials in private office and mail boxes within departmental offices.

(5) <u>Paper trailing</u>: Ron, via mail, departmental memos, and conversations planted negative and false information on professors, mixed in with routine mundane matters. For example, this paraphrased quote explains: "John, I hear you are reading a coauthored paper at the annual meeting. I have approved your travel request but have heard and noted from a very reliable source that you do not want your coauthor, Bill, to go with you. Well, he is going if you go. We have had difficulties with you before about such matters which have been noted; and, I also hear that you do not like any criticism from the hearing audiences when you present papers at professional meetings. This will have to stop. You should be more gracious. After all, you are representing our department in a way when you read papers. Of course I have chided you about this before (a lie). Please act a little more modestly. Maybe you forgot about this. I also hear you drink a little too much at meetings too. Good luck

on your trip and be nice to Bill." Most of the foregoing would be false and contrived, and Bill might have been a friend. The head would be building up a case against the victim with a false paper trail record. Should a victim confront him about this, he would shrug it off with remarks like, "People talk, you know. I listen, note, and record. Shucks, I'm busy; let's not talk about this trivial matter today." Such "trivial" matters did not appear trivial to his victim later on when confronted with an official negative paper trail as part of an investigation.

Ron the Con did not even have to deal in trivialities, and remarked to a victim one day after paper trailing him for two years thusly: "If this stuff keeps piling up about your behavior, I'm going to have to nail you to the cross and you sure aren't Jesus, and I'm no Roman soldier." When this targeted victim tried to verbally defend himself in a deferential reply Ron countered with: "I have at last got you by the balls! I don't have to stick a fork in you. Your are done. Get yourself a lawyer or still better an undertaker." Ron showed no mercy. According to several confirmed reports, Ron employed the best criminal lawyer in town on retainer to protect himself from any unforeseen charges that could be made against him; and, to help him do whatever he wanted to do with whomever. Usually the retained lawyer helped him support those he liked, or bring charges against professors he was trying to run out of the department, or squelch.

(6) Theft: At certain times when a victim was being investigated Ron or one of his students, cronies or clerical staff would either break into the victim's office or use unauthorized keys to enter in search of any useful derogatory information, or to find out what the intended victim was up to.

(7) Reconvening and Re-voting: Ron, at times when departmental meeting votes did not go his way, for example, on the tenure of a favorite, the imminent faculty's removal of an undeserving favorite student of his from the graduate program, failure of his favorite student on prelims or PhD finals), Ron would recall the involved committee members (and/or all departmental members) for a "revote." His excuse would go something like: "I have received new vital information about this case, which we must discuss further." Those who had voted contrary to his wishes were likely to get a call announcing a new meeting. He would, (knowing who they were), drop his usual interrogation methods and render opening remarks like: "I know you voted against John. You never liked him anyway. I want you to come to our new meeting about him with a more open and cooperative mind. After you hear the new facts in the case from me, I hope you will come to your senses." At times when

the votes or "re-votes" were unacceptable to him, he would pace the floor before committee members, stomp his feet, rail and shout. For example (paraphrased): "We must pass this man for political reasons. You people are dumb about real politics. He will be the first one of his kind to get a PhD with us. Think of what a good necessary representative he will make. We have to graduate PhDs like him. He's no great scholar and neither are any of us. Look at him (the student is awaiting his second reprieve PhD orals exam vote), he's got a good front and a good heart and academia must have more professors like him."

He would occasionally pressure one to reconsider his negative vote with a veiled verbal threat like, "You better wise up and vote right." Sometimes he would have the dean call and make his case to negative voters when one of his favorite PhD students failed, or when one of his favorite professors was not voted for tenure.

(8) <u>Flagrant discriminatory socializing</u>: Ron played basketball during so-called lunch periods with favorites (particularly, would-be jock students, professors, graduate students, and teaching assistants); socialized in his office behind closed doors with favorites; held private parties at his house with favorites; and he socialized exclusively with favorites at professional meetings.

(9) <u>Violations of other university rules</u>: (a) Ron overlooked the sexual violations of his favorites (for example, dating students), but punished others for the same conduct; (b) He pressured some of those he did not like to retire early by offering them questionable monetary rewards (for example, adding a year or two to their career service papers); (c) He selected all graduate school candidates for admission and assigned them to specific professors of his choice; controlled all graduate student reassignments; (d) He recommended and helped place weak and very marginal PhD graduates in positions for which they were not qualified (which hurt the department's professional image, probably his biggest mistake); (e) He forbade any professor or student to see the dean without notifying him in advance. (And the dean knew before any visitor reached his office from Ron's department who was coming and about what); (f) He took some disliked professor's favorite courses away from them, and assigned them to MA graduate students teachers. (This was one of the most demeaning and punishing things that he ever did.)

(10) <u>Hiring discriminations</u>: Ron never seriously considered hiring anyone from the upper Midwest, Northeast, or California, or those with PhDs from Ivy League or Ivy League type schools (like Chicago, Duke, Emory or Vanderbilt) or even some prestigious state universities (like the University of

Michigan, University of California, Berkeley, University of North Carolina, University of Virginia, University of Texas). He stated one day to a group of professors and students: "We will hire one of them when they hire one of us. You know, our PhDs are just as good as theirs" (a bad joke). Finally his personal relationships with some female MA and PhD students were in question; and, according to some reliable respondents he had sexual relationships with some of them.

Ron obviously resembles a classic antisocial personality disorder type that, many have said are rare in academia. And some have questioned the actual existence of such a type. We disagree. Ron would have probably been detected, fired, and jailed had he been employed in many other social institutions or first rate research institutions. Psychologists and psychiatrists have used different terms for those like Ron, and disagree about their number in the general population as well as their number in academia. The DSM-IV-TR uses the appellation antisocial personality disorder; H. G. Eysenck used extreme extravert or antisocial; Harvey Cleckley, who studied this same type all of his career, used psychopath (Clekley, 1982). Some use the term sociopath. The DSM estimates their number to be 3.6 percent in the "clinical population," or from 0.7 to 1.0 percent in the general population; Cleckley 3-5% in the general population; Eysenck 16% in the general population. We agree here with Eysenck and think it is easier for this type to avoid detection in academia than does any other personality disorder type. According to some scholars intelligent, highly educated persons of this type function sometimes successfully in certain segments of society (politics, business, and entertainment) but because of the difficulty in identifying them, we do not know their incidence in the general population (Widom, 1977; Barlow and Durand, 2009). "Subclinical studies" of psychopaths are not extensive or properly recorded, but some do indicate that intelligent, educated psychopaths do exist and prosper at the expense of others in highly placed positions. These have not undergone psychological therapy, and have not admitted they need to be treated.

Perhaps there are only a few as bold as Ron the Con in academia, but in our opinion many somewhat similar to him in personality type exist there. We suggest that all applicants for positions in academia be required to: (1) take standardized personality tests (as administered by clinical psychologists); (2) that a social background history be constructed for all; and, (3) that all candidates be interviewed by professionals without as well as within the department to which they are applying. The results of these three procedures and tests would be made available to those doing the hiring. Additionally, the results of the foregoing procedures could be used to detect not only those like or similar to Ron the Con but other personality disorder types as well.

Ron's negative social background factors and the weak structural educational settings he operated in were conducive to his serious deviancy pattern; however, his apparent entrenched antisocial personality disorder appeared to be the crux of his deviancy pattern. Structural or situational stress problems were not in evidence. There is no known treatment for "psychopaths" like Ron, because for one reason they do not relate to therapists, and their personality appears to many scholars like H. G. Eysenck to have a strong genetic base. Some mellow out at middle age, but this is of little help to academia. Those like him should not be hired, and when they become criminals like Ron they should be fired.

(7) Eve, the Vamp

Eve was born and reared along with her older brother in an upper class southern family in a small city in the deep south, where upper class members associated with upper middle class people because there were only a few of either of these two classes around. Her father who had inherited oil money, practiced law in his own law firm, and was known as one of the best trial lawyers in his county. Though a somewhat flamboyant and aggressive, extrovert, he possessed a stable, agreeable, outer-directed personality; and, he was an affectionate, dependable father and husband, but was overprotecting and controlling of Eve. Relationships with his wife and his well adjusted son, Tom were congenial, though he dotted on Eve, who reminded him of his mother (he said). Eve's mother, also an extrovert, held an AB degree from the same prestigious, private southern university as that of her husband, and like him she was a conscientious, intelligent conforming parent. She favored her son, Tom, who was also an extrovert. The harmonious wealthy family travelled together throughout the United States and Europe during yearly vacations.

Eve was an energetic, curious, temperamental, emotional, high strung, intelligent, attention seeking person as a child, youth and adult, who made and lost friends easily. She loved her brother but vied with him as well as others for continual praise and the center of attention. She frequently shifted relationships with decent interesting people in her own social circle whom she had sought out but became bored with them quickly and considered many ordinary people dull and provincial.

Highly suggestible, she agreed with significant others on different topics for brief periods, but was quick to change her mind, become equivocal and disagreed with them later on. Though charming, intriguing, articulate and amusing in a theatrical, acting-out way, and in her approach and reactions to mundane or serious subjects and happenings, she was simultaneously provisional and vague in her opinions and views on almost everything. She had an evanescent quality about her evocative of an alluring exciting romantic. Mercurial she was hard to read, and many said she was a bit flighty and flashy, a "social butterfly type" who was forever acting on a make-believe stage for adulation. From childhood she liked to dress up for her parents and guests, and play like a charming, seductive, beautiful lady, or beautiful heroine— using plenty of make-up, high heels, rich gold and silver shiny garments, exotic bracelets, earrings, and customized jewelry (an attire she tried to perfect as an adult). Though praised frequently and lavishly by her teachers, parents, brother, classmates, and friends for her good looks, intelligence, good grades, apparent suaveness, and dancing and acting performances in school and community plays (wherein she had to be the protagonist), she was only a fair actress without star stage presence élan, discipline or dedication. All this showmanship for praise and adulation was not enough. She wanted also to be a beauty queen as well as a diva, and was envious of her classmates who were crowned beauty queens. Her mother, father and brother tried to explain to her that though she was attractive as well as intelligent, there were others who had been judged prettier and more physically attractive (in terms of the fickle prevailing norms on what beauty was) than she; and, that she could not be superior to all females in everything all the time—especially the ever changing norms of feminine beauty. She would not listen because that was exactly what she wanted to be and consequently spent much time and a lot of daddy's money on expensive cosmetics, sexy exotic clothing, expensive jewelry, perfume and beauty-parlor treatments of one kind or another. Most of her female classmates shied away from close contacts with her because, as one said: "I like Eve but don't feel at ease around her. She has to be the best in everything. And she flirts with all the boys, even my boyfriend." She did have fleeting congenial relationships with a few, especially a number of her brother's friends. One perceptive male friend (she did not have boyfriends) told her once she had read too many novels about the old south (which she had), but that the southern bell she aspired to be was no longer de rigueur. She would not agree to the evident, and though admired by males, they considered her a to be a flirt and a tease as well as a superior person to them intellectually, and above all unattainable. She flirted with her classmates' boyfriends, and dropped them abruptly when she thought she had them psychologically hooked without permitting much physical intimacy—a restrained kiss was a maximum expectation from her. Normal and sensual in her sexual drives, and knowing that she looked sexy, she worked hard, and successfully at maintaining control of her urges. She really wanted to playact as a pure provocative virgin as well as a beautiful charmer, a femme fatale, an exciting but dangerous role, as she discovered later on.

At high school graduation she enrolled in her parents' almamater and like them graduated four years later with honors (magna cum laude). As an undergraduate she adapted, though most of her classmates thought her an attractive conundrum, who dressed up too elegantly at times, and too provocative at others. Most of her university dates were with freshmen, although she did go out occasionally with TAs, who dropped her quickly because she refused to go to bed with them, an expectancy they thought (erroneously) she had indicated. She flirted with two different married assistant professors during her junior and senior years who were initially interested, but quickly saw through her sexual game playing and shied away without any physical contact. Eve could never understand why she was dropped and wondered why males desired only shallow relationships with her, but contrariwise she never examined her reasons for suddenly and inappropriately dropping out of friendship relationships with them. "I just did because I could and wanted to," she would say when asked why she suddenly dropped a male friend with no apparent reason. For example, one of her roommates asked her once, "What in the world do you get out of these games? You turn eligible men on, and then off like a spigot without doing them. What is the point"? Eve replied, "Oh, it would take me forever to explain, and I really do nothing wrong. I don't hurt anybody. Some other girls do the same thing. And what's wrong with getting my silent kicks"? This was one of Eve's chief problems; she never could see that her erotic game playing and attention-seeking behavior was perplexing, unseemly, shabby, immoral and morally wrong. In her mind, she was only having fun as a part of her nature; and she answered her critics with exclamations like: "There is nothing wrong with me! Other girls do it." Had she sought some counseling or preferably professional psychological help, which her brother suggested, she might have avoided some of her difficulties. Female friends and her brother chided her about her shallow flirtations, and told her she was no longer in high school (where she had played the same charade) and that she must get more serious about her relationships with men. Instead of conceding, she justified her actions and disclosed the mental superiority she felt to most of all the men she met with a sexy but haughty mien which exacerbated her problem. In brief, she was conceited, emotionally flighty, romantic and immature for a person of her age and intelligence. Daddy had overprotected his little girl who was, to him, too good a catch for any man (which she agreed with, and she was for more intelligent than most of the men she met). Daddy had been a very strict and overweening father who had to pass on all of the boys she dated as a teenager, before she could go anywhere with them. When away at the university she still remained in close contact with her father; and, ask him for advice even on trivial matters. One male classmate told her, "You remind me of the old-pop song, *My Heart Belongs to Daddy.*" She did not disagree.

At graduation, bored and not wishing to return to her "provincial" home town, she said, without a desirable prospective mate, and, not ready to go to work, "a boring drab thing to do," she enrolled as an MA candidate in her university's English department, and explained to her parents: "After all I like novels. Maybe I'll learn how to put one together." When asked about boyfriends she explained with something like: "I can get one anytime. I'm just not ready to become involved and settle down." Her mother and brother (now in law school) expressed displeasure to her and to her father, about her flippant attitude toward males and the future. Her protective father told all: "She is a free spirit, leave her alone to work things out." Her brother retorted, "You mean give her more time to go find herself." "Something like that," her father replied. Despite her frivolity she was an excellent student in graduate school but her seductive and provocative habits at department socials and off-campus university parties continued. She would enter a social gathering or party dressed in a bejeweled, sexy, chic fashion and try to impress all the attractive males; that is, by utilizing her same old "turn on and off" tactics, which became a "dog and pony show" to many. She had to be not only the sexiest and most beautiful female there, but also the most intellectual and charming female present—forever the bell of the ball, a very tall order for any female.

Finally she hooked and consummated a shaky and very unrewarding sexual relationship with a PhD candidate, whom she persuaded herself to think an acceptable and easy catch—and it was high time, she said, for someone. She claimed the men she really preferred were already married or engaged and there was a gist of truth in her prospective (The authors have known some such females who typically married men far beneath them just to get a man). She knew her parents wanted her settled down or married; and, at the time there did not seem to be any eligible male prospects around. In brief she contemplated marriage for the sake of getting married under what she thought was family pressure, and chose a man whom she later called a ninny and a loser. "He was just there," she said later by way of explanation. She married following her MA in a civil ceremony away from home, because she said she and the groom were atheists which she admitted later was a lame excuse. Her parents were not pleased with the groom whom they considered (correctly) a wimp, but coped, persevered, and lent her moral and financial support, before and after her marriage. But, her father grieved over her misguided marriage for a long time. Back in school after her marriage she began work on a PhD as a graduate assistant, and continued her flirtatious masquerades which angered her weak willed, timid, anxious, jealous, and introverted husband. Consequently, he left her, dropped out of graduate school, and fled the state never to return. Eve explained to her family members and to anybody else who would listen, that her nerdy husband turned out to be a "sexless, hopeless, cold neurotic." "Then why did you marry him"? her parents and brother wanted to know. Silence was her first passive-aggressive answer. Later she told some classmates, "I'll never know why I married a jerk. Probably because, he was a weakling whom I could dominate and I thought I had to marry somebody." She was a female who several friends of her father told him she would make an excellent happy second marriage.

When Eve took her PhD she had coauthored two journal articles with her major professor, a fatherly figure; and, being a noted TA, she secured an assistant professorship in her state's major, public university. She then tried to cease open flirtations (she said) and dressed more conservatively, but remained discreetly seductive without trying (she said); that is, ostensibly concealing but simultaneously revealing with the sedate little black dress with its low-cut blouse exposing ample, well shaped breasts; the enticing smile, the slight undulation of her hips; and an occasional "accidental" brush against an eligible male target, etc. came about as second nature beyond her control (she claimed). She "dated" two different professors in her department (one married, one single) at the same time secretly; she thought, during this period, but the married professor's wife found out, and spread rumors about what she called, "The affair." Eve stopped seeing either of the two, and insisted she had not had sexual relationships with either (probably the case). The rumors eventually subsided and no formal complaints were made, but the department head and the dean warned her not to "date" anyone in the department, anymore. She complied.

Thenceforth Eve relieved of the fear of losing her position, worked hard, matured, somewhat and published three articles and one book. She developed into a good scholar and teacher, and dated men from out of the department occasionally whom she called, "innocuous scholars;" kept her office hours; mentored coeds who wanted to be professionals in one field or another; lectured authoritatively on southern writers, her specialty (for example, Eudora Welty, Thomas Wolfe, Mary Flannery O'Conner, W.G. Cash, William Faulkner, Edward Reynolds Price, etc.). She attended departmental faculty meetings regularly, showed no interest in academic politics or bureaucratic minutiae, belonged to no factions, and associated with only those who published. Female department members were polite but envious and wary because they knew about her past reputation and were not very forgetting or forgiving. "Few women are forgiving when it comes to sex," Eve said. However, their avoidance was depressing because she had tried hard to control her attention-getting behavior, which though subdued, continued when attractive males were present (she had wisely sought the help of a clinical psychologist who had treated her regularly following her divorce.)

When tenured, several colleagues thought it was too soon, and openly voiced disapproval, to which in response, Eve proclaimed she felt the envy of excellence. One year later a disgruntled female colleague with a scanty and mediocre publication record spread a rumor that Eve was having an affair with a married, full professor in the department. With pressure from inside and outside the department, and with a written complaint about the rumor on the department head's desk, and in the dean's office, the head reluctantly investigated the matter as quickly and secretly as possible. Both accused parties denied any physical sexual affair (though they had seen each other), and there was no official determination of the complaint's veracity one way or the other. However, there was a bitter split in the department regarding the head's and dean's indecision. Some clamored for Eve's dismissal in lieu of her past, and some others supported her and suggested the charges be discredited. The gossip continued, but no one seemed interested in the male professor's responsibility in the reported affair excepting his wife. Eve determined that too much damage had been done to her, the accused, and the department for her to remain. Therefore, she resigned under some attenuated pressure from the dean; and, secured a position in another prestigious university in the state. The dean said later, "Eve is an excellent professor and scholar but the Vamp had to go" (see Benedict 1992; Marcus 1989; Paglia 1994; May 2007).

Eve with the help of her clinical psychologist's professional help while in this new position; adjusted, matured, remarried to an older professor, mothered two children; and became a tenured full professor. Finally, she curtailed her flirtations though she never completely ceased her seductive mien. Her second husband's intellect matched hers, and according to her he understood her problem, and was a real man, like her father who understood her too. Certainly her inability to find a man of her stature (for a long time) was a part of her problem which many females in such situations face. Some of her type marry losers and like Eve even lose them. Eve's saga finally ended with near success, though she never could empathize with colleagues who expressed complaints about her seductive and flirtatious nature. "I'm only acting natural," she continued to say and she was in a personal way. (Eve's success has not been the case with several other females apparent, histrionic personality disorder types we have encountered in academia usually females.) The source of Eve's deviancy pattern seemed to be rooted in an apparent histrionic personality disorder. The negative social background factor of her relationship with her father contributed to her difficulties and to her deviancy—one and the same. Biological factors were also significant in her relationships with men. Unattractive females do not usually have her problems. Many males, especially those from traditional backgrounds are ambivalent about sensual, beautiful, intelligent, highly educated females like Eve whom they know to be superior to them. And many females of this type find it difficult to find suitable husbands in western cultures. Contrariwise in many eastern Asian cultures this problem is either nonexistent or attenuated by customs whereby parents play a significant role in their children's choices of marital mates.

Eve, though never denying her sensuality and her sexual freedom, suffered in what she termed, a chauvinistic society, but she did acknowledge her personality flaw, and tried to correct it. She also faced structural and situational stress problems: (1) cultural chauvinism; and (2) sexual dating problems tied-in with her intelligence, beauty, and her insatiable crave for attention. This type is hard to identify during the hiring process, and even later on. They appear to be intelligent, friendly and outgoing, dedicated people with a dramatic flair, who apparently would be good teachers. Over time, however, they may become seductive, showy, emotional, flighty; and, begin to play games that please them but distress others. Further they may create jealousy among department members, and real physical sexual affairs may or may not ensue. However, it is the banter, dramatic and emotional exhibition, flirtation, jealousy, and attention-getting game-playing that foster most academic disruptions which vamps engage in rather than sex per se. Professors are adept at game-playing and need not be burdened with attention getting sexual charades engineered by vamps like Eve. Histrionic types should not be selected in academia; and, those who are selected, when and if discovered in problematic situations should be dismissed, should they not seek professional psychological treatment and cease their antics. Those like Eve should be retained; that is, should they be mistakenly hired.

(8) Todd the Stud, the Sexual Deviant

Todd, an only child was born and reared in a lower middle class family in the urban upper south. His parents had a high school education; worked regularly in blue-collar occupations; possessed normal, extroverted, stable personalities, and were well adjusted in a working-class neighborhood. Todd, mesomorphic in body build, was a physically strong, extrovert, and a leader in school in contact sports. He was proud of his nice looks, physique, and success with many girls; and, his friends admired his athleticism, leadership qualities, and sexual successes. His teachers looked upon him as an exceptional youth among rowdy others in his neighborhood.

Despite his so-called successful sexual behavior (so defined by some) his parents did little to modify it beyond verbal disapproval, because they reluctantly abided this conduct as a negative cultural expectation among many of their peers. He made good grades in school, and was obviously an intelligent, pleasing, friendly youth. Both parents were proud of him because of his overall obedience and good grades, and performance as quarterback on his high school football team. Todd was a very special person to them and his relatives because he was good with books as well as sports which was not usually the case in his milieu. He liked girls; girls liked football players, so he made out well in the dating game, perhaps too well. During his senior year he was caught in consensual sexual dalliance with a couple of girls beneath the football stadium, and although there was some talk, and the girls' parents complained to school authorities, his coaches and the principal hushed and covered up the incident, thereby avoiding school or court sanctions. Further, Todd's grandmother, who lived in his area, disciplined him verbally for "entertaining" girls in his room at her house occasionally without a chaperone. She did caution him about these episodes, but according to Todd: "It was really no big deal." Again, Todd's parents beyond a little scolding took no firm disciplinary action concerning these sexual escapades.

Following graduation, he was recruited to play football at a liberal arts college nearby where he adapted academically, but not conduct wise. He played football and basketball; made above average grades; and made out with several coeds simultaneously. The latter resulted in trouble when he and a teammate were accused of sexually molesting a coed in a men's dormitory. As in high school, the case was fixed; that is, the coaches along with campus police, and the school administration cooperated with the coed's attorneys and her parents in settling the case out of court. Beyond a warning no school sanctions were applied. His parents paid the steep bill.

After completing his undergraduate degree Todd became somewhat more discreet in his risk-taking sexual behavior; enrolled in a respectable university graduate school; made above average grades; and, became a teaching assistant. An average graduate student he completed an MA and PhD in United States History. Though no untoward sexual activities were reported, he was still known to be a promiscuous playboy, which was never noted in his school records. However, the glamour of the stud role in undergraduate school had worn thin and many of his classmates did not approve of his promiscuous lifestyle, however, they remained silent as did his professors who also knew his story line. To him, his lifestyle was normal, so he said. "Girls liked it and I liked it," was his rationale. When his father cautioned him about this behavior, he responded with, "Don't worry pop, I use protection most of the time, but most girls prefer the real thing and I don't hurt anybody." He had to know better.

Upon completing the doctorate, Todd was recruited again, this time as an assistant professor by an acceptable state university. Throughout several years as an assistant and associate professor, he apparently made a good adjustment; married and sired two children; performed well in the classroom, and was considered an adequate professor; however, his publication record remained too thin for further promotion. So "Seeing the writing on the wall," as he said, he applied for and obtained an administrative position as an assistant dean, though still teaching a few undergraduate courses. Two years later, he and two professor friends were reported to a vice president for renting and using jointly a three bedroom house as a sexual playpen where female students and staff members went for sex with the three renters. The vice president conducted a secret investigation after which Todd and the other two renters were forced to resign without further official sanction, and the case went away without fanfare.

Todd soon took a position at another university as an associate professor and associate dean rumored to be lenient about campus sexual conduct. Reportedly, he became well adjusted and a good teacher and administrator. Todd never denied his extramarital conduct that caused him trouble, and maintained consensual sex between two adults, married or single was normal. However, he stated to close friends that all couples should be discreet and that not being so was "morally wrong." Many believe he had received a "golden parachute" from the university that had forced him to resign. He was finally forced to resign again over another scandalous affair with a married colleague, another administrator. Then he dropped out of academia.

In summary, Todd was an intelligent and competent teacher though a flagrant womanizer, who had been promiscuous since youth, and was not sanctioned or corrected for what he called, "being a normal male." His "problem" had been glossed over, and at one point had lent him prestige as a stud. Stubbornly and persistently he denied the "stud image" and argued that he was only acting out the role of a normal male. His movement from one sex partner to another defined his indiscretions rather than sex act *per se,* and fostered most of his problems. Perhaps he should not have been hired in the first place, and he would not have been, had his mentors been more open and helpful about his record. Factors in Todd's social background, such as permissive attitudes toward sex, and lax parents and mentors who failed to educate and discipline him regarding his frivolous attitudes toward, and conduct with, females augmented and sustained his deviancy pattern. Structural factors, like the permissiveness of his college and university professors and administrators also contributed. Todd's stubbornness in his failure to perceive a different cultural view towards sexual conduct other than his own was crucial to his maladjustment. He probably had a narcissistic personality disorder. He never really appreciated females as equal sex partners. Females to him were primarily sex objects.

There is much talk about sex in academia, and it is difficult at times to determine which rumors are true, and whose sex norms are being violated. Though sexual conduct norms vary from one campus to another, professors and administrators, who practice sexual promiscuity on campus, are deviant trouble makers. Those with Todd's lifestyle, attitudes toward females, and narcissism do not belong in academia. Should he have received professional counseling about sex early on he might have lived a more careful and wholesome life, and had a healthier attitude toward females. He should have been directed to psychological counseling in high school and in college. His type if mistakenly hired in academia should be directed to psychological counseling when first detected, that is should the decision is made to keep said type. Those who do not improve by ceasing their promiscuous lifestyle following treatment should be fired.

(9) Sky Pilot, Teacher the Preacher

Teacher was born into an upper middle class family of five in the suburbs of a deep southern city, the eldest child of a retired, prosperous farmer, a college-educated, conservative, religious, man with many friends. His mother was a happy, adjusted, housewife, who held a bachelors degree from a liberal arts college where she met and married his father. A well adjusted ambivert, she deferred to a traditionally dominant husband (an extrovert), thereby making for a congenial family life. She had more to do with her three daughters than her husband who provided more guidance for Teacher. Discipline was strict and puritanical, and at times overbearing. Teacher from childhood assumed the role of a secondary domestic leader to his father, and tried to help micromanage his sisters' and household affairs which amused his mother and her friends, but not his sisters. Things had to be just right, his way, including the mode his mother's and sisters' dress style. As a youth through high school, he was an avid and regular churchgoer, and took biblical percepts literally—which his friends thought too fundamentalist for membership in his family's mainstream Protestant church. Some perceived his quest for his self perfection and that of others did not spring solely from pious good will, but also from a rigid, perfectionist personality. Others observed that despite his known about above average intelligence, he became distressed or angry when mundane household decisions did not meet with his stubborn preciseness and moralistic standards. For example, his sisters wore too much lipstick; their dress though sedate in style was too revealing; someone said "bad words," or did not show up on time. All family members hoped with time and education he would mature out of some of his "silly, rigid, and puritanical notions." He did not, and discounted any rational scientific, explanations that negated his literal religious interpretations of the Bible. Church goers therefore refrained from religious discussions with him.

Teacher graduated with above average grades from high school, where he adjusted, but was known as stiff, formal, serious minded loner who spent little time on the playground, though a mesomorph. He then went on to earn a degree in Theology and Sociology from a local noted Protestant seminary, where he was known again as a loner and serious boy. He married young, at the age of twenty-one, which prompted some of his classmates to opine in a jocular fashion: "To assuage the sins of misplaced lust." Some others disagreed with the remark, "What sins"? they asked. Following graduation with an AB and later with a BD he preached for two years, but found this to be "unrewarding both spiritually and monetarily," he said. Bookish and politically conservative, he then sought a PhD in political science at a respectable state university in order to teach somewhere at the college level, where he made average grades and took a MA and a PhD in Political Science (that is, with the financial aid of his parents). At graduation he had a wife and three children, and his mother said he had a short childhood, and appeared much to grown up even when a teenager. Though intelligent, his wife was traditional and just submissive enough to abide his rectitude, monolithic, rigid moralistic views and demands. With the PhD he secured an assistant professorship in a neighboring state's respectable university, though some department members there were dubious of a "sometime retread preacher." Hardworking, bureaucratic, and politically savvy within a few years he was a full professor and department head, and then said to some close friends: "Now I can do things my way." When the school's administration began to require publications for promotion which he did not have, he applied for and received a full professorship back home at his almamater. His teaching area, the Sociology of Religion, matched what the department was looking for, and he replaced a womanizer whom the department had forced to retire. Teacher's moral credentials loomed beyond reproach, however one perceptive department member said later on, "We replaced one deviant with another, though of different stripes."

Teacher initially made a satisfactory adjustment in his new position but over time he began to show what he really was: a smooth speaking, formal, rigid, overzealous, detail man who did not express empathetic feelings and was envious of those more competent than he. As a strong family man and a deacon in his church, he was work rather than pleasure oriented, and respected in his off-campus community. He became the department head's unofficial assistant, and the departmental paper-pusher, a detail man who was at his desk every morning at eight o'clock when he stayed until four or five, Monday through Friday when not in class. Not preoccupied with students who found him fair but too strict, dour, dull and tedious, he occupied himself with a mass of paperwork (budgets, supply orders, class schedules, travel requests, etc) and a multitude of forms that had to be filled out every day and routed to various campus administrative offices.

The former head of a Political Science department, Teacher claimed that he had "stepped down" from head in order to devote more time to research and publishing, a claim called an inside joke even among his supporters. The real reason was that as a perfectionist, he demanded that everything must be done his way, especially matters pertaining to rules, class schedules, course requirements, regulations and routine departmental forms and reports. This behavior pattern persisted and irritated many who could not understand his obsession with trivia (to them) and paperwork (called housekeeping chores by others). His sobriquet, Sky Pilot was bestowed by "intellectuals," a department faction that published. No one called him anything other than Dr. Teacher, some called him Dr. Teacher the Preacher because of his stiff mien and inability to take a joke, especially should he be the object thereof. Most called him Sky Pilot behind his back. His usual response to jokes on himself was projections such as: "Oh no, not me, you." And all would understand from his sober facial expression, tone of voice and defensive body language, that he was not amused. No laughs, no smiles, no signs of physical relaxation; therefore, few were humorous in his somber presence. When one professor remarked to another that Sky Pilot needed a joke book, the other retorted: "No, even if Sky Pilot reads it, he wouldn't get it with his rigid frame of mind. You can't teach a sense of humor."

Sky Pilot was the self appointed leader of the department's "home boys" (insiders from the region who published little), so named by a group of outside publishers from without the region and insiders, southerners who published. All who published were called "intellectuals" by those who did not. Southerners who did not publish and some outsiders and independents (outsiders and insiders) made up a mixed group of non-publishers, and mediocre teachers, called "weak sisters." Homeboys, the most powerful departmental bloc, were full professors who got most of what there was to get.

Sky Pilot's job as he saw it was in addition to that of presumed assistant to the head was that of: keeping his bloc in power by massaging the head's ego (convincing him that the preservation of the status quo was in his and the department's best interest); and, keeping the homeboys and their supporters in line. Accordingly, Sky Pilot tried to convince the head that: there was too much emphasis in academia on publishing; and that those in the department who devoted their time to publishing, and attending national meetings regularly were intellectual snobs and poor teachers, and "not one of us." He could not see that research results gave one something to teach. The head did not accept this point of view, but he respected Sky Pilot as a senior department member who knew how to do his paperwork.

Sky Pilot wrote only in-house printed statistical reports and treatises which he erroneously claimed as publications. He and his bloc prevailed because the head thought he needed their support to keep his job (which he did not). The head, a scholar and a competent administrator, was a homeboy only by birth. One of Sky Pilot's tactics was an attempt to discredit all intellectuals. For example, he befriended and praised them to their faces, but damned them with faint praise in the company of his club members, minor administrators, graduate students and independents (but, rarely put anything negative on paper). Further, he trashed them to the head and to the dean when in private protected settings.

One of his sneaky rouses was to pressure department members to reconsider votes on matters he did not agree with. For example, he would say: "Let us reconsider, pray and reconvene, and vote again. We must not just routinely throw this poor boy out (one of his favorite losers who had flunked his prelims before and now again). We might ruin him if we kick him out." Prayer and reconvention gave him more time to convert opposing professors. He occasionally made late night telephone calls urging colleagues to change their initial votes at reconvening. He would say something like, "You know the department head doesn't agree with you. He sees things our way, you better wise up." One of his sneaky tricks backfired, when he proposed in a departmental meeting that each professor grade each and every other professor on a list of thirty items that supposedly could be used to rank all on professional competency; that is, render colleagues' evaluations of one another the results of which would be given only to the head. Of course, Sky Pilot and members of his bloc had already done their ranking, giving themselves very high scores, and very low scores to the intellectuals. After perusing the silly, skewed rankings, the department head destroyed them and without open comment, refused to discuss the matter further. Sky Pilot also tried to persuade the department head to call important meetings early in the morning (before eight), when he figured the intellectuals would not be around. He tried to persuade graduate students not to vote for some proposed visitors (outside scholars at times invited and paid to speak to the students) he disliked. Additionally, he had his "sacred cow" graduate student TA do a little spying for him now and then. When caught in one of his ruses, he remarked one day: "You can't blame a man for acting in his enlightened self interests." He expected homeboys to drop by his office for occasional chats; that is, by way of paying him homage as their leader.

Sky Pilot's shenanigans and deviancy pattern reminded one author of some of the students in the School of Religion he had known as a graduate student. For example, it was okay for Sky Pilots to go out with your girl, but betrayal should you ask one of theirs out. The ministers he knew had remained men of the cloth and did their preaching behind elegant pulpits in large prestigious urban churches, where they had jockeyed around and "politicked" to preach in. Finally hitting the jackpot they found status in a large church that paid their ministers high salaries along with attractive fringe benefits.

In summary, Sky Pilot herein appeared to be a rigid moralistic, obsessive-compulsive, personality disorder type. To him his dishonest means were justified by moralistic ends. Such personality types are disruptive, troublesome characters in academia as well as in other formal organizations. Perhaps in their own minds they do no wrong. For example, Sky Pilot turned in a formal report charging a single colleague (supposedly a friend) with having an affair with a mature coed in his class whom he later married. Said colleague resigned. Sky Pilot, the squealer, later had second thoughts, and though he had finally gotten religion, pertaining to this matter, he could not be consoled. A colleague to whom he cried and confessed suggested: "Go see your preacher." Sky Pilot's kind is unacceptable in academia where professors should have open inquiring minds. Self contained he faced no remarkable structural or situational, stress problems throughout his "saintly" life; that is until his last academic betrayal, which gave him misgivings. Serious rule violators like Sky Pilot should be fired.

(10) Peter, the Rabbit

Peter, an only child, was born into a middle class, mainstream Protestant minister's family in the upper south. His father held an MA degree in theology from a noted private university, and was ordained to preach and did, in a medium sized church in a medium sized city. A mild mannered introvert, he was pleasant, conscientious, and emotionally stable. His parishioners considered him to be a moderately successful minister, a good solid husband, and a wholesome, easygoing, caring father. Peter's mother, an ambivert, a housewife and former church secretary in a large urban church, held an AB degree, and functioned as an honest, efficient, and affectionate wife and mother. The parents' relationship was equalitarian and Peter grew up in a harmonious, stable, economically modest, but adequate home. However, he had no close friends, and felt isolated from his father's parishioners and their families. Introverted and shy, he opted for the study of music and books, and avoided rough and tumble play activities for which he was not equipped either physically or emotionally, and associated with a few male and female acquaintances of his own shy type, whom he met at church services. Moderately physically handicapped in that he did not see or hear too well, he was timid and withdrawn, and was nicknamed Rabbit because of his soft, flexible personality. He also had a tendency to avoid conflict situations (verbal or physical), and a need to please others even when he knew he was right and they were wrong about any discussion or situation. When faced with a problematic situation or conflict, he procrastinated, retreated, gave up, or ran away rather than take a stand, for fear of being rejected or discarded as a friend. These traits appeared in childhood and remained with him throughout adulthood. His assets included above average intelligence; a gentle, kind, helpful, cooperative disposition; consistent and industrious work habits as a loner, a drive to "do right;" and, wishes to please others.

Negatively, he could be stubborn and passive-aggressive when he sensed (emotionally) that he was under attack, even when facts to the contrary were obvious to interacting others. Not preoccupied with ambition he preferred to take follower rather than leadership roles in play and work situations. He married young, age twenty one, sired three children; and thereafter was emotionally supported, protected and dominated by an intelligent, ambitious, strong-willed wife, a marked stable, extrovert. The backbone of the family she did a good job including: shopping and running the household; cooking and entertaining his colleagues, and work superiors; rearing three sons; taking care of finances and staying off creditors; standing up for him in situations which he tried to run away from; protecting him from discreditors; bolstering his ego when he felt defeated; and politicking for him among his peers and supervisors. She was a remarkable dominatrix.

With the encouragement of his parents and wife he took three degrees (AB, MA, and PhD degrees) from a prestigious, private university in the upper south where he made good grades and studied under two noted scholars in a Sociology department that specialized in Demography. He made no close friends among his classmates though they accepted him as a passive studious little man; confined his social activities to wife and family where he felt safe and comfortable; and, eased his way along with a retiring self deprecating persona. Following the PhD he secured a position in a first-tier southern university's Sociology department headed by one of his former professors where he was eventually promoted to an associate professorship. When this eminent head took a position elsewhere, the new head considered his teaching competence so-so, and his publication record too thin. New professors were hired, old ones left, and Peter no longer felt secure. Realistically fearing eventual expulsion or no further promotion, or favorable salary increases, he sought another position elsewhere in the south. The only position open in the region that he thought he could qualify for at the time was a headship in a known about troubled department in a nearby state. Never wishing to be a department head, Peter nevertheless applied for the opening, because (so he thought) he had to have some job in academia somewhere. He knew full well the hiring department was split between twelve-month survey researchers and nine-month liberal arts types (the former referred to as "seed bags," the other as "nerdy flakes.")

Both blocs viewed Peter as a short, pudgy, shy, sensitive candidate who was weak in leadership qualities, and research; and, that his publication record was very thin. However both admired his quiet scholarly front, and his prestigious degrees. Moreover, they thought, "this weak introvert" could be manipulated. The two blocs were endemic to many southern Sociology departments at the time: (1) those who considered the discipline a science requiring professors trained in and proficient in quantitative methods whose research endeavors centered on statistical measurable data samplers, polls and models; (2) those who did not view the discipline as a science, but rather as a subject devoted to the study of sociability and group relationships, and society that required ethnographic, biographical, historical accounts, case studies, and participation observation in gathering and analyzing qualitative data. This division had split the discipline into two camps nationwide into "numbers crunchers" and "observers." Peter was hired as a compromise number-crunching-candidate among several more competent applicants for the position that department members could not agree on. Being a southerner helped. Initially he tried to straddle the fence by appeasing both blocs, but this did not work because each membership supported him (privately and publically) when he approved and signed off on policy and procedures that satisfied its agendas. To them then he was viewed as a democratic, easy going administrator; but when he acted otherwise they railed against him to staff, professors, students, and administrators. Then he was a would-be dictator.

Sometimes his policies and procedures were questionable or ambiguous, and therefore unacceptable to either side which made for further splits, mixed loyalties, and disapprovable among members of both camps; then, he was a wishy-washy to both sides and called behind his back Peter the Rabbit; and, then ridiculed, mocked and laughed at by some. To the students, staff and other campus dwellers, he was at all times known as Peter the Rabbit, a sweet and tender person who never wished to hurt anyone, but one who could not lead anyone or stand up for his rights.

Following three years of this "schizophrenic" situation, the Rabbit threw in his lot with the "seed bags," those whom he thought had the most pull with the administration, and did receive more funds from the state and Federal governments. Thenceforth, he became a "seed-bag" puppet, of those who ran the department "their way" and punished others. Consequently and subsequently the liberal arts professors, "flakes" rebelled after five years and demanded redress from the administration. After eight years of academic hell the Rabbit was removed from office, but remained on in the department as a full professor with tenure and the same salary he had received as the former department head. He had been awarded premature tenure when hired, so desperate was the administration to find someone to head a long time leaderless department. All liberal arts professors were finally awarded twelve month appointments, should they so desire; and, an outsider was eventually found to head the department. Peter the Rabbit, drifted on as so many rabbits do in academia, with a low profile in a vacuous career. Therefore, not really a loser (monetarily) but a winner by default who smiled as he went to the bank, relieved of his former administrative problems; was situated in a cushy position for the rest of his life, a tax payer's burden who could not teach well, publish or administrate. Some of his kind flourish in academia.

In summary, "rabbits," like Peter tend to be frail physically, intelligent, wishy-washy, dependent, passive-aggressive personality types, who are apparently easygoing but stubborn when they feel cornered. He probably had a dependent personality disorder. As a rule Rabbits do not purposefully hurt others and tend to be tentative, unsure of anything, uneasy, edgy, anxious, and unable to stay on course for long periods. They are not usually good teachers, writers or researchers. For example, Peter told a colleague once that he wrote only one or two drafts when preparing a manuscript for journal publication consideration. "I get tired of it after that," he said. No wonder he had a thin publication record. One can quickly see that these uncertain weak sisters are frequently strongly dependent on significant others such as their wives, manipulators, and bosses—and bullies. As administrators they try to be too nice to everybody at all times (as the Rabbit attempted) and wind up pleasing nobody. Easily pushed around they do not belong in academia. Peter did face severe departmental structural and situational stress problems which contributed to his dishonest, wishy-washy deviancy pattern—primarily deviancy of omission rather than commission. His wife tried to take care of his many situational stress problems by bolstering him up; and placating his detractors. Candidates like Peter should not be hired in academia and if so when detected they should be required to undergo psychological treatment or dismissed should they not comply. Retention would depend as with other cases on treatment success.

(11) Byrd the Nerd

Byrd was born into an upper middle class family in the deep south where he grew up in a pleasant, stable, affectionate and comfortable home in the suburbs of a medium sized city. His father was a well adjusted introvert, a successful orthodontist, and a kind, quiet, unassuming, serious minded man who stayed home and read books (primarily professional, literature) when off duty. His mother, a former CPA, was a very intelligent, attractive, extroverted housewife. Both parents doted on their only child Byrd, a wiry in build, intelligent, stable, well adjusted introvert. Self contained and with only a few close friends he developed into a quiet rather restrained person who preferred to read and play alone at home, with educational toys. He adapted to home, community and school situations, though his parents and friends noted that he was a little too tidily dressed and his clothes had to match, and always be neat and clean. His mother thought he made undue efforts to keep his room and possessions orderly; that is, things had to be always put away in the right place. He liked and associated with classmates who were like him: nice, obedient, quiet, peaceful and serious minded people who were interested in science and books.

Byrd was overly conscientious about, tasks and school lessons; and wanted his mother's or father's help in double checking all of his school reports from elementary school through high school. Homework (essays, book reports, etc.) were carefully and studiously prepared and turned in late at times. Leisure time objects and school paraphernalia had to be kept in a proper order; however he had a problem with completing school and everyday projects, and his mother at times had to force him to finish schoolwork and home projects. Though strong and healthy, he shied away from physical contact sports and all risky behavior, and he liked demure, sedate girls; and, he avoided contact with rowdy and risk-taking classmates. Throughout high school, college and graduate school he experienced special friendly relations only with females with whom he had mutual caring relationships. Though sexually normal, he was not promiscuous.

With high grades, and SAT scores, and good study habits he took an MA and PhD in Economics from two different private, prestigious universities in preparation for an academic career as a professor. He adapted well to university life, and was accepted and admired by his classmates and professors who considered him to be very scholarly, ambitious, reserved, "straight" (meaning square) who was occupied with only a few close friends. He dated quiet, serious minded girls occasionally; drank a few beers with classmates at student hangouts, but avoided "night life" and any earmarks of an exciting lifestyle— carousing males, promiscuous females, and feminists frightened him. Sexual relationships could wait.

Following the PhD he married a modest, petite, attractive former schoolmate an ambivert who held an MA degree, and secured a position in a first-tier public state university. He adjusted well during his first year, during which time he taught undergraduates and prepared journal articles to read (and later to publish) at professional meetings. He continually worried about balancing his time between teaching, research, and publishing, and spent most of his time in his office at school or in his home office. He spent considerable units of time in his university office with students out of class beyond office hours. His wife, now pregnant with their first child, told him that he could not educate all of them to be scholars like himself, but he tried to do just that and worried about students poor performance, as he put it. His preciseness and expectations encouraged students not only to study, but to depend on him unnecessarily.

Of medium build, and fairly nice looking in a nondescript way, he did not stand out in a crowd or on campus. Well prepared with a serious mien he lectured adequately, but his forte was the individual scholarly attention he gave students in his office after class. Students quickly found this out and swamped him with their class needs in his office (for his classes and their other classes as well). He found it hard to let go of anything—teaching, tutoring, researching, or office educating.

Colleagues paid little attention to his problem because he was not in their way; did not compete with them; did not teach graduate students; and, he was not interested in departmental affairs. In brief he was just another assistant professor to them who was trying to get along.

When promoted to an associate professor, things changed. Although no polymath, he could and did teach well, crunch the numbers, do case studies, construct tables, schemas, graphs, and models; and, do the rest of what economics professors engage in. His fields of interest required both qualitative and quantitative methods that usually required two kinds of professors, but you got two in one with him. He could, and did, do it all. In time he published a lot on his own and coauthored with others in the department, though he did not really like to coauthor for two reasons: (1) He had always preferred to work alone and thus accept full responsibility for his work; (2) He knew he was being used by some professors who could not publish without him. On the other hand, he did coauthor with some colleagues because he thought he had a moral and educational duty to help others. He also received an internal reward for teaching others. In brief, he was a born teacher and sucker for his students and colleagues—quiet a burden. He was busy in his office all day when not in class, and most weekend days at home in his hideaway den, a detached lair attached to his garage, where a door-mail slot provided communication with his wife, children, and the outside world. Every now and then he would exit for his kids, and romp with them, his dog, and his mate briefly; and, then back to work. A friend would drop by every once in a while for a chat, but no one else was let in except his dog (for an occasional pat on the back). He wrote at an old roll-top-desk that filled most of his scanty work space. There was no phone to run him crazy as there was in the other part of his domain and "at work in the mind' factory," as his wife called the university. His TA did a lot of his office paperwork, but never enough. The problem was not his alone, but his students' needs and the aid he gave to some of his colleagues. The labor involved in putting things together for them, and then the interminable explanations that had to be made were too much. At times he felt like all were devouring him. In short, he loved the chains that kept him from his other loves, and his family. He never could balance the time required for his different academic duties and responsibilities; that is, as he envisioned needs and time. His uncommon willingness to serve students and professors rendered him acceptable to all departmental factions; however, much of his aid to professors was not really appreciated, and some he helped grew envious of his talents, which he could not understand.

He was even tempered, comfortable in his own skin and not involved in department politics. His attitude was: "Run the show any way you want to, just leave me alone to do my thing." This seemed more than just pleasing to most of his colleagues who did not have to worry about him one way or the other; unless and until they needed his research help. The point is that in brains and knowledge he outstripped most of them by far. In brief his colleagues possessed a compulsive sucker. Even when an associate professor with tenure he stayed away from bureaucratic departmental decisions; did not compete for graduate students; did not insist on salary raises or summer teaching; did not compete for anything there was to get. A humanitarian or a sucker (or both) he stood ready to give academic aid to anybody in any way. Moreover, he was modest and actually self effacing. His wife did not approve of all of his "humanitarianism" and wondered why he was really all that nice. Maybe something else was driving him, and she asked him once, "If you are so damn smart and helpful, why don't you make more money and spend more time with your family? We have two children and they are more important than your precious students and so-called colleagues." This question amused Byrd in a way and reminded him, he said, of a line from an old pop song he had heard once wherein a female sang to her lover: "Get out of here and make me some money too," a song by Patty Page.

His chief, pressing problem involved both undergraduate and graduate students who complained to the department head that he did not give them enough after-class time. They had grown use to his out-of-class-time and wanted more—especially for his help with their research needs. In brief, he was an out-of-class professor whose services were always in demand. He tried to explain to them and to the head of the department that he was only one man with a limited amount of time and energy to help all students, some of whom were not taking his courses. The head, as usual, tried to please all parties with a snow job that made no constructive decisions about the matter. He should have lent help to an idealistic, compulsive, workaholic, a real departmental jewel, both a do-gooder and a sucker. For example, he could have hired an assistant professor to help him or directed other professors to extend him aid.

Byrd's graduate students thought him a better classroom teacher than his undergraduates, but they had basically the same complaint. One outspoken one reported to the head, "Dr. Byrd knows his stuff, and I know he's a scholar, but when he is out in the field, or in his office writing his stories, or at some damn meeting, how in the hell do I get somebody to direct my dissertation? Dr. So and So sure as hell doesn't have the know-how to help me. Why don't you hire another Byrd man"? No matter how hard Byrd worked to meet the needs of his students, other professors and simultaneously do his research, he could not. He found himself in what he called, "a double bind." He tried to ease his problem with the help of his TA, but that was not enough. One TA remarked, "I don't mind helping the undergraduates, but why in the hell should I help some grad student on his PhD dissertation? Shit, man, I haven't finished my MA thesis yet." The problem escalated and Byrd's colleagues finally exemplified their jealousy and lack of concern when the head asked two of them to help Byrd out. One said: "I would like to help, but it is not my fault that he chewed off more than he can swallow; and, I myself am overloaded. You gave him a reduced teaching load, not me, and I asked for one. I think the problem is that he wants to be a full professor before his time." Another professor spoke: "Byrd is good, but so are the rest of us. You have given him more privileges than us, hell; he's been out of the country twice. If I had his teaching load, I could publish like hell too. Let that exalted genius come down to earth. He has been flying too high; I can't do anything for him. I can't even take care of my own red wagon; he is too damn popular and nerdy anyway."

The pressure mounted, and finally at his wife's insistence, Byrd consulted a clinical psychologist who interceded for him with the departmental head. Byrd, overwhelmed and mentally exhausted, was given a half year's leave with pay, a sort of sabbatical not yet earned. Finally, another professor was hired, and when Byrd returned to the campus, the new hand was there to assist him. Byrd found out the hard way that no man is indispensable; and, that anyone can be overworked and face mental exhaustion. Byrd's clinical psychologist found no serious underlying personality disorder that could not be modified and that his obsessive-compulsive disorder could be assuaged, with treatment and the cooperation of others. Structurally his department head could have provided for a more equitable workload. Situationally his colleagues could have been more cooperative and less envious. His obsessive-compulsive personality evidenced by his work habits and perfectionist demands upon himself had to be tampered down. Such types do harm to themselves and their family, as well as incite the envy of colleagues; and, thereby contribute to the drama of deviancy. Despite this; academia could use more of these over committed types in an attenuated form. Perhaps some of Byrd's uncooperative colleagues should have consulted a clinical psychologist about their extreme envy and unwillingness to help a fellow teacher. Byrd eased up somewhat in his work habits but remained a compulsive workaholic. Should such personality types be hired and become problematic, they should be required to undergo psychological treatment. Retention would depend on adjustment following treatment.

(12) Farmer the Foreigner

Farmer was born and reared in a southeastern Asian developing country and emigrated to the United States on a student visa, though he already had two degrees from his native country (a bachelor's degree in Sociology and an MA in Geography). He was reared in a stable, respectable upper middle class, rural family and conformed in his family, local community school and state university. His developmental history was normal for one of his class and local, physical, and cultural environment. One among five siblings he was well built physically, intelligent, studious, mildly aggressive, and a very ambitious extrovert. Now he is a professor in a respectable southern university's graduate school of Agricultural Economics where he was initially recruited as a PhD student by his current senior colleague (whom he met when both were doing research in his developing country on a research project sponsored by a US federal agency). Farmer switched careers from Geography to Agricultural Economics in order to obtain a graduate student assistantship in the department where he now teaches. Brilliant, congenial and industrious, he took a PhD in Agricultural Economics within five years, during most of which time he was his recruiter's TA. Moreover, as a graduate student, he unofficially tutored fellow students in statistics and methodology, and helped them with their theses and dissertations—in brief he was a subrosa professor for five years without pay. Staying only on student visa he was supposed to leave the United States upon graduation, and according to university rules, under no conditions was he (or anyone else) to teach in a department from which he or she had received a PhD. Notwithstanding the rules, he urged his professors to find him a position in the United States; because the alternative of returning to his country would block his career ambitions; stymie his goal of becoming a citizen of the United States; and prevent him from rendering required economic aid to his family of orientation.

The department head under pressure from Farmer's mentor, a noted scholar, and, in need of someone with Farmer's credentials in the department, with the aid of the university administration and legal help, persuaded the Immigration and Naturalization Service (INS) to issue Farmer a green card, which paved the way for employment in the department, and eventual citizenship. This action broke the inbreeding rules of the university against hiring its own graduates which were suspended in Farmer's "special case." He was hired as an assistant professor in a tenure tract teaching position. Subsequently, he became a full professor with tenure and a US citizen. He married and raised a family; and, brought his parents to the United States, as well as some foreign students from his country of origin. In so doing, some university and immigration laws were either broken or severely bent. Though a competent researcher and publisher some of his students initially complained that they had some difficulty in understanding his colonial English in class lectures, though he had no problem otherwise.

Farmer pointed out to the authors that the emigrating student and his or her family (who usually extended financial help for the emigration), knew aforehand the move to the United States was likely to be permanent. The emigrating student usually pledges to send money home after completing his studies and securing a job; that is, to help other family members and friends there, and, to help some to enter the United States later on. He also explained that many foreign students switch majors when graduation time nears in order to remain here, and avoid deportation. During his student and early teaching years, Farmer appeared to be "outer directed" and exuberant about the United States and western culture, as is the case with many immigrants. Later he continued to take a keen interest in US current events as well as what was happening back home.

Farmer's case is fairly representative of many other student emigrants the authors have known in academia, and presents a ubiquitous controversy and "immigration problem." Some say when the foreign student on a student visa takes the first degree in the United States, he or she should be required to return home. Others say foreign students return should not be forced to leave, should the political situation back home be unstable or dangerous, or, if their services are needed here. What to do then poses a problem. Certainly universities and the INS should keep better records so authorities can tell who is here legally or illegally. Perhaps some should stay because their services are needed here; and, perhaps some should remain because of political or humanitarian reasons. Others argue with some justification, that international students should go home immediately after graduation regardless, because they might someday replace US would-be graduate students, and later professors in American universities; and, still some others question their English language skills, and even their presence here in the first place. However, the reasons for keeping some foreign students after graduation are substantial in engineering and the sciences because US universities can no longer find enough American applicants with the mathematical and science skills required for admission that are possessed by some international students, desiring to attend US universities.

The Patriot Act and other US security measures have reduced but not resolved the problems of foreign student visa entanglements: foreign college and university student records are not carefully kept and monitored; and, enforcement procedures concerned with who stays and for how long have not been worked out. Therefore the INS is a joke to many citizens. These authors agree with the sentiment that the INS should not issue student visas to: students from countries that knowingly produce terrorists; countries whose governments are openly hostile to the United States; and, to students from unstable countries where violence prevails. At present some graduate programs in the physical sciences would have difficulty in functioning without foreign Asian professors and students. What to do about this in the future is another matter and beyond the scope of this study. Certainly most Asian students who remain in the United States have made valuable citizens.

Farmer, though in many respects a sterling character without any personality disorders or stress problems, represents one with a deviant educational (structural) pattern. He has a normal personality and has adjusted very well in the United States. And foreign professors like Farmer contribute much to US higher education. As Georg Simmel (1858-1918), the famous fecund German Sociologist, pointed out in his frequently quoted essay, "The Stranger" in 1908, the *stranger* is a particular social type who plays a special and significant role in a society or subgroup (in this case US higher education). The stranger is not an outside wanderer who comes today and goes tomorrow, but rather one who comes today and stays tomorrow. Initially an outsider, the stranger has the benefits of mobility, objectivity, freedom of thought, new perspectives, and skills, which are beyond the realm of insiders. Despite "otherness" and not being of the group, he becomes an organic group member via a reciprocal conditioning element, namely simultaneous amounts of (a) nearness and of (b) remoteness. "Though both of these qualities are found to some extent in all human relationships, a special proportion and reciprocal tension between them produce the specific form of the relation to the *stranger."* Said relationship renders the stranger a better observer, judge, trader, emissary, tax collector, sometime lover, middleman, and even personal confidant than insiders—though calculated, an appreciative reciprocity. It is likely that the individual becomes aware of the "other" when he or she first sees its image when first looking into a mirror and realizes that said likeness one sees is something absent from, or lacking in one's self. Thenceforth one tries to close the gap between its self and the "other"; and, thereupon assumes various selves to meet different situations throughout a life history (Simmel 1908). Conversely, the stranger is in a precarious situation at all times.

Simmel notes another type of strangeness between two parties (which is frequently overlooked) wherein the very individuality and "being human is disallowed to the other. The stranger here has no positive meaning, the relation to him is a non-relation; he is not what is relevant here, a member of the group itself." He gave the example of the relation of the Greeks to the Barbarian. The position and role of the *stranger* throughout history has been ambiguous; that is, simultaneously enviable and vulnerable. For example: (1) the envy of the high status and wealth of the court Jews under the Hapsburg monarchy in central Europe; and, (2) the vulnerable Walter Rathenau, the German Jewish prime minister of the Weimar Republic, who was murdered by the Nazis. The court Jews, *strangers,* succeeded as negotiators; but, Walter Rathenau, a *stranger,* obviously failed (See Hannah Arendt, *The Origins of Totalitarianism.* New York: Hartcourt, 1951, Section one: Antisemitism, pp. 1-117).

We think the stranger as a professor helps students, widen and deepen an understanding of themselves and their cultures in reference to identities and cultures of others; for, as Simmel concludes, "Not a thing or event has a fixed intrinsic meaning; its meaning only emerges through interactions with other things and events." Nevertheless, as Simmel explains incommensurate cultures are permeated with innumerable irreconcilable differences and ambiguities. Therefore, conflicts inevitably ensue (this factor is frequently denied or overlooked). Simmel concentrated on forms of social interaction and the delineation of social types (for example, "The Stranger," "Sociability," "The Adventurer" etc.) which aligns with the purpose of this study (See Simmel 1908, Lepadatu 2010). We too have attempted to construct social types.

(13) Glad the In-breeder

Glad was born and reared in a lower middle class, intact, stable family located in a small town in the upper south. Her father was a healthy, sturdy, sober, conscientious, serious minded outdoor working class person; and, an outgoing, friendly, self-educated electrician who worked for a local power company. He held a high school diploma and was proud of his status among peers, and of his large, respectable and harmonious family (a wife and five children). Her mother, also a high school graduate, was a modest and efficient, well adjusted housewife who met the emotional and caring needs of all family members. Both parents were outer-directed stable extroverts who shared a simple, ordered, congenial, lifestyle in keeping with that of provincial neighbors—all family members were honest, hard working, and church going people. The nearby nationally prestigious state university, though not derogated, had no significant meaning in their lives.

Glad, a slightly aggressive extrovert was the youngest of her siblings and throughout her grade school and high school years she shared the simple lifestyle of her parents, siblings, and working-class neighbors. Red headed, gregarious, attractive and moderately androgynous, she played basketball; made above average grades; conformed easily and assumed leadership roles in schoolyard and neighborhood play activities. Intelligent and ambitious and on the practical rather than the intellectual side, she took the commercial high school educational track rather than the academic route, excelled in typing, business and secretarial courses. She dated occasionally and had a normal sex drive, but for reasons family members and friends could not understand, she did not form romantic relationships with any local males. She was curious, imaginative, and adventurous, read novels, and considered herself a cut above her complacent schoolmates in world view. Therefore, she decided to look beyond the local scene for dates, a career and lifestyle, while still retaining close family ties—not easy.

At graduation she decided to seek a typing job at the "exalted" but socially isolated, nearby university, and well aware of the social cleavages between herself, her town and the land of the "gown," she dressed in her best and applied for a clerical position in the university's Sociology department. She knew something about Sociology which she had picked up from one of her history teachers who had talked about it in one of her high school classes. She got the job and within four years became the department's head secretary. Two years later she was the head's private secretary; and then rented an apartment on the campus where her lifestyle changed along with an elevated vision of success. She began taking free courses on the side in the department, and two years later she married the head of another department on campus, an older, widowed and attractive scholar. With his advice and that of a Sociology professor mentor who admired her drive and class work, she continued taking classes, and became one of the head's administrative assistants. Thenceforth, despite specific prohibitive university rules, she took over time an AB, MA, and PhD in the department. Then despite specific departmental and university rules against inbreeding, she resigned her position as an administrative assistant, and, was then appointed as assistant professor. She had strung out the completion of the PhD fearing as she told friends, "I'm educating myself out of a job." She knew the university rules that prohibited anyone from teaching in the department who had been awarded a PhD therein. However, she knew the rules, rule makers, rule enforcers, and rule breakers. She and her husband had socialized with many involved with the rules and decision making at the university.

In the PhD process she failed one preliminary exam containing difficult theoretical questions, which she thought had been carefully contrived to "flunk her out" by two professors who did not think she should be granted a PhD degree. Fearing that this would be tantamount to her appointment as an assistant professor in the department, Glad lodged a formal complaint against the two professors who had flunked her with the Vice President of Academic Affairs, who called these two in for what he called, "a discussion of the problem." He then shoved her graduate school record of A's and B's in front of them and exclaimed: "This lady deserves a PhD, now what shall we do about it"? One professor replied: "She will have to take the test over like everybody else." The Vice President responded: "Oh no, she is not taking the test over. Give her a lengthy term paper, and have her write out the answers to your questions she did not answer well; and, then we will see about her further work on the PhD. This conference is adjourned gentlemen, and I do not want to hear any more about the matter from anyone." On leaving the Vice President's office, one of the two professors remarked to the other: "That SOB had a lot of gall. He didn't give us a chance to disagree, or explain our position. I wonder if he is a friend of Glad's husband. Those damn administrators stick together. I like Glad, but she should have to take the test over." The other replied: "I know but there is nothing we can do. And I don't have tenure yet." Glad complied with the Vice President's stipulations, took the PhD, and was appointed an assistant professorship in the Sociology department as a special exception to inbreeding rules.

She taught (primarily) undergraduate courses until retirement as an associate professor, and along the way gave birth to three healthy children; published a few journal articles; functioned as a congenial colleague; was an adequate teacher and a good mother; but, she was still problematic nonetheless. She was not an intellectual and did not do much empirical research, and most of her students were undergraduates. She was placed in charge of Women's Studies after she reminded the head that she was the senior female professor in the department. Many faculty members and some graduate students thought she spent too much of the department's library allocation money on books in her teaching area, and one graduate student asked her: "Three-fourths of the stuff you order is trash. Do you have to be a female to write and teach about women"? Further on this subject, one professor asked her in a departmental meeting if she had ordered any of Hanna Arendt's writings, for example *The Origins of Totalitarianism*. She answered thusly: "Who in the hell is she"? And when the questioner tried to tell her, and explain his inquiry, she cut in and retorted: "No, why in the hell should I order anything that German woman wrote, or taught about at Berkeley"? The prolific publishers, so-called department intellectuals, were somewhat wary and all called her, "a very savvy girl." She was also recognized as a good poker player in the department's poker club which met once a month, presided over by the department head. One so-called intellectual player remarked once: "Glad is not an intellectual, but she could be. And how would we distinguish ourselves from the upscale rednecks if she weren't around"? (See Roebuck and Hickson, 1984; Roebuck and Murty, 1996).

Glad was knowledgeable about university rules and operating procedures; budgets, retention, and tenure regulations, etc. which she shared with the head. An adequate undergraduate teacher in the field of women's studies and social stratification, she was admired by her students; was congenial and civil to all others; minded her own affairs, and did not belong to faculty factions. Though somewhat intellectually limited, she enjoyed social relationships with many across campus groups and filled an important niche in the department where she was the department head's "Girl Friday" (and advisor about university rules, regulations, and clerical procedures). Most importantly she mentored coeds across departments on the campus, who were interested in becoming professionals (in any field); and, when she did not know the answers to their questions and problems, she knew the professionals and places to refer them to.

Glad was a diligent (apparent) obsessive compulsive workaholic who should have sought psychological counseling when in graduate school where she felt intellectually inferior to other students, if not before in high school, when she became very social class conscious. As she said, "I did what I had to do, with what I had, to get what I wanted to get." And she did well considering the rigid local southern social class structure. Her professional problems inhered in the dangers of inbreeding that may: (1) encourage or permit the employment and retention of incompetent professors who do not publish; (2) "provincialize" a department; (3) enable the formation of sectional and ideological cliques (for example a cable of good ole boys); (4) give the department a mirror self image; (5) block students' exposure with different schools of thought, and association with different social and personality types from without a particular region; (6) foster nepotism and empire building; (7) disrupt competency and fairness in hiring, firing, tenuring, and promotions;

and in salary standards and procedures; (8) engender the ill will of some who resent them as insider inbreeders.

Glad's deviancy pattern was grounded in the structural deviance of the Sociology Department and the university administration where she was employed at two administrative levels, and permitted to break many rules and regulations pertaining to employees who take courses while working and teaching in a department where they take PhDs.

In summary, Glad was a conscientious, efficient person and honest in most situations. She was also very ambitious and broke rules that she was well aware of in order to get ahead. A workaholic she appeared to have a obsessive-compulsive personality disorder including a mild inferiority complex; and, she should have been directed to psychological counseling (Brown and Gillian, 1992). However, she had managed to cope very well. Further, she was a problematic case in other respects; for example, she did not engage in empirical research, and was limited in her intellectual interests, and teaching areas. Though most of her colleagues liked her as a congenial and efficient person in specific departmental work areas; some colleagues never fully accepted her as an equal professional, and could never overlook the fact the she was somewhat of an "interloper and in-breeder who obtained an easy inside PhD."

The authors have seen several departments weakened academically by inbreeding and think it an ill advised practice resulting frequently in infighting and the discrediting of the in-breeder among other things. The weaker the graduate school academically, the more damaging inbreeding. No inbreeding should be permitted on a permanent basis. Glads should never have been hired as an assistant professor in a tenure track position.

(14) Ryder the Outsider

Ryder was born in a northern California beach town near San Francisco into a middle class family descended from an upper class family. His father, a self effacing, shy, introverted, intelligent man, ectomorphic in body build, projected a placid presence and shy persona. He loved his son, but was deprived of a close relationship with him by an aggressive, domineering, overweening, and socially ambitious wife. Holding a law degree from a prestigious state university, he practiced law in a real estate firm from nine to five. Ryder's mother, an extrovert, was a very sensual, physically attractive, seductive, emotionally charged, impulsive, intelligent, arty, attention seeker who had met his father while both were students at the same university—where they were married following her graduation with an AB, and his with an AB, and a JD. The only child, Ryder was pampered and over protected by both parents, especially by his mother, who made sure that he played with children from the "right" social class and those who had good manners. Ryder preferred to play alone at home and loll around. Medium sized though frail in physique, whinny, anxious, edgy, temperamental, and quick to anger as a youth, he presented an aggressive front with his playmates at school who were amused at times by his showy, but obviously unsubstantiated masculinity. Though involved in frequent minor physical altercations, he was a "bantam rooster" whom his schoolmates and teachers tried to overlook; but, they did note his moody, disposition and unprovoked violent temper which was expressed at irregular intervals. He changed shallow "friendships" frequently and was dropped frequently from play groups during grade school through high school and university; he devalued those left behind, did not appeal to girls, and engaged in sporadic, unsuccessful and brief courtship relations. Though he appeared to be sexually normal in a physical sense, liked girls, and pursued several during high school, females thought him too edgy, peculiar, disagreeable, and wimpish.

Most of his leisure time was spent at home with his parents where a large number of couples paraded in and out during frequent parties where ample amounts of alcohol were served; and, where intellectual conversations were encouraged. Educational books, magazines, and periodicals were at hand. Classical painting reproductions, and representational art and cloth tapestries hung from the walls of a modest house. Despite his unstable relationships with peers, an unstable self-image, inappropriate, sporadic temper tantrums, and occasional intoxications, he made a shaky so-so adjustment at home, in the community, and at school—probably because of strong parental supervision, and excellent teacher support, and mild, sensible disciplining measures. (For example, removing his car keys for a week when he drove recklessly, or after drinking, though no DUIs resulted.)

Sporadic highly-charged verbal battles took place occasionally between his parents over his father's jealous outbursts, when he accused his wife of overt, provocative sexual moves on male party guests; for example, dancing too close to them. These petered out peacefully however, because she was able to convince her husband that her "moves" were not intended to instigate affairs. And there was no evidence or likelihood of any affairs transpiring. Ryder stood up for his father in these bickerings, and at other times when his mother wore clothes and jewelry much too expensive and showy. She was a provocative attention seeker rather than a seducer.

Though Ryder was only slightly above average intelligence both parents had high hopes for his success in something, and pushed him hard in school to make good grades. He studied hard, but made only slightly above average grades which was a disappointment to him and his parents. Nevertheless, he and his mother decided he should be a high school teacher. Without adequate grade point averages and SAT scores at high school graduation to enter any first-tier university in his state, he matriculated in a second-tier state university, where he again made barely average grades. He initiated friendly relationships with peers which did not last long because for some reason or another, for example, his feeling, they did not give him enough attention. These shallow relationships petered out. Additionally he displayed anger should classmates not help him with classroom reports, or agree with him in arguments with others. He also threw occasional temper tantrums when intoxicated for no apparent reason which friends could not figure out. At irregular intervals he also engaged in binge drinking when and where he provoked minor physical altercations—but was never sanctioned or arrested for these temper outbursts. Occasional dating relationships with females resulted in infrequent sexual relations that were not judged satisfying by either party.

He had started out in his state university with a major in Sociology but when he discovered this subject was not generally offered in high schools, he switched to History that he found boring, but acceptable. His mother agreed. He later opted for a double major in Sociology and History, and spent an extra year in school to meet graduation requirements. Because he did not have to work he had ample time to study, but found it difficult to compete with many of his classmates. This exacerbated angst, mild depression, anxiety and a poor self-image. By his senior year, it became obvious to his professors and others, including his parents, that he was only an average student academically; and, that his sporadic binge drinking, temper outbursts, mood swings and irritability indicated a conduct, and a personality problem.

Following graduation he decided again with the counsel of his mother, but not with university counseling services, to switch career plains, and prepare himself for teaching in a junior college which he said would offer more money and prestige than high school teaching. Without a required MA degree he had to continue in school, and therefore, applied for acceptance in his school's graduate program. Not accepted, he applied for admission to a weaker graduate school program in another out-of-state state university, where he was accepted. Finding his coursework easier than that beforehand, he graduated with a MA in Sociology in two years with the help of classmates and tutors in theory and methods. While there, his conduct improved, though he still experienced mild mood shifts, questions about his identity, and at times a poor self-image—all accompanied by occasional drinking binges. However, strong relations with his parents continued; friendships with his peers though shaky lasted longer than those before; and though still not attractive to females, he managed a few so-so casual sexual encounters. At graduation, unable to secure a position in high school or a junior college, he stayed on in the weak graduate school program and took a PhD, again with difficulty five years later. Knowing that his overall school records would not qualify him for a college or university position in his home state, where all records were carefully checked, and where the competition for positions in higher education was keen, he decided to make a fresh start elsewhere, and applied for positions all over.

A Sociology department in the deep south had been looking for four years for an acceptable "outsider" to teach Marriage and the Family. Several competent candidates had applied and been interviewed, but all had been rejected by a fractious faculty, for an assortment of reasons: too young or old, too liberal or conservative, too regional or cosmopolitan, too religious or secular, too this or too that. The head, hired a few years earlier to restore a once respectable department, could not persuade any faculty member to teach Marriage and the Family. Further the department was inbred with PhDs from the department, or with southerners with PhDs from southern schools (many within the state). New outside blood was demanded by the university administration. Ryder, a compromise candidate (other more competent professors had been under consideration) agreed to teach Marriage and the Family, though it was not his choice or study area. Someone had to be hired that academic year or the department would lose the open assistant professorship position. Ryder, an unknown, presented a pseudo sophisticated, charming front fortified with phony intellectual prattle, shallow glibness, and strange west-coast story telling. He also assumed an apolitical position, and indicated that he was too preoccupied with research, teaching, and publishing to be concerned with politics and culture wars. This was what many listeners wanted to hear, but he had never published anything which should have rung a bell, nor read a paper at a professional meeting. After intense departmental bickering, Ryder was hired without a close checking of his references or school records.

During the first five years he made a so-so adjustment, cultivated a few "friends" quickly from different departmental factions (but as usual, changed them often or was dropped), attended professional meetings where he read three inane qualitative papers; co-authored two published articles in second rate journals; displayed a quick temper when drinking at a few departmental socials (for which he later apologized); received passable student evaluations; and, continued to teach Marriage and the Family (a burden no one else would assume). More importantly he married a former student, an intelligent homely daughter of a local wealthy businessman. His mother had taught him something well. At the end of his fourth year when he came up for tenure he had published three additional articles coauthored with more competent colleagues, again in second rate journals; and read four more mediocre papers at regional meetings; chaired two or three more regional paper reading sessions; aligned himself with a "good ole boys" faction of full and associate tenured professors; continued to get passable student evaluations. Sporadic mood shifts, irritability, and inappropriate outbursts of temper continued. He also engaged in departmental political game playing, favoring the "good ole boy faction." Further, verbal altercations with colleagues in the department and at professional meetings increased. Moreover, he began to engage in more frequent binge drinking bouts, and started hustling women at professional meetings. He had no real affairs for obvious reasons (who would have him), but just wished to display a macho image to his drinking buddies. Nonetheless this overt improper conduct was observed and gossiped about by many.

Meetings on his tenure at all levels were lengthy, conflicting, tedious, and tumultuous. It came down to provable reasons why he should not be given tenure, rather than why he should be. He had not engaged in any worthwhile research or published any "I found" journal articles. What he had published with coauthors was rehashes of past prosaic drivel. Critical questions raised apart from his weak qualifications were: "Who is going to replace him?; Nobody wants to teach Marriage and the Family;" "Remember how hard it was to find Ryder;" "He is an outsider which we need;" "He will damn sure sue if not tenured;" "Perhaps he could be tenured should he sign an agreement to stop drinking;" "He is not an alcoholic so we cannot force him into counseling;" "He certainly acts crazy sometimes but he is not psychotic." Finally with the support of the "good ole boys," and the dean who feared a legal battle, Ryder was tenured. Conveniently he had married the daughter of a rich powerful business man.

According to customary academic requirements, Ryder was not eligible for tenure because: he was not above average as a teacher; his publication record was weak (he had not published a single book, nor published any articles in top-ranked journals); and, he did not exemplify much interest in future research or publishing. Moreover, graduate students did not rank him as a good scholar or teacher. In brief he was a very problematic professor "who also ran" (at the race track), and who never should have been hired in the first place. Additionally, he had weak impulse control, especially after a few drinks, which led to verbal and near physical altercations with colleagues (in the forms of angry outbursts, devaluations of other professors, and alternate cynicism and adulation of social institutions without factual basis in either case). Some professors noted his unstable social relationships; disruptive political game playing; instability in work relations (eagerness to participate in collaborative projects sometimes and passive/hesitations at others). Students noted his occasional swift mood shifts; irritability and defensive and hostile reactions when his opinions were questioned.

In summary, Ryder was weak academically and a temperamental, aggressive, mercurial, unstable, violent trouble maker with poor impulse control who resembled those diagnosed as borderline personality disorder types. Further, he was not intelligent enough to ever become an intellectual; and, had accumulated a poor academic record. Despite his middle class status his social background variables were negative in that his ambitious parents pushed him to excel beyond his capabilities. He also suffered situational stress throughout his life because he could not measure up, and an unstable personality did not sustain him. His case indicates, among other things, the time and care *required* in the selection of university professors. Compromise candidates are always highly questionable. Tenure should be based on academic performance (teaching, research, publications, and team playing) and, decent professional conduct. Unstable personality types and binge drinkers have no place in academia. Outsiders should never be selected just because they are outsiders; or hired because they agree to teach courses others will not teach. Finally his case illustrates how political influences (like that of his wife's father) can sometimes in some places help retain incompetent professors. Ryder's type should never be hired in academia, and should they be mistakenly employed, dismissed as soon as it is feasible when found to be trouble makers unless they undergo psychological treatment; that is, should the foolish decision be made to keep them.

(15) Fred the ABD (All But Dissertation)

Fred was born in an industrial factory city in the northeast into an upper lower class, dysfunctional family. His parents were divorced because of his father's drinking problem and inability to support a large family of five children and a wife. Due to his frequent absences, Fred saw little of his father, an aggressive, extroverted, jealous (without cause), abusive, violent man who beat his mother at frequent intervals; and, engaged in street and bar fights for which he served jail time. A bitter factory worker, often unemployed, he saw little of his family. His mother was a very intelligent introvert but emotionally broken woman, who worked steadily at different blue collar jobs (from secretary to waitress) to support her family sometimes on welfare. She loved Fred, the eldest sibling who helped support the family by taking odd-time blue collar jobs until he went to college. A physically robust, aggressive, suspicious, irritable, moody, vengeful, disgruntled, angry youth, with self image problems probably related to his unsuccessful attempts to form a proper relationship with his father whom he loved and hated, he had no play time or friends. Life for him was a grind, unstable, quarrelsome relationships at home, dull, dirty, part-time jobs, and, squabbles with his mother and father about finances. Co-workers shied away from Fred, an intelligent but troubled man.

Fred's only solace was at school where despite intermittent absences he made good grades, especially in math and science. Despite his status as a student he was bossy with his teachers, particularly with males with whom he wrangled throughout high school. Teachers found him to be intelligent, curious and eager to learn, but difficult to manage in class where he was argumentative. He had no male friends, and had only casual, meaningless, unsatisfactory trysts with sexually promiscuous girls, brutally known as floozies and losers. Despite his all over precarious social and economic situation he was ambitious, and wanted to be a teacher. Occasional conferences with his family priest may explain this unexpected (by others) and questionable occupational choice. With hard earned money from summer jobs, a scholarship, and help from his church, he enrolled in a first-tier Pennsylvania university at high school graduation where he took a BS in Political Science five years later. He had no time for social life at school and was called there a nerd. Sporadic off-campus jobs (e.g. bartender) kept him busy with little time to brood, though he was a worrier just about everything. At graduation with above average grades he enrolled in a prestigious southern state university where he took a MA in Political Science with honors; but, from the jump he wrangled with his professors about common place moot academic points. His PhD was placed on hold because he could or would not agree with members of his dissertation committee. When his money ran out he applied for an instructorship in another nearby respectable state university, where professors were impressed with his academic record. Officials there replied that they only hired PhDs and wanted to know about his progress on his dissertation. He did have very high grades and his specialty, methodology, was the area they were looking for in a candidate. Though some reneged, his PhD committee recommended Fred for the position and stated that his dissertation would probably be completed and accepted by the end of that academic year. He was appointed as an ABD instructor with the promise of promotion to an assistant professorship pending the completion of his dissertation, and the attendant PhD. Communication between him and his dissertation committee faltered, and he never completed an acceptable dissertation.

From the beginning Fred proved himself adept at helping MA and PhD students with their quantitative and research design problems in writing MA theses and PhD dissertations; and, in teaching introductory methodology courses (extraordinary for instructors). He did have minor problems with some males who were weak in quantitative methods, but strong in qualitative methods (which Fred disdained). He did not complete the PhD dissertation on schedule or at any other time; although, he was given two one-year leaves of absences to finish. Then he should have been dismissed or reappointed as a temporary instructor. However, he excelled in his role as an unofficial thesis and dissertation adviser (in a technical sense); though over time without promotion and departmental status, he became bitter and disgruntled, and disdainful of his male students and assistant professors who were exponents of qualitative methods. Consequentially verbal classes ensued, and were talked about. The department split over, "what to do" with Fred. Most wanted him ousted, but by now the department head had made him his flunky (running errands and doing much of his paperwork), which insured his continued employment for twenty years as an academic technician and a gofer. His ambiguous status irritated him and some colleagues.

Without a doctorate, he was never promoted or given tenure, and was known as just another ABD, who had slipped between the cracks, and become a "supposedly" necessary cog in the department's wheel of technical operations. Ambitious and a would-be scholar, he attended professional meetings where he posed as an important professor representing his university. Further, he submitted numerous manuscripts to professional journals throughout the years, none of which were accepted for publication (probably because he did not have a PhD). Frustrated and unwilling to accept his junior, shaky and anomalous status in the department, he acted out in all sorts of ways to attract professional attention; for example, he argued with many young assistant professions openly and questioned their scholarship—and at times his acerbic criticisms were valid but only augmented further wrangling with some professors and students who began to detest him.

Frequently he walked around with a number of books and recent journal article publications under his arm, and explained their contents and findings to anyone who would listen, and spouted out critiques about these "scholarly props," as he called them. Further, he criticized the publications of the department's junior faculty, especially those he did not like and tried to pull rank and seniority that he did not have. Also, as a would-be self-appointed leader of some assistant professors, he tried to turn them against senior professors he envied. A busybody, mischievous troublemaker, and rumor monger over mundane and inconsequential matters, he tried to be a pivotal wheel in departmental decisions concerned with routine schedules and everyday functions. Mercurial, testy, defiant, stubborn, and quick to take offense over mundane matters, he was civil at times, but verbally combative at others. Additionally, he played favorites among students and colleagues on an ever-changing basis. Most tried to avoid him, and those who had to interact with him tried to keep relationships on a formal, impersonal level. One never saw his wife (no children) who some locals reported to be a "cipher."

A disgruntled wannabe, Fred vented his rage and lack of academic success (based on unrealistic expectations), on those he was jealous of and could victimize, by putdowns or blockages of one kind or another. For example, he held up temporarily some students' theses and dissertations on technical quantitative grounds. Consequently many formal and informal complaints were made about him to weak department heads and dismissive deans, to no avail. Some were afraid to intervene in what they knew to be a "messy case." Others said: "We have more pressing problems to attend to, later for Fred's case." Cleverly Fred had made himself into a useful nuisance and a deceitful troublemaker, but yet a "necessary" technical tool. That is, many students depended on his statistical skills and time related to their theses and dissertations which their professors did not take the time to give them. He could never complete his dissertation, but helped many others complete theirs. One professor on his PhD committee that never accepted his dissertation reported thusly: "Fred might complete a dissertation written in heaven and approved by Saint Peter; but, I would never sign off on it. I will never give him a ticket to teach because of his *rotten personality*."

Finally, due to a number of serious complaints made by full professors, steps were taken by the administration to terminate his service. He pressed with the legal aid of an attorney for retention on the basis of twenty years of service. His case was finally settled out of court, and he was moved to another academic department where he taught statistics until retirement—still a very frustrated and bitter man.

In summary, Fred the ABD was an intelligent and industrious teacher who helped many others, but did little for himself because of a serious personality problem. He appeared similar to those with a borderline personality disorder. Unstable in social relationships and self-image; moody, miserable, angry; what relationships he had were shallow; and, he displayed erratic responses to others at times in problematic situations. Quick to shift from apparent congeniality to anger, he was an impulsive puffed up "wannabe," and ambivalent in his attitudes toward others; and, he was an angry bitter man.

To this day some of his former students swear by him and are appreciative of his help, while others detest him and claim he held up their dissertations by insisting on the use of "too many fancy statistical techniques and models." Former colleagues express similar mixed views. The structure of the department he taught in and "busy professors" who did not have or take the time to guide their students with theses and dissertations provided him a niche and a shaky academic career. Fred's dysfunctional, emotionally cold, and economically deprived family background including the dearth of a father's love; and, a miserable, broken, ambivalent mother contributed to the makeup of the man he became. His overall unsupportive and negative social background was detrimental to his negative development and necessary difficult social adjustments as a youth. He also faced a multitude of structural and situational stress problems with an underlying unstable personality.

Fred's profile further illustrates the problematic situations that ABDs face in academia as well as the problems they may create for those who hire them. To reiterate all ABDs are iffy products and academic departments would probably be better off without any of them. All instructors without PhDs at whatever educational level should be hired as temporary employees for definite periods of time. Finally, instructors like Fred are to be pitied rather than detested, but his personality type is not needed in academia. He required psychological treatment earlier on in his shaky career, if not before. When detected as troublemakers, Fred's type should be dismissed.

(16) Luke the Kook

Luke was born into a staid middle class Lutheran family located in urban Connecticut where he grew up with a tall, sturdy domineering father (an extrovert), a nourishing and dependent mother (an introvert), and a devoted younger sister. His father, a college graduate, worked as an accountant in a small-town business firm from nine to five; and, his mother also a college graduate, taught in a local, public elementary grade school. Discipline was strict, and though the father was an honest, straightforward, family man, he had difficulty in expressing affection, and caring feelings. No clowning around, or disagreement was permitted in his household, and mealtimes, study, playtime, and bedtimes were highly structured and enforced. Visiting playmates and acquaintances had to pass his muster; and no drinking, card playing, smoking, loud talking, frolicking or joshing were allowed. Therefore young people did not feel comfortable in his house. His mother, an intelligent and warm introvert was dominated by her husband, and reacted by spending her time and attention on her two other children.

Luke though average looking, intelligent, well built and strong doubted his physical alacrity and looks, and was somewhat of a "lounge lizard." He steered away from the playground particularly body contact sports. From childhood he had a retiring, secretive, suspicious, emotionally flat disposition, and was not interested in making close friends. Those who sought his company interacted with him briefly, because they found him edgy and doubtful about their friendly intensions. His unwarranted doubts and fears drove them away. Bookish and aloof, many considered him dull, dour, and lethargic and a killjoy.

Relations with his parents, submission to his father and a protective stance toward his mother and sister, appeared to fall within a shaky range of marginal adjustment. Luke was an unhappy child with no apparent reason other than that of a strict domineering father with whom he did not relate. He was at ease with his mother and sister. Somewhat reclusive, he preferred to be alone at stamp collecting, watching T.V., reading, and playing with educational toys. Though a loner, he adapted in school and made above average grades. Girls admired his physical appearance, but quickly lost interest because of his stiffness, indifference, moodiness, taciturnity and apparent lack of emotional affect. He liked girls but was suspicious of their infrequent overtures; and, did not think they liked him—for what reason he could not figure out. He had a few dates throughout high school which were not emotionally fulfilling to either party; and, he went to a few parties where he tried to fit in but did not, because he did not dance, did not smoke or drink, and could not engage in bantering conversation. "Girls," he said, "can wait until I have a career going." Actually though a "normal" heterosexual, he never expressed much interest in sex, then or later. Notwithstanding his cool and aloof nature and obvious dearth of élan or stage presence, he wanted to teach science courses somewhere—probably because his father had said: "Science is the way to go." But, confusingly his father disagreed with his career choice and stated: "There is no money in teaching." Suffering from a shaky self-image and self-resolve, he succumbed to his father's will and gave up the idea of teaching science in high school; and, switched interests to social studies (a copout).

Following high school graduation with high SAT scores he enrolled in an Ivy League university; majored in Political Science and History; and, again made above average grades. Upon graduation with a high grade point average he entered a graduate school program there. Though only an average student, he earned a MA and a PhD in Political Science with a minor in Sociology in seven years. Again, he was suspicious of his classmates; failed to confide in others; expected too much from acquaintances and sometime "friends," and lashed out verbally against those whom he (unwarrantedly) thought disloyal. He avoided group study and research projects when possible, and when required to do so, thought classmates took advantage of him. For example, he once said: "They expect me to do too much of the work." Further he held grudges against those he thought had slighted or maligned him in any way. Despite his above average grades he had no interest in teaching or research, and was never awarded an assistantship or a TA appointment. This he resented and complained about to department heads along with (unwarranted) reports that his classmates were jealous of his skills and solo projects. Some classmates and professors described him as a problematic, nut, and called him behind his back, "Luke the Kook." Puritanical, unpopular, rigid, cold, suspicious, edgy and envious (characteristics that began to show in elementary school), Luke began to question his identity and his ability to function as a professional in any field. Relationships with females as with males remained tenuous, brief, and unstable; though, his relationships with family members remained strong, and all members gave him strong emotional and financial support.

Upon receiving a PhD with the help of a politician, a family friend, he found a middling position with a Civil Service Parole Board. He had taken a few Criminology courses during his MA and PhD study programs, and had worked two summers as an assistant case worker in a state prison. He succeeded in the parole board position because he functioned in a protected environment, and worked primarily with parole progress reports, and clerical procedures (paperwork, not people). Here he met and married a coworker, an attractive, highly intelligent, emotionally stable widow five years his senior, a social worker, who gave him thenceforth professional and emotional support. Bored after four years he said, "This has nothing to do with rehabilitation." Next he applied for and received an assistant professorship in a west-coast state university Sociology Department where the head was looking for a PhD to teach Criminology, and help develop a study area in this field at the undergraduate and MA levels (as demanded by the university administration) but had not been able to find a suitable candidate with a PhD (a requirement of the position); and, Luke was the best qualified applicant he could find. After six years of acceptable teaching and five journeyman articles published in Social Work journals Luke was tenured and promoted to an associate, and later to a full professorship. Teaching in this applied social work area he was not expected to research and publish extensively. More importantly, his position became that of a Criminology subhead administrator within a Sociology Department. Students and colleagues noted that he was an average teacher, but, an eccentric administrator, a loner who associated only with the department head on and off campus. Moreover, he was suspicious and kept his office door closed when talking to students and visiting professors. Stiff, formal and demanding in class, and somewhat strange, he claimed to have extrasensory perceptions at times. To his advantage, the number of students seeking a major in Criminology and Corrections increased with amazing speed. Therefore, he was directed by the administration to hire three new Criminology faculty members with PhD degrees with the consent and help of the Sociology Department Head.

Luke hired three from a list of competent candidates following a long and tedious selection procedure, due to his fractious, persnickety, indecisive decision-making. One was a southerner who impressed the Sociology head and dean, but not Luke, who disliked all southerners whom he termed "useless rednecks." Despite Luke's reluctance the southerner was hired on the orders of the Liberal Arts dean. The southerner and two other recruits, like the students, found Luke to be a weird, suspicious, and foreboding enigma. Luke arranged to share a two-man office with each of the three recruits on a one-semester rotation basis. "This way," he said, "I will be better able to fit you into the program." Of a stingy and aloof nature, he complained if anyone of the three touched anything on his desk, which he locked each day before leaving. Further, should a colleague look too closely at some item atop his desk (such as a mundane class schedule), Luke would give the observer a long, hostile look, and immediately tuck away the object in one of his desk's locked drawers.

Luke came first with the clerical help and complained to his underlings frequently about their shoddy clerical procedures. Without speaking, but with a nod to the door, he indicated a desire to be alone with incoming students or visitors, which often interrupted officemate's work. Each stepped outside in the hall until Luke opened the office door at the departure of his visitors. Sometimes he took considerable time before opening the door, allowing colleagues to reenter the office. Frequently people walking up and down the hall would ask the recruits why they were standing in the hall, which proved embarrassing because they had to makeup some excuse for an awkward position. Sometimes they overheard Luke's strident voice, giving some visitor hell in conference. His day-to-day moods and behaviors were erratic; that is, sometimes he was more civil than at others. For example, on some days he shared greetings before discussing professional matters, but on others, he walked in, sat at his desk without a word; stared out the window with a dreamy look, and nervously picked dry skin from his fingers which were always mottled up with small raw spots. When Luke answered the phone he turned his back on his colleagues and whispered during conversation. When a colleague's student whom Luke did not like came in, he expressed displeasure by giving him/her a hard hostile look.

One of the three assistant professor recruits remarked to Luke one day: "I hear your brother was in town this past weekend," to which he responded: "Who told you I have a brother? Let's get to work." On another occasion a colleague said, "I hear you collect stamps. Would you like to see one from Belgium I got last week"? Luke responded, "Who told you I collected stamps"? "No." Not a publisher, but jealous of those who did, he told one office mate, "I hear you got a paper published. I saw you working on it all this semester. I wish I had time to write articles, but you know, somebody has to run this program. You young bucks have the time to seek glory." Graduate students feared Luke because he got upset in class when they disagreed with him; and, they were keenly aware that, without his approval, they would never finish their MA degrees, and therefore showed him deference at all times, which they knew he expected. He was very wary of colleagues, thinking they might gang up and try to get rid of him on the basis of one thing or another (and there were many things). His obsessive need for privacy was obvious to all, and his graduate students wondered, as one asked: "How did that old kook manage to get such an attractive wife"?

When one of the three received notice that one of his articles had been accepted for publication, he hid it, because he knew if Luke found out, he would explode with envious, negative remarks. When one's wife delivered a child at the same time he had a paper accepted for publication, Luke exclaimed, in a derisive manner: "So you had two children born this week, big deal"! (Luke had no children.) He also pitted each colleague against the other and praised and devalued each in different encounters at different intervals. He also berated and praised them to his graduate students. One of the assistant professors was so afraid of him that he stood up in his office each time Luke entered. The southerner sought scalp treatment from a dermatologist when his hair started falling out in circles following Luke's downgrading. For example, Luke claimed that this southerner showed bias in student grading; set too high standards; expected too much from students; lectured too much; gave too many hard tests and poor grades.

When the three recruits came up for tenure, all at the same time, Luke announced to several tenured professors, "I'm going to keep out of this because if I offer any comments one way or the other, people will think I'm biased." Of course he knew as well as others that it was his obligation to pass judgment on each. After two were tenured, Luke told a few colleagues in what he thought was secrecy: "None of them should have been tenured." He knew that those not tenured were dismissed at the end of the following academic year. In this instance, the southerner, the one not tenured, on advice of three full professors appealed his case to the administration and was tenured. All three found out later that Luke had voted against all of them, and bragged about it to two other tenured professors who were asked to keep his negative decisions a secret. He did remark openly: "We got too many damned tenured professors in this department already."

Luke also made negative and untoward remarks about professors he did not like off campus. For example, once at a professional meeting he prefaced a joke about the south in a group including one southern professor: "Now we are going to excuse you John, because we know you are from the south." One other southerner from another campus retorted: "And who is going to excuse your ignorant ass, Luke"? Again he commented once to a group of west-coast professors: "You see, in Ivy League schools where I come from (Yale), we send our bottom of the barrel PhD graduates down south to teach the rednecks. Did you know that"? "No" said one respondent, "And if so, what are you doing out here, Luke"? He had had enough of Luke the Kook.

On one rare occasion Luke and the department head hosted a party at Luke's house where no one except the department head had ever visited.

Feeling safe, Luke had a few drinks more than was his custom; sat on a large sofa overlooking a crowd of professors; and, patted his two aged German Sheppards fast asleep at his feet. When several made complimentary remarks about these pets and asked questions about them, Luke exclaimed: "You see they are sleeping, but only I know they are dreaming." One brave visitor remarked: "We can't tell, but we accept your claim they are dreaming because you know them. But I wonder if you can tell us what they are dreaming about." After a long silence on all sides, Luke gave the following paraphrased answer: "Yes, I can. But then you will ask me how do I really know, and how can I tell, and a bunch of other inane questions. This would be difficult and require a long complicated answer. Yes, you should know, I've extrasensory perception, a gift that only few of us have. With it we can read many conditions and thoughts that most intelligent animals have, as well as people. I know this is difficult for you to understand. So, let's change the subject." A long silence ended, and the dogs dreamed on.

Luke hogged the library orders and travel fund budgets, and frequently attended professional meetings off campus even when not reading a paper, or being on any program committee. At times the three junior members in his unit were not allowed to go even when they were to read papers, unless at their own expense. Luke would explain: "There is not enough money for all of us to go, but as the administrator of the Criminology Program, I must go." And of course he would take his wife, his protector.

In summary, Luke represents an aloof, oversensitive, suspicious, envious, sour, rigid and argumentative personality who resembled a paranoid personality disorder type. He remained under occasional outpatient psychiatric care, and taught with some personal success until retirement, though he remained an unhappy disgruntled and suspicious person. After retirement he secured employment in a government job where he said: "I work harder now than ever before." His type does not belong in academia, and Luke should have never been hired in the first place; and, he should have been dismissed early on when he started exhibiting a deviancy pattern (the violation of many serious university rules and regulations concerned with faculty civil rights). There were negative factors in his social background, though his personality defects were paramount and crucial. Edgy and suspicious at all times since childhood, he demonstrated situational stress problems that he created himself throughout life. Further Luke behaved like a paranoid mentally sick person at times. The academy is not equipped to treat those with serious personality disorders; and those like Luke when unmasked should be dismissed.

(17) Sarai the Princess

Sarai was born in New York City into an upper middle class, Reform Jewish home situated on Long Island within a predominantly Jewish neighborhood inhabited by professionals, business, and commercial types. Her father practiced law in a nearby personal injury law firm, and her mother, a PhD, taught English part-time in a local liberal arts college. Both parents were extroverts and possessed stable, conscientious and agreeable personality traits. She and her older brother grew up in an equalitarian, harmonious, affectionate, secure and congenial family circle. Though the parents were secular in attitudes and lifestyle the Jewish Holy Days were observed in an intellectual, but conservative arty atmosphere. She listened to recorded classical music (Brahms, Mozart, Beethoven, Chopin, Mendelssohn Tchaikovsky, Rachmaninov, Verdi, Gershwin), and a little swing, jazz and pop. House walls were decorated with alternating reproductions of representative art paintings by Degas, Manet, Renoir, Cezanne, Picasso, Van Gogh, Modrian, Matisse, Munch, Edward Hopper, and a few modern paintings by Felice Casorati, Max Ernest, Andy Warhol, and Kadinskly. The New York Times, The New York Review of Books, The Harvard Classics, the Hebrew Bible, encyclopedias, atlases and science, philosophy, and history books were at hand or shelved in a large library room. Her amusements were trips with friends to Rockefeller Center, the Zoo, The Metropolitan Art Museum, MOMA, operas, ballets, The New York City Public Library, off Broadway theatres, Greenwich Village, Central Park, Soho, Coney Island, and to a number of theatres, restaurants, and museums. Voluptuously attractive (but never fat) she was a Mediterranean physical type of medium height, straight, black coarse hair, dark brown eyes, a prominent nose, olive complexion, moderately sized breasts, and well shaped hips and legs. She wore very little makeup and perfume; and, she walked in a slightly sensual undulating way which she kept under control. She had an occasional date in high school, but most leisure time was spent with female classmates, family and friends at home and at a Jewish community center.

Sarai conformed well and pleased her parents and teachers intellectually and conduct wise. Her excellent grades were no big accolade among her peers because everybody else made good grades in her crowd. And at graduation she entered Hunter, arguably the city college with the highest academic standards, where she was a Phi Beta Kappa member; and, from which she graduated summa cum laude. By this time her peers knew she was a superior person, but again there were many other bright, intellectual, attractive, females around; and, she did not feel different or superior, nor did she showoff her assets. Expectedly by all she decided to pursue an academic career as a professor of English, which she knew required a PhD; and, she could have gone to any of several prestigious graduate schools nearby; but (unexpectedly and disappointingly for many), she chose an Ivy-League type school's English department located in the upper south for several reasons. Her house seemed vacant since her brother had gone off to law school; adventurous and curious, she desired to leave the city for a while; some of her friends were going there; one of her uncles and his family lived there; and, she thought her parents were a little too protective and it was time, "to get out of the nest and away from an affectionate but overprotective and demanding mother."

Living in a dorm, she found her classmates from home, agreeable and pleasant; however, some students from elsewhere, especially the locals (those from the south) appeared provincial, strange and standoffish—and they talked so slow and funny. Her classroom work went well, but, she noted a fierce competition among the department's graduate assistants for the few available teaching assistantships, in which she was not interested, because the work involved would restrict her study time. Some of her classmates who were graduate assistants demonstrated envy of her, thinking correctly that she was the best scholar and potential teacher among them. She was use to competition, but not this kind because some began cutting her socially, and others did not invite her to group-study sessions. Still others made snide unwarranted remarks behind her back; for example, "She thinks she is superior to everyone else." "She is the professor's pet." "She is too nerdy to date." "Perhaps she would fit in better back in New York." "She flirts with our boyfriends." "She thinks she is too good to go out with Christians." "She is too ethnic." Sarai did not know how to handle these reactions to her scholarship, ethnicity, and background, which she had taken for granted as common place back home. Consequently she moved out of the dorm, and shared an apartment with a girlfriend from Long Island. To exacerbate matters her professors pressured her to accept a TA position which she finally did during her second year. This further increased the competition with and social distance from some classmates. The young men she dated occasionally were Jewish New Yorkers, who acted like protective brothers, so she treated them as such. Now the competition shifted from who was going to be a TA to who might become an instructor. Some male classmates told her she thought she was too good to go out with Christians which she brushed off. Finally, Sarai saw the light. She was very attractive physically, exotic to the locals, and at the same time an intellectual; and that this combination even in graduate school enhanced the envy of many females, and engendered ambivalence in many traditional males. Southern males found her to be romantically alluring, but mysterious, and out of reach which drove some of them "crazy." One she had turned down for a date told her she was preparing for the wrong profession. She slapped him in the face and moved on. The snide remarks continued and some of her young professors' wives began to give her quizzical looks. It was necessary that she spend a considerable part of her time in close contact with professors in doing her job—writing papers, grading papers, preparing research notes, etc. which kindled the envy and/or suspicion of some others.

She had planned to return to New York after the MA, but unexpected financial considerations for work on her PhD intervened. Her father had to take sick leave, and her professors urged her to accept a lucrative instructorship in the department while simultaneously working on a PhD. She accepted reluctantly, and now competition shifted to which instructor would finish the PhD first. The soonest would be eligible for good positions in prestigious schools now available, but things could change in an ever shifting academic market. Further, the word was out that her department had decided to hire its next PhD graduate student instructor as a temporary assistant professor. This action would negate the department's rule against hiring one's own, but according to the dean, scholarly professors from good schools were now hard to find, and the addition would not be a tenure track position. In any event Sarai knew that a keen race was on among the PhD students to finish first, a very pathetic race to her which she would not enter. Scholarship rather than time was her interest, and she was already reading papers with her professors at professional meetings and coauthoring a few articles in scholarly journals. This further whetted the envy of some older PhD graduate students. One southern male PhD student remarked to her once in a joshing manner but meaningful intention: "You are just too young and luscious and wise to be in academia. Look around. How many PhD women do you see who look anything like you? What about television or Hollywood"? She responded with an icy smile.

Three instructors and one temporary assistant professor ganged up and tried to push her out of the department the first year of her instructorship by spreading false rumors, and advising students not to take her courses, because, they said, she was a flirt of easy virtue who dated her students; that she was a radical, a socialist, and a feminist who demonstrated biases in her lectures. Following an investigation by the Dean the cabal was broken up, and the guilty four were forced to resign, but damage had been done. Some envious female TAs and instructors rumored: "Where there is all this smoke there must be some fire." Sarai did not try to explain or placate her detractors, but soldiered on as a competent instructor.

Sarai's case illustrates how a prevailing male dominated culture can in some places impinge negatively on what goes on in a citadel of higher learning; that is, a very prestigious private university. Sarai married an associate professor who taught at another prestigious school nearby one year before taking her PhD, and she then moved a few miles away and taught in the same school as her husband, but in another department. She had been offered a high salary to remain on after her PhD as an assistant professor, but said: "I had had enough academic envy in one place." Her problem, the mixed blessing of superior intelligence, scholarship, beauty, and a naturally controlled sensuality, had not been completely solved, but marriage, children and her stable well integrated personality, assuaged her beneficent burden. Her husband, a Unitarian, was a hard sell to her mother who wanted to know why she could not find a nice Jewish man (an often repeated, sad and hackneyed story). Sarai explained that she had been considering males for a husband, not a soul brother, and had just happened to find a nominal Christian.

In summary, Sarai's profile illustrates the problems that very intelligent, attractive, and sensual females frequently encounter in academia as well as in other professions. The stereotype of the dominate male professor lingers on; and some look askance at an attractive PhD female professor. As one upscale bubba remarked to these two authors once: "By the time that good looking girls graduate from college they are married or soon thereafter. The culls go on after the MAs and PhDs, and by the time she gets a PhD, all femininity has been drained out." Perhaps, but hopefully, such male chauvinism will die out. There are more females in colleges and universities today than males. Most women have to work and want to after marriage, and therefore they will eventually reach par professionally and economically with men. Men must realize the inevitable and that attractive, intelligent, females are as good in the profession as their male counterparts, and must have equal privileges without harassment. Obviously, Sarai had social background advantages and a well integrated extroverted personality that helped her face situational and structural stress problems which she overcame. Her profile illustrates how and why she was envied as a problematic anomaly by some unenlightened others. Academia is in need of more Eves.

(18) Beecher the Incompetent Teacher

Because scholars and researchers have listed various common classroom deviant behaviors engaged in by professors (see Braxton and Bayer, 1999), we preface our deviant type, Beecher, with one deviant list which appears to be typical of current findings in this area. McPherson, Kearney, and Plax (2006) have observed what they refer to as "college teacher misbehaviors" in the classroom, and categorize some 28 into four general types. We consider all of their four types to fall into one category, the incompetent teacher, however we record them here in McPherson, Kearney and Plax's format; and, then render our comments on them. McPherson *et al.* deviant behaviors include being absent or tardy for class, returning homework late, sarcasm and putdowns, unreasonable and arbitrary rules, sexual harassment, inaccessibility to students outside of class, unfair testing, and unfair grading among others. Their four general categories are the incompetent teacher, the offensive teacher, the unfair teacher, and the indolent teacher.

The Incompetent Teacher

The incompetent teacher is one who does one or more of the following (among other things): reads material from the book; talks too fast; tries to cover too much material; lacks interest in the students; never allows questions. Some of these mistakes may be those of new teachers, who do not yet have enough material to teach. They may also be attributable to "dead wood," a person who is merely collecting a paycheck but no longer cares about teaching, students, research, promotions, or even salary increases. Finally, they may be the behavior of disgruntled faculty.

College professors, some say, are not educated or trained to be teachers *per se,* and that most have not received any formal training in how to prepare lectures, or how to manage a class. Many of those considered incompetent by students are knowledgeable about their fields, but may not know how to teach ... so the story goes. Many student complaints are about *how* teachers try but fail to transfer their knowledge to them. Some administrators who know about poor teachers allow them, and are themselves deviant in these two authors' opinion. Some professors on the other hand maintain that education courses are of no value, because they say: "You cannot teach students how to teach." Most educators, at least PhDs in education or EdDs, maintain that a teacher should take a wide range of education courses ranging from 20 to 30 credit hours. We take a moderate view on this issue, and think that a minimum number of education courses, two or three at the most including "the methodology of teaching" may be required. We think knowledge of the subject taught and the natural ability to communicate are the two essential requirements. Many teachers with a plethora of Education courses have neither in these two authors' opinion.

The Offensive Teacher

The offensive teacher puts down students. Some belittle the class as a whole, while others target specific students. One administrator in discussing offensive professors drew a distinction among them, separating sexual harassment and sexism. For example: "Perhaps you should return home and cook for a living," "Maybe you should just make babies." While sexism borders on sexual harassment, in that here is gender discrimination, there is usually no untoward intentions toward individual students. The sexist may believe that teaching some women is a waste of time and energy; whereas, the offensive teacher may believe that teaching itself is such a waste. Sexual harassment is usually directed toward a specific student. Harassment occurs when a professor directs put downs to individual students, groups, or the class as a whole.

The Unfair Teacher

Teachers must assign grades to students, and some assume that grades are assigned fairly and impartially, however this is not easy. The authors knew an instructor who taught a class where students presented oral reports. One student went to the instructor's office to argue for a higher grade. The next day, the instructor signed a grade change form for the chair to "rubber stamp." When the chair asked the instructor why the grade was changed, she said that the student had provided some good arguments. The chair however refused to sign the grade change, explaining that the rest of the students had not been given that opportunity. They may have had some good arguments as well. Testing in college is of two types "subjective" and "objective," but there are no purely objective tests. What students and professors mean by objective is short answer—multiple choice, true-false, matching, and the like. Subjective measures comprise essay questions on a test as well as papers, oral reports, and performances. Students more frequently challenge these latter grades because they are more "subjective" than objective tests and are typically given in smaller classes where the professor knows the students by name. Bias is often charged in these cases. For example, one male African-American complained to the chair, "He likes black girls."

Administrators often advocate the subjective type because it also "tests" the students' writing, critical thinking, and qualifying abilities. Administrators usually want classes to be as large as possible. Most faculty members who teach small classes in the junior and senior years use subjective tests. Professors who teach large, introductory classes typically use multiple choice and true-false questions. The authors recommend that all teachers should explain their grading procedures to their students and tell them: "I may not be able to grade you completely objectively, but I can grade you more objectively than you can grade yourself," and then stick to your guns with no further explanation.

The Indolent Teacher

Traditionally, universities have been known as harborers of "dead wood"— professors who have been tenured for some time and lack the fortitude to do anything much are called "dead wood." They use old notes and reuse the same tests every semester. Rarely do they update their approaches in any way.

Typically, they use the same textbook, even if out of date. Generally some assign fairly high grades in order to prevent complaints.

Beacher

Beecher was born and reared with three older siblings in the upper south. His parents owned and operated a profitable family-owned and run tobacco farm (an intensive agricultural operation which requires year-round careful tending, knowhow, hard labor, farm machinery, and some technological knowledge). Beecher was a strong, healthy, outer-directed, intelligent, extrovert, an outdoor type who when not in school or working as a field hand with other male family members, hunted and fished with his siblings and local farm-boy companions in the woods and on a river bank, and in the low-grounds of a tidewater river. His parents, high school graduates, married young, worked hard, and inherited land from both sets of parents; and they lived a respectable, upper middle class, harmonious, rural lifestyle. Both were stable, extroverts and leaders in their local church, and, community. His father had attended a business college in Virginia for two years, and was well read.

Beecher was a popular serious minded youth in his school and community and he avoided hard drinking, gambling, smoking, unnecessary risk-taking behaviors, and promiscuous females. He made good grades in high school where he was mentored by a history teacher who inspired him to be a teacher. Following graduation he enrolled in his state's most prestigious, public university where he majored in history; made good grades; fitted in; and continued dating a coed from back home who had matriculated with him as a freshman. At graduation he married her; returned to his local community and lived on the family farm. He taught successfully and farmed for two years, and earned the reputation of being an excellent teacher and farmer. Then he returned to his almamater and took a MA in History. Returning home again he resumed teaching and farming. Three years later two of his former professors, his parents, and those of his wife, encouraged him to return to his university and work on a PhD. He was happy with his high school students, two young children, and his local lifestyle, and really did not aspire to a PhD and college teaching (because he was primarily a teacher rather than a dedicated researcher and scholar). But a number of people including his and his wife's parents pointed out that with a PhD he could teach in a noted, four-year, liberal arts college only ten miles from home and still farm simultaneously. Obviously they wished to have a PhD professor in the family. With some misgivings he returned and took the PhD five years later while still working on the farm during summer intervals. Schooling however which earlier on (while working on his MA) had been exciting and rewarding had by now become tedious and arduous. With a PhD he obtained an assistant professorship, at the nearby college (which by that time offered two or three MA degrees); adapted; enjoyed teaching; read papers at professional meetings; published four journal articles; and, enjoyed the camaraderie among his colleagues.

However, when promoted to an associate professorship and attaining tenure he was faced with more farm work (his family had purchased more land and diversified their operation) and then he began to lose some of his zest for teaching; and, now felt it was time to recapture the summertime rapture foregone to attain a PhD. However, he tried to meet his obligations pertaining to teaching and farming, but slipped into a holding-on mood and lassitude, foreign to his nature and professionalism. Though he refrained from most of the deviant misconducts listed in the researchers' statistical findings noted in the introduction above, he began to lose a zest for teaching. He acquired a mindset found among many middle aged associate professors who become comfortable and too relaxed in their teaching. Beecher found himself with a disease lassitude problem: less interested in preparing his lectures; more permissible in terms of his class standards (such as required homework, book reports, classroom participations, corrections in returned test papers); less strict in requirements for student class attendance and their promptness in arriving to class on time; less demanding in requiring silence while lecturing; less firm in prohibiting eating, reading other class materials, and in other classroom diversions. Now he became more dependent on old notes in lecturing; became more lenient in changing grades; assumed a more passive attitude and response to students' phony excuses. He also eased up on historical research and publishing which he had never really enjoyed. In brief, his relaxed, comfortable and vague frame of mind, and his relaxed position and standards regarding his professional duties comprised his problem; rather than the statistical conduct violations listed by McPherson et al. He had never wanted to be a research scholar, but he thought he should be as a college professor. He was not, and this bothered him.

In summary, Beecher was a decent person with a stable and well integrated personality who should probably have remained a high school teacher. The pressure of two professions with added farmland was also baffling, stressful, and finally too much. Promotion to an associate professorship and a secure comfortable lifestyle contributed to his disquietude and professional disease. He remained for sometime a fair professor comparatively speaking in his particular teaching position, because he was not teaching in a research university. Nevertheless he was still teaching and his lassitude devolved into a deviancy of neglect and omission. Then he began to feel guilty and consequently retired from teaching. Too many professors try to pursue educational careers insincerely and the academy suffers as a consequence. We do not think that professors or administrators should assume additional careers outside academia, and that perhaps there should be well-defined rules prohibiting this practice. If and when professors or administrators become problematic cases of any kind when trying to hold down "two jobs" (one within and one without academia) they must be required to discontinue the extra outside occupation or be dismissed.

(19) Greene the Mean Assistant Dean

Greene was reared in several suburbs of the deep south in medium sized cities. He was the son of a peripatetic Protestant minister who at the discretion and direction of a bishop moved every three or four years to a new church congregation. Generally newly ordained ministers of his father's denomination start out as young men in a village or small-town congregation and move up the professional ladder to larger urban churches that pay more in money and prestige until reaching the upper rung of their competence and/or popularity. Green's father moved more frequently than most because he was good at building up small beginning congregations into good sized ones, and, then moving on to another less established church. A tall, strong, muscular socially aggressive, extrovert, he was outwardly friendly effusive, and somewhat of a glad hander, who presented an exuberant mien. A handsome carpenter and sometime amateur contractor, he literally (physically) helped build beginning churches. He also headed a family of a well integrated, modest, introverted wife, and three healthy and well adjusted children (two daughters and a son). Greene was the youngest. His mother married his father while attending the same denominational liberal arts college. She studied nursing after her AB, and became a registered nurse (RN). She temporized between a puritanical father and her lively children. Greene, like his father, was a tall, sturdy, intelligent, outer directed extrovert—somewhat of an Elmer Gantry type. He had strong, normal emotional relationships with his mother and two sisters, but stood in awe of his father; and, relations between them were ambivalent because of his father's strict disciplinary measures and pressures. For example, he pressured Greene to teach Sunday school; refused him a car on weekends, and never for dating. Greene conformed but felt deprived of the freedom and ease his peers experienced, many of whom had a car of their own. He fitted in at school where he made above average grades, and where teachers viewed him as a well behaved, serious-minded student who wanted to be a leader in classroom discussions, on the playground, and in gym classes. Classmates found him to be straightforward, conscientious, but too serious minded, and "straight." They also thought he was a little too stuffy and precise in his language and preachy. He rarely used slang or expletives; acted a little uptight around girls; and did not hang around with the boys after school or on weekends—too busy at church assisting his father. Girls liked his looks, gentle manners, but thought him a little too polite, self contained, and dull; and, most of all he did not have a car!

Greene had conflicting views on a career choice. His father counseled him to be a minister and his mother wanted him to become a teacher. At high school graduation he enrolled in a so-so denominational, four-year college and graduated with a double major in History and Religion. He fitted in well, made above average grades, and socialized with his peers who were products of the same religious background and social class as he (middle class Protestants). As in high school he was considered a square, though not obnoxious, who did not "turn girls on." He was a little too preachy and formal. All his classmates thought he was seminary bound "where he belonged," said many.

At graduation with an AB he surprised all by enrolling in an upper southern state's premiere state university noted for a strong liberal arts program, and high academic standards. For one year he took undergraduate and two graduate courses in preparation for an MA program. His father supported him, still hoping he would eventually enter the ministry. At the end of two semesters and summer-school classes he enrolled in an MA program in History and Education. His classmates considered him to be a serious minded student who, "what you saw was what you got," a "so-so guy," but too puritanical and a "square" who did not drink, go out much with the girls, or even with them after exams. Female graduate students and coeds thought him provincial, and one said, "Dullar than paint on the wall." He had always liked girls, but found females in graduate school even harder to get a date with than with those back home. Females looked upon him as a cipher, professors saw him as an industrious and well behaved student.

Following the MA Greene returned home and taught history in a local high school for two years, and married a high school teacher he met at church, a member of his congregation. Then with his father's support, he went back to another state university (with his wife) and enrolled in a PhD program. His former professors advised him not to pursue the PhD, but rather a D.Ed. or a seminary degree. Finally he was accepted as a History and Education major, and in five years took a watered down PhD in Education and History. Still disregarding his father's advice to enter the ministry, he applied for and received an assistant professorship in a southern state university's History department, where he was no avid researcher but an adequate teacher. His colleagues, younger than he, were succeeding as researchers and publishers. Students thought he was a kind, fair but very dry teacher. He tried for three years to publish and did so in education journals, but was unable to in History journals. His department head knew he had to do something about Greene who was getting to be known as a non-researcher. He talked to the dean of arts and sciences, who at the time thought he needed another assistant to help him with an investigation of several sexual harassment cases that confronted him. Greene by this time knew the only chance he had in academia for success was in administration because he could not publish in History journals. He also reasoned that his double major in Education and History had prepared him for an administrative position. Following a meeting of the three, Greene, the History department head, and the dean of arts and sciences, he left the History department, and moved to another office as one of the dean's assistants on a temporary basis, ostensibly to see how things would work out. Greene was now on his way on another career plan, thenceforth he was one of the dean's gofers and investigators. Though a good errand boy, paper pusher, and bureaucratic office aide, he was too moralistically monolithic and zealous in investigative techniques, and too prosecutorial in his approaches to those charged with sexual harassment and other sexual offences as the following examples demonstrate:

(1) When one professor was charged with sexual harassment by a female graduate student at a party hosted by faculty and graduate students, Greene asked him to meet with him and an examining committee of faculty and graduate students in a room where recordings could be made, without telling him the meeting proceedings could be recorded. The accused professor smelling a rat appeared accompanied by his lawyer who was also ignorant of the recording possibilities. There was no proof in a "she said, he said" case; and, further it was disclosed that the female student accuser had made other unverified sex charges against another professor previously. (2) He on his own without instructions to do so investigated several former graduate students who had been charged with past campus sexual misconduct but now lived elsewhere. (3) He interrogated several students and professors about the sexual conduct of a professor who had been charged with embracing a coed at a party "in an untoward sexual way." Some walked away from these interviews. (4) He frequently queried students and professors about negative stories he had heard concerning some professors' "sexy lecturing content," though they were not under investigation. (5) He himself roamed one department's office halls at night during weekends, surreptitiously to check on professors who had reportedly been using their offices for sexual trysts with female students (but never discovered such trysts). (6) He called one professor who had been falsely charged but exonerated with sexual harassment to his office, and interrogated him about some previous participant observation study he had engaged in with others, and published (which included some sexual content). This savvy and disgusted professor left without giving him any information.

(7) He queried yet another professor about some drug and sexual scenes he had reported in a published book. This professor laughed in his face. (8) While investigating one sexual misconduct case he asked interviewees about other past and pending cases. (9) He told several professors who had been charged in different cases and exonerated on sexual misconduct charges that: "We know you got off, but we didn't believe any of your story then or now, but we could not prove it conclusively and decisively, so look out." (10) When investigating one case, he would ask some professors and graduate students to spy on professors in other cases; (11) He and another church member visited some other professors' homes without invitations and tried to persuade them to switch their churches to his. (12) He queried a campus MD about a report that he was treating a professor employed on the campus for a venereal disease. (13) When sent by the dean to help investigate a troubled departmental split into warring factions, and peopled with a number of disgruntled professors, he irritated many by asking all kinds of personal and unnecessary questions aside from the issues at hand. For example, he asked one professor: "What salary do you think we should give you next year"? (This professor laughed at him). When he finished this investigation, he left more of a shambles than had existed beforehand. (14) When one of his former colleagues who had just published a book on the south dropped by his office to chat, Greene argued with him about his findings; and, told him that his book would not get him promoted. (15) On one occasion he visited a professor's summer-school class while in session to find out if the required number of students were actually in the class. When he told the professor that the number was slightly deficient, but he would recommend that he could teach it anyway, the professor expressed his appreciation. He needed the class to survive during the summer, and ask Green in a joshing manner if there was anything he could do for him in return. Greene answered in a very serious way: "Yes, I understand you grow good watermelons. You can give me two or three." The students who heard this dialogue laughed. The watermelons were never delivered despite the fact that Green ask about them a short time thereafter. Reportedly the dean disciplined Greene verbally on several occasions, and demanded that he ease up on some of his charges and investigations. Greene eventually retired as an associate dean. Whether or not he "eased up" is unknown.

In summary, Greene represents an apparent obsessive compulsive puritanical conundrum, and certainly a mischievous, nosey, dangerous deviant. He claimed he thought he was always doing his Christian duty—and maybe so from his spiritual prospective. In reality, he was a self-righteous, sanctimonious, overly conscientious, inflexible, nosey hypocrite who though not too scrupulous about his own ethics and moral values, tried to impose some on others. Such people are inimical to academia because it is impossible to change anyone who believes he or she is always right, and others always wrong. Green's social background was too puritanical, and his father was too demanding and authoritarian. More significantly he was probably an obsessive compulsive personality type and did not belong in academia; and, his dean was also a deviant for permitting him to stay in place. Greene convinced of his Christian virtues, experienced no recognizable structural or situational stress problems, properties he attributed to others in his milieu. Again we see that weak, flawed, non-scholars do not necessarily make good administrators. Perhaps Greene needed some other form of religion. Those of his type are serious violators of one's civil rights and university regulations, and they should be dismissed when detected in these violations.

(20) Stuart the Career Student

Stuart, an intelligent only child was born in an upper middle class family in the urban mid-south, the son of a successful merchant who owned several clothing stores in a medium-sized city. His father was a serious minded, outer directed, efficient extrovert and a firm but reasonable person in the way he supervised his employees and his son. At home he was an open-minded, agreeable, dependable, affectionate father whose relations with his wife and son were stable and congenial. A "solid citizen," so his peers said who was highly respected in his community, and a liberal thinker in a mainstream Protestant church. Politically conservative, as was his wife and neighbors, he was a member of the Republican Party. Stuart's mother was a modest, neat, intelligent, well adjusted ambivert, who like her husband held a BS degree in business. Stuart was a quiet, reserved, intelligent introvert whose developmental history at home, school and in the community was problematic. He made above average grades in school where he was marginally adjusted, too tentative, indecisive, and bookish about things that were not modern. Though heterosexual, he was uptight and diffident about sex, and not popular with girls who said he was too prim, aloof, and too flighty from one subject to another. Nor did he speak playground lingo or express interest in popular music, dance or listen to rock and roll. He did listen to jazz, a thing of the past to classmates, and at the urgency of his parents he did listen to classical music which classmates did not understand or care about. He also liked art, which is not in line with the taste of his classmates either. One of Stuart's male classmates reported: "I guess Stuart is all right, but he is dated and has no balls. He belongs to another century". Girls were indifferent toward one who was not very interesting or exciting about anything, but jazz, old movies, and poetry.

Though of medium build and physically healthy, he was solitary in habit and preferred books, art, and poetry to playground activities. Classmates voted him: "The most unlikely to succeed." Unlike his father, he expressed no interest in making money or business, but voiced some early vague interest in teaching. Both parents reluctantly accepted his choice but suggested he keep engineering in mind as a second career choice. His father's older and favorite brother was an electrical engineer. Stuart's parents wanted him to choose a more lucrative, and to them a more solid career than teaching. Desiring to please them, but undecided about any career he enrolled in his state's flagship state university as a engineering major, despite the fact that he had never been proficient in math or science. Understandably, his grades as a freshman were barely passable in either math or science, so he switched to a double major in History and English, and said, "I can abide liberal arts." At graduation five years later, he belatedly found out he could not teach in his state without a number of education courses he had not taken. While attending summer school to obtain the necessary hours in education to teach, he found the coursework in this discipline interesting, so he continued in school, and took a MA in Education, which took four more years. Then, still not knowing which discipline he liked best, he took a MA in History. Still in a quandary he entered a graduate school program in English and Communications, and took a MA in English. Four years later he took a MA in Communications, and five years afterwards he took a PhD in this discipline. During summer breaks he returned home and read books on a number of topics. Finally his parents realized he had turned into a nerd and a professional student. He went out with girls when he could get a date, but most females still found him dull, too much into old fashioned stuff like jazz, and neutered. One female said: "He has no masculine flair." Hearing about this, Stuart asked a male friend who was popular with girls, "What does she mean by masculine flair"? Understandingly he received no answer.

With a PhD he secured a teaching position in another southern state university where he taught Communications and took a MA in Sociology on the side. This took several summers more to complete. During this period he married one of his instructors, an older, more sophisticated person than he who said to him before marriage: "I'm just a step in your education." (His problem was there were too many steps in his educational career.) Soon after marriage he and his wife moved on to another nearby state university where they taught in separate departments. Two years later he divorced her, and moved on to yet another university and explained to her: "You were right on but you aged out." He explained his divorce to his parents thusly, "She was a wonderful woman at first but she got too old for me." Later he married one of his students, ten years younger than he and moved on to still another university where he taught by day and took law courses at night. Six years later with a JD, he taught law in yet another university's Criminal Justice department. When asked if he ever took the bar exam following graduation from law school, he responded, "Oh no, why should I take the bar exam. I never wanted to practice law. I just wanted to learn about law; and, I thought I would please my favorite aunt who always wanted me to be a lawyer." Now middle aged he had several degrees and was working on a BA in Art History, while he still taught, and was ostensibly responsible for a wife (who said later she married him because he was a scholar). Without the continual financial support of his parents, his protracted, compulsive career as a student could not have been. When his parents were asked why they kept on supporting him in his study of one thing after another, his father answered: "Oh, well he is our only child and we know he will never grow up, but what else can we do? Fortunately he never sired children."

When quizzed by his parents and acquaintances about his penchant for a student career, school and job changes, and his divorce and remarriage to a second much younger wife, Stuart gave no plausible answers, but verbalized the following long paraphrased excuse, "Oh, I am just a normal person with curiosity and a drive to learn about many different things. When you stop studying you atrophy. The degrees don't mean much, just a means to a study end. The marriage thing is just one of those things one goes through. My first wife grew too old and domineering. My present wife meets my needs. She thinks she understands me. What else can I say? I get bored in one place with one woman too long." (Was he bragging? Certainly he was no Casanova.)

Obviously his frequent changes in subject areas; accumulation of various academic degrees; changes of employment; flippant attitudes and behavior relating to females and marriage; financial dependence on his parents; and, his presentation of self as an intellectual indicated a pompous, emotionally immature, unstable, undirected, insecure dependent personality. He was described by his employers as a "marginal dreamy teacher" who got along with his colleagues and students but demonstrated no real interest in scholarship or his students. He told some colleagues once: "I have no flair for teaching, and most of my students are not worthy of me. But what can I say, I have to do something. Long ago I thought I might like to teach, but it became a drag." Additionally, his publication record was thin, and he signed off on his few publications with a string of degrees following his name—real strange to publishers. When several administrators chided him about his limited publication record, from time to time, he answered with statements like: "How many faculty members do you have who have one-half the degrees I have? Publications are not everything, and most of them are drivel and worthless props." More seriously, Stuart was nonchalant about keeping class rolls, attendance, grade records, report cards, etc.; and, he frequently forgot to return test papers, essays, and book reports; and often turned grades into the registrar's office late. Further he kept irregular office hours; and, students noted that "He joked around when we found him in, and he is a good teacher and fun." Perhaps he left serial positions before he was pushed out or fired, but still he was popular with students. Reports on these issues were not clear, though his flighty nature and desire for change were paramount problems. Despite all this, his students praised him and said he was interesting and fun to be around. (Perhaps some students, like children, like Peter Pans.)

Professors like Stuart who continually wonder if the grass over the hill is greener than where they stand; have difficulty in choosing one discipline of study; chase one degree after another; are remiss in their classroom duties; and have no serious interest in students or teaching; and who are dependent financially and emotionally on their parents do not belong in academia. Stuart's parents were enablers who made possible his career as a professional student; but, his apparent underlying dependent, immature, and unstable personality disorder appears more significant as the source of his cavalier deviancy pattern. He should probably have been dismissed from several positions.

He sailed blithely through life with no evident structural or situational stress problems. Though beyond middle age, he gradually grew morose, and often quoted the following lines from Johnny Mercer's lyrics to acquaintances:

The days of wine and roses

Laugh and run away

Like a child at play

Through the meadowland

Towards a closing door,

A door marked "Nevermore"

That wasn't there before.

—see Kimbell *et al.*, 2010

Stuart's parents and second wife gave him continuous emotional and moral support despite his persistent childishness; and, their love and loyalty probably held him together emotionally, but simultaneously enhanced his dependency and deviancy. Counseling with those like Stuart is difficult for any therapist, though his parents should have sought psychological help for him early on. Unmasked administrators and professors who appear to have a dependent personality disorder and who become problematic should be required to undergo psychological treatment or dismissed. Retention would depend on treatment success.

(21) Bruiser the Successful Loser

Bruiser was born in a lower middle class farm family in the south and reared there and in a large northeastern city. His intact family migrated to the north when he was twelve, and thenceforth he lived during intervals with his parents in the city and his grandmother on a small family farm down south. Bruiser was a strong, muscular, highly extroverted, self-centered, aggressive, unsympathetic, guiltless, rebellious youth who was predatory in his relationships with his five younger siblings, playmates, classmates, and others he could con or push around. Sightly above average intelligence he picked up conning street tactics from his corner-boy associates in the city. An ambitious wannabe, he was always willing to do most anything to get what he wanted—"An easy life with a briefcase," as he explained to a classmate.

Following a marginal adjustment in an urban high school located in a working-class neighborhood where he played second string basketball, he enrolled in a southern university (actually a college) where he had conned coaches about his exaggerated athletic prowess. A height of 6'3" helped along and he played basketball two years as a second stringer before his coaches belatedly discovered they had been bamboozled. His pseudo-sophisticated city-street lingo, mesomorphic body structure, friendly façade, swaggering gait, sporty macho dress style, and vaunted athletic skills impressed some of his classmates and professors, and he was a "cock of the walk" with some naïve coeds (who wrote his term papers, book reports, take home exams, etc.), and a do-gooder Sociology professor his mentor. He made average grades and graduated with an A B degree in Sociology. Then his Sociology mentor persuaded his erstwhile professor (who taught as a full professor at one of the state's public universities) to get Bruiser accepted in his school's graduate Sociology program. Said professor with great effort, persuaded reluctant department members to accept Bruiser with the proviso that his mentor "monitor his pet." Shortly after Bruiser's admission his undergraduate mentor and sponsor was charged with sexual misconduct involving a coed, and asked him to come to his rescue as a character witness. Simultaneously, the dean of Arts and Sciences at Bruiser's almamater (where the changes were made) persuaded him not to appear; and, provide him a written negative character report on his former champion. Bruiser complied with the tacit understanding that this dean would repay him with job recommendations following his PhD graduation. With Bruiser's help his former undergraduate major professor and mentor was pressured to resign. Nor did Bruiser lend this former mentor any emotional support.

From the beginning of his PhD program Bruiser had grade problems despite the aid of his new sponsor. Additionally, some female undergraduate and graduate students rumored that he was a stud and a sexual harasser. He had led a promiscuous sex life since puberty and though now married with one child, he still continued a promiscuous lifestyle. Things were somewhat iffy for him until another super mentor appeared during his second year in graduate school in the form of a new Sociology department head, a would-be jock, who took Bruiser under his arm as a useful spy, and a star player on the department's basketball team. Despite faculty attempts to drop him from the graduate program following his marginal grades on his MA examinations, the head countermanded such action and Bruiser stayed on. One year later, the head made him an instructor, after he was awarded a marginal MA, and assigned him to classes heretofore taught by professors with tenure. Bruiser no longer spoke to his former mentor, the one who had initially managed to get him accepted in his PhD program, because this professor was now disliked by the head. Bruiser made only passing grades in his PhD program with the aid of tutors and the department head's cronies, and flunked initially his MA preliminary exams, and later his PhD orals, and the defense of his marginal dissertation—passing all the second time under pressure from the head and a weak dean. The head actually bullied his PhD committee to pass him. (Bruiser's dissertation was removed from departmental files and the library, and is now lost.) The head argued for Bruiser's retention and eventual graduation on political grounds and said: "Academia needs more regular fellows like Bruiser, rather than snobbish intellectuals. Other schools are graduating students like him and, we cannot fall behind."

Following Bruiser's PhD graduation the head recommended him for three different successive positions in good, respectable universities where he did poorly in teaching and research. Under pressure Bruiser resigned from the first two before coming up for tenure because of weak teaching (really preaching) and no publications. He obtained an administrative position in the third—and had been also recommended for all three positions by the dean of his former undergraduate school. He was removed from the administrative third position he held during the second year following two sexual misconduct charges; the first by a female coed on campus, the second by a female colleague at a professional meeting. Both cases however were hushed up by the university's legal staff, and Bruiser remains on this university's payroll as a full professor with tenure in the Sociology department (where he now "earns" more money than the department head). He is now married to a second wife reported to be economically independent yet he provides no income for his two children left behind. The university claims it did not have enough evidence to convict him of the sex charges … so the story goes. Furthermore, he had lawyered up with a high powered, noted attorney who practiced criminal law, and the university apparently wished to avoid scandal. The administration did remove him from an administrative position, and placed him back in the classroom where he remains as an incompetent professor and a potential sexual predator. Therefore in a sense Bruiser is a "successful loser." We have seen several incompetent professors kicked upstairs to administrative positions only to be kicked back downstairs when they failed again. To reiterate, weak and deviant professors do not necessarily make good administrators.

Bruiser appears to be a successful antisocial personality disorder type who probably could not have survived in many other social institutions. He illustrates the case of how some professors with rotten personalities can do more than survive in academia even with marginal credentials, and con their way (in some places) with the help and acquiescence of weak and/or corrupt administrators. No known about professor or administrator with an antisocial personality disorder should be permitted to remain in academia; certainly not those who become trouble makers.

(22) Don the Don Juan

Don grew up in an upper south village, the only child in a middle class family dominated by an intelligent, extroverted, well adjusted mother, who taught English in a rural, public high school, and an introverted, functional alcoholic father, a county librarian, who wrote and told short stories at home which were never published. Don, an extrovert, remembers with nostalgia these adventurous sagas, and of asking his father questions about them. His mother told him later: "I married your father because I loved him despite my knowledge that he drank too much, and thought he was the Gods' gift to humanity." She ran the household and took good care of Don, a healthy gregarious, well adjusted youngster, and her husband, a quiet, dreamy man who spent his off-work-time drinking, reading books, and writing, and telling stories. No one ever saw him drunk because he held his liquor well and was perceptibly sober most of the time, although inebriated a lot of the time but always had time for discussions about books with his son. Harmony prevailed because his father was an agreeable, pleasant, mellowed out sot who only wanted to pontificate occasionally. A widowed paternal aunt lived next door with her five children, one son, and four lively, attractive, well adjusted girls, all a little older than Don. He played with all of these double first cousins (two brothers had married two sisters) and brought up their family's side by side. From childhood, Don remained close to all of them particularly to his aunt and female cousins.

Don remembers listening attentively to these female cousins' accounts of their courtships, and how dense males were at the "dating game," as they called it. These discourses reminded him, years later, of opera buffet that disclosed, he said, "A lot about males' and females' differing perspectives." He discounted most of what his older male first cousin told him about females as dross, but treasured the girls' stories and insights as very entertaining. His male cousin warned him (metaphorically speaking), "Do not forget the whip when going to see a woman." His female cousins cautioned: "Always remember that the female is three steps ahead of you in dating relationships … her intuition and subtlety matches the males' physical superiority and more." He also recalls how these voluptuous cousins would say to him at reaching puberty when they were lolling about scantily dressed next door in the summertime: "You better go home now Don, your mother is waiting for you." As a friendly, precocious, intelligent, handsome youth, he conformed at home, in his community of farmers, and retired farmers, and at school where he made good grades, and was admired as a well behaved boy by his classmates and teachers—particularly by females who called him, "Such a darling boy." He tried, but was only fair at contact sports; and, though he did some hunting, a requirement of males in southern rural communities he detested shooting animals or anything else. Don explained to a group of outsiders once: "Southern males when growing up must drink liquor, chase women and rabbits; hunt deer, bears, ducks, turkeys, squirrels and coons with hunting dogs, and bark at the moon." Of course this was partially metaphorical, but his outside audience got the picture (See "Savage Ideal" in Cash 1941; Cobb 2005).

Nice looking, intelligent, curious, energetic, verbal, fashionably dressed and well read (and shod by his mother) with instructions from his next door cousins, and knowledgeability of the local culture, he had no difficulty in getting dates. From childhood he much preferred the company of girls over boys and related to females easier than to males throughout his life. Not rich or upper-class, nor a hunter, or an athlete, and bookish to boot, he was not considered too eligible by popular girls but this was fine with him, because he said: "I prefer girls nice, intelligent with class who are physically attractive." Those with the whole ball of wax, as his mother and female cousins advised; and as they pointed out: "Nice girls like to have a good time too." Therefore, he avoided promiscuous and risk-taking females, who smoked and drank to excess, and slept around. He denigrated nobody but was selective in the company he kept at and away from home. As a high school senior he had consensual sexual relationships with a few girls (within which it was mutually understood that no strings were attached); and a plausible rumor floated that he had a brief affair with a young, single English teacher the summer following his high school graduation. Girls called him a "smoothie" because he drank only wine and beer moderately; did not smoke, gamble or carouse with the machos or rednecks; used few expletives or obscenities; and, talked elegantly. He is a "good boy" his mother said; and, others commented: "How could he miss out with his assets, intelligence, good looks, gentleness, and precocious sophistication."

Following high school graduation he enrolled in his parent's almamater and graduated magna cum laude five years later with a double major in English and History. He conformed and the tenor of his university life was similar to that he had left behind. He made good grades; made friends; and his professors (especially female professors) admired him as a handsome, studious, mannerly, friendly, ambitious, smooth-talking, polished student. Classmates admired him, but males wondered why he did not spend more time with them at student hangouts and other bars. He did as his mother and female cousins had advised; that is, when not in class he spent most of his time in his dormitory room, or in the library, or on the internet; and, studying. "Time out behavior," as he called it, was spent with "good intelligent wholesome girls" similar to those back home. He dated coeds and TAs (slightly older than he), and his sex life was actively normal for his age, place, and time. Females chased him and consequently he had several affairs, and some called him a "silent player," a label he denied. A routine physical exam revealed a high testosterone level which he dismissed as unimportant and kept quiet about. At graduation his professors recommended him for a graduate school assistantship in the English department of a nearby prestigious, private university which he applied for and received.

He studied hard, made good grades, and took a MA and a PhD in six years. During the PhD process he coauthored two papers which he read at professional meetings and published with his major professor. Noted as an ambitious TA, he ran on a career fast-track. Upon graduation he was invited to stay on as an instructor which he did for two years. During this period he was applauded for his teaching performance and scholarship, however he had several affairs with single female professors, and single female TAs, which were accompanied by rumors which did not bode well for the future, though no complaints were made. Females chased him as they had in high school and in undergraduate school and he complied, but did not exploit. Rumors spread and Don was tagged "Don the Don Juan," a sobriquet he denied. Consequently, he decided to leave (though he was asked to remain for another year), and found employment as an assistant professor in another prestigious university, where he hoped to escape the label, "Don Juan."

When he had completed his PhD his mother, aunt, female first cousins, and friends wondered why had he not settled down with one female partner. Patiently he explained that he was not a womanizer, but rather a normal male who preferred the company of females, was not ready for marriage; did not hurt anyone in his affairs; and, that he experienced friendly relationships with several females of different ages devoid of romantic relations—well maybe, but the question remained, how did he juggle all of these "friendly relationships" in the air without offending someone?

In his new position in an English department, disproportionately female (as the one he left behind) he attended to his professional duties assiduously; researched and published, and, was popular with students and colleagues. Importantly, he avoided close friendly and/or sexual relationships with female professors, as well as with other females on campus though he knew several from his graduate school days. Things went well until he was promoted to an associate professorship, and erroneously decided he could now initiate new "friendly relationships" anywhere with females again; and, renew those of the past without stirring up past rumors. "After all," he reported, "I had clearly demonstrated that I could refrain from romantic relationships on campus." However, he made a colossal mistakes when he engaged in a close "friendly relationship" (devoid of romance or sex, he said) with an attractive narcissistic flirtatious, disgruntled female colleague who scolded him when he unknowingly ventured into a simultaneous "friendly relationship" with this disgruntled professor's rival (one promoted when Dr. Disgruntled thought she should have been promoted instead). Dr. Disgruntled insisted that Don cease contact with her perceived rival (now her enemy as she read it). Don refused and tried to explain that he could be friends with both (impossible as his cousins would have told him). Dr. Disgruntled disagreed, and with the help of another female colleague who (unjustifiably) thought Don had refused her friendly overtures, spread rumors that Don was a playboy and sexual harasser. Don thinking (correctly) that he had been had, lost his usual composure, lawyered up, and demanded that his department head reign in or sanction the two spiteful rumor mongers. Both refused to retract their frivolous charges, now in the dean's office, therefore, the head reluctantly investigated the matter as quietly and quickly as possible. During this investigation, past rumors resurfaced and spread about Don's so-called womanizing; and, two other female professors he had dated before reported that he was, "A romantic cad who loves you and leaves you." Despite no pressure to resign, and no negative official decision, Don nonetheless found a suitable position in yet another university and resigned. Here Don earned a reputation as a teacher and an all around good professor; and, he finally took his mother's and cousins' advice and selected (or was selected by) a mature, attractive, stable, strong-willed, intelligent, extroverted colleague and married her. Under her eye, charm and grace he refrained from further "womanizing"—so he and she said. Had he sought psychological help from professionals earlier on he probably would have learned that it is difficult and counterproductive to engage in romantic relationships with several women simultaneously—and psychologically risky for oneself and the females involved.

Many claim Don had always comported himself as a normal male in relationships with females, and that he had been a victim of some women's jealousy and scorn. Others argued he had conducted such relationships deceptively and motivated by salacious goals.

The question remains open about "sexy" male and "sexy" female relationships in academia. That is, at what point do they become deceptive, promiscuous, selfish and predatory? The sexual norms of particular academic groups within particular institutions must be considered. However, colleges and universities do not usually provide written rules concerning sexual conduct of specific campus groups, or those with specific academic rank. Most rely on vague unwritten customary rules such as "should you bed her, be prepared to marry her, etc." However, it is a generally accepted rule that professors and administrators refrain from sexual relationships with students (particularly with undergraduates), which the authors think is a necessary and must stipulation which should be written down and enforced. Violators of this rule pertaining to undergraduates should be: (1) fired or (2) required to cease the sexual contacts, and (3) undergo professional psychological counseling. Those refusing either (2) or (3) should be terminated. Many factors would determine options (1) or (2) and (3) above; for example: age, impending marriage, marital status, maturity, extenuating circumstances, etc. The rules in this area pertaining to graduate students would vary with the values of each individual institution; the social status of the actors involved; and, the circumstances of the sexual relationships.

Don probably represents a narcissistic, obsessive compulsive "mama's pretty boy" personality disorder type who displayed immaturity in his shallow (though not purposefully harmful) relationships with females. He did not show good judgment and must have known his relationships with females in academia embodied problematic, risk-taking behavior which was detrimental to departmental peace and harmony as well as to bruised female egos. And he should have sought professional psychological counseling from a clinical psychologist or a psychiatrist early on. He did not and his problem lingered and became more serious. Obviously he was not a replica of his namesake "Don Giovanni" as portrayed by Wolfgang Mozart (Forman, 1994:151-168, 877-881). "Don Giovanni" (1757) in Mozart's tragic comedy who was an obsessive-compulsive, unscrupulous pursuer and seducer of women, a pathological case and a "beast" (so-called by critics), who engaged in no self-analysis and in the end was consigned to hell (friction).

On the other hand, Lord Byron's (George Gordon, 1788-1824) "Don Juan" (written between 1818 and1823), an unfinished epic satire and a portrayal of Byron himself, portrays a more normal, brave, sensual, compulsive, womanizing adventurer; and, a brilliant sardonic literary critic of English events, poetry, women, wealth, power and politics (See Don Juan in Briggs *Great Poems of the English Language*, 1941: 511-516). Our Don Juan (herein), though deviant, is more likely tilted toward Lord Byron's portrayal and that of Casanova (See Casanova, 1726-1798) in Giacono Casanova's autobiography, *History of My Life* (never completed), an account of Casanova's more than some four-thousand pages of eighteenth-century sexual adventures in Europe (a masterpiece compared by some scholars to Mareel Proust's works). Casanova, a historical figure above all, was a smooth operator, the archetypal man who loved women, and who seduced (and was seduced by) many females (aristocrats, servants, divas, actresses, nuns, courtesans, virgins, etc.). He was a masculine, connoisseur and Renaissance man (classical scholar, historian, librarian, mathematician, magician, soldier, translator, diplomat, con artist and womanizer among other things who hobnobbed with the beau monde and famous philosophers; e.g., Voltaire, nobles and scholars, artists, priests, novelists, scientists, as well as with charlatans con men and the hoi polloi). Gentle, kind, considerate, caring, protecting, thoughtful, and very generous with females, he courted. He loved women according to his dictum: "Ultimately giving pleasure is far more important than receiving it" (See Trask 2007). Nonetheless Casanova was admired, loved, and deplored simultaneously in his day and henceforth to the present. Casanova is still a metaphor for successful male lovers. Lord Byron and Casanova's autobiographical portrayals illustrate the ambivalence toward womanizers in society at large, and make the distinction between immoral and acceptable sexual behavior difficult to make. The distinctions drawn between the sexual behavior of Don Juans and Vamps and that of the prosaic and less adventurous of those in the United States have been somewhat blurred since the sexual revolution of the 1960s and the pill; however, the societal ambivalence toward Don Juans and Vamps though somewhat attenuated remains. Changes in sexual attitudes follow in the wake of changes in sexual behaviors.

The question is when does a male who enjoys the company of females like our Don become a Don Juan? And when does a Don Juan become a deviant? If one does not seduce under false pretenses, is he deviant? Who seduces whom? We suggest that the movement from one friendly or romantic relationship to another is the crux of this knotty academic problem. The situation with a Vamp, the Don Juan's counterpart, is similar though she is more likely to be labeled and scorned as a deviant than the male in most U.S. academic subcultures. Physiologically and psychologically speaking, what's fair for the goose is fair for the gander, and neither males nor females are inherently monogamous. Some scholars claim that the female is less promiscuous and more demure and selective than the male, however the gap between the sexual behaviors and attitudes toward sex of males and females in the US has narrowed since 1960s, and the pill.

Don's profile illustrates the problems with Don Juans in academia: (1) Don Juans and/or those so labeled frequently engender envy, distrust, and negative moral judgments in the minds of colleagues who might react to them with deviant acts of their own; that is, of one kind or another; (2) Don Juans' movements from one female admirer and/or sexual partner to another creates departmental problems. To reiterate this movement rather than the sexual acts *per se* produces the real academic problems. Don Juans and Vamps who act out the parts of "playboys" and "playgirls" have no place in academia; and, should they be selected and begin to play they must be required to stop and seek professional psychological therapy, after which if they still play, they should be terminated. Rules and sanctioning procedures pertaining to them should be spelled out in writing and enforced.

Further the view of some that consensual sexual relationships between single professors and single adult students are permissible, and frequently result in happy marriages, is highly questionable. Our experience has been that very few of these sexual relationships eventuate in either congenial friendships or in happy marriages—but more frequently in grief, wounded egos, scandal, conflicts and/or problems for all concerned. Finally to reiterate sexual relationships between professors or administrators and undergraduate students should be prohibited because they tend to endanger and/or destroy the purpose of learning, and teacher-student respect and trust, among other negative consequences.

(23) Pat the Dilettante

Pasquala (Pat) Junior, the grandson of a deceased prune orchardist (an immigrant from Naples, Italy) was reared in a big house on a fruit-growing section of land in northern California owned and inherited by his father, Pat Senior and his aunt Jean, his surrogate mother (Pat Senior's sister). His mother died when he was six and he lived with his father, his aunt Jean and her daughter Judy. Aunt Jean, a well adjusted extrovert and a high school graduate, had married a spoiled brat and divorced him before her daughter Judy was born. Pat Junior and Judy grew up like brother and sister. Aunt Jean was his father's bookkeeper and business confidant as well as a conscientious, stable mother who helped her brother, Pat Senior extend and develop his and her land holdings. She and Pat Senior also owned and operated a clothing store, and a storage-space company. Pat Senior was a muscular, handsome, well-built extrovert, who as a youth worked for his father at all sorts of manual jobs including the planting and tending of fruit trees, and truck-driving produce to market. He too had only a high school education, but was a very intelligent, verbally smooth individual with a pleasing, personality. He dressed stylishly, drove expensive cars and was quite the sport and big spender around town. A charmer and a real Casanova, he was very popular amongst women, other orchardists, business men, and politicians. Additionally, he was a successful businessman with the help of his sister Jean who co-hosted his many business meetings and house parties.

Pat Junior (our subject) loved and respected his father, though their relationship was somewhat ambivalent because he actually saw little of him. His father tried to be a firm disciplinarian, but spent most of his time working or at upscale piano bars and restaurants socializing with many other Italian Americans. A good actor, he was also gifted with a rich baritone voice and was pressured to sing American and Italian pop songs; and, was even offered an actor's contract by a famous Hollywood producer which he turned down—and was quoted as saying, "Why should I leave this valley of delight (Santa Clara Valley) for smoggy and phony Los Angeles"? Jean frequently accompanied him and sang, all for fun, at several different piano bars. She had a boyfriend for many years, but never remarried, and devoted her life to the wellbeing of her father (while he was alive), her daughter Judy, her brother Pat, and to his son Pat Junior. Pat Junior's life was spent with Jean, her daughter Judy, and later on with Judy's husband, Dick an electrical engineer at an auto company in San Jose, California.

Pat Junior (Pasquala) did not completely approve of his father's playboy lifestyle; and, tried throughout the years, with the help of his aunt Jean, to reign him in without success. Pat Junior was a handsome, intelligent, well adapted extrovert who made good grades without much effort in school, and projected a pleasing personality similar to, but not as flamboyant, as that of his father. He made easy and pleasing adjustments in and out of the classroom, and spent some of his leisure time in high school and undergraduate school surfing in a wet suit on the beach at Santa Cruz, California, and in students' hangouts in San Jose and on up the peninsula to Half-moon Bay, and on to San Francisco. He drank only beer and wine, and like most students, he had a fake ID. The bar-age thing of 21 was a joke to all high school and college students then in California. Unlike his father, he spent most of his time reading at home and listening to all kinds of music including jazz. In body build, he was muscular like his father, a mesomorph, and appeared mature beyond his age because his black hair began turning iron gray prematurely when he was 21. Many friends said this feature enhanced his already good looks, and "made him appear more distinguished." He played tennis, danced, and swam at the family's country club, but shied away from contact sports, which he thought a waste of time. Though not a nerd, he read historical novels, went to plays and art galleries, and the opera in San Francisco with girlfriends occasionally. He liked upper middle class arty girls, and avoided serious relationships, as well as rowdy, risk-taking behavior and wild company— nor did he speed though he had owned a sports car since high school. He also worked occasionally at all kinds of odd jobs in the family's fruit orchards, and in his father's office. He even modeled suits and men's wear in the family clothing store, but never become seriously interested in business. He liked school and did not avoid the rough and tumble of the playground, but preferred to read and study at home. He was also very much interested in art and classical literature and traveled in Europe (primarily Italy) occasionally with his family during vacations; but, had no idea of what to do following high school, but knew what he did not want to do, become a business man like his father.

He made good grades in all subjects but preferred art; painted some oils; learned how to play the piano without lessons; acted in a few high school plays; took a few voice lessons; and sang pop songs with his aunt Jean and his father. The problem was his interests were too wide and ever changing, and though good at many activities, he was not exceptionally gifted in any one, but he had a good baritone voice (bel canto singing) and knew some art history. However he did not wish to be a professional musician, an art historian, or a museum curator—or for that matter a professional anything. All he knew for sure was that by temperament he was arty rather than pragmatic or scientific. At high school graduation, some suggested: "Go to Stanford, you are a good student and Stanford is the Harvard of the west." Others said: "Not Stanford, it's a class-bound school for snooty people." Still others said: " Go to Berkeley, you have the test scores." Most said, "Go to Santa Clara University, where most of your friends have gone." The latter was a respectable school and in keeping with his Catholic background and tradition, but he told himself and others that he did not wish to lead a derivative lifestyle shaped and bounded by others. He meant an orchardist or store owner. Half heartedly he thought about becoming a classical scholar, a Renaissance man. Finally he opted for Berkeley, where he made good grades and adapted, but thought he was "on a strange cold cultural island full of nerds immersed in a radical atmosphere," he said. He made good grades, but the only courses he really enjoyed were Philosophy, Art History, Anthropology and classical literature (of Greece and Rome). Pushed by his family to take solid courses he could use for something to do following graduation, he majored in Sociology, which his family and some of his friends thought was some kind of social work. After all he pointed out, "I'm a good observer and reader of social scenes, and that's all Sociology is about." He had taken a course in social stratification and one in deviant behavior at Berkeley that kindled his interests, but as he said: "They didn't really turn me on." He also liked Philosophy courses dealing with Schopenhauer, Henri Bergson, Husserl, Heidegger, Albert Camus, and even Nietzsche, but the popular and frequent discussions he heard in and out of class on Marx, Michel Foucault, Louis Althusser, and Jacques Dierrida and abstract painters like Francis Bacon dismayed him (especially Derrida whom he called a postmodern fool)—"They were so cold, detached, and blatantly false," he said. He admired Monet, Matisse, Picasso, and Cezanne and all the impressionists. Renoir was his favorite painter and when one of his "sophisticated" artistic classmates sneered at him and said: "Renoir was just a so-so vase painter," he cringed and became fed up with the whole Berkeley scene. At graduation, he returned home still not knowing what to do (not really wanting to do anything but read, write and paint) and balked at his father's offer to work with him. He enrolled in another University of California nearby in self defense where he entered a graduate school program in Sociology halfheartedly—and explained his rationale thusly: "I will always love the classics and art, but I want to know a little more about Sociology. You know about people's leisure time activities and deviant behavior." His family and friends asked him, "For what"? He answered: "Well you see I may become a writer, and Sociology may give me a good base for short stories and novels." "Really," replied his aunt Jean—and some said "What a crock!"

For the next six years "He lived the life of a scholarly gentleman," as some of his friends put it. With the support of his father and aunt Jean, he set a leisurely pace: attended classes; made good grades; socialized with his classmates at Del Mar beach nearby; wrote a qualitative MA thesis and a PhD dissertation (both minus any quantitative or empirical data) and took a MA and a PhD from a University that was no Berkeley but respectable. Then he rented a house on Del Mar beach near Santa Cruz and settled in for what he thought and hoped would be a good scholarly life. Now he could enjoy the best of several worlds: surfing at the beach; trips to nearby San Francisco for culture (classical music, art galleries, the stage, opera, ball games, culinary pleasures)—and discuss philosophical discussions with friends. Work and marriage could wait. The family finances were fine, and his monthly allowances were secure. He explained to friends: "My life is similar to that of the English gentry, you know, like that of a country squire only I don't have to chase foxes on a horse and holler tallyho. I don't have land yet, but I might purchase a small winery with some grape acreage, and I have my eye on a piece of land in the Livermore Valley. Maybe not Pinot Noir grapes, but certainly

Cabernet Sauvignon." But protested one friend: "Livermore is nowhere Pat," to which he responded: "Everywhere is somebody else's nowhere." When not trying to write, he tried water coloring and a few more oil paintings. His sex life remained in the normal range of his peers.

After one year of this "intermezzo" as he called it, his father and aunt Jean told him he must do some kind of work. To them writing and painting (which he claimed he was doing) was dreamy pie in the sky, because they did not think (correctly) he was good enough at either to become a professional artist. His father counseled him again to come to work in the family's business; Jean suggested (as she had before) that he seek a teaching position in some college or university, and, some of his friends also coaxed him to teach. One exclaimed: "What in the hell is your PhD for? You sure cannot find a job doing anything else with that degree you got in Sociology. Away from the campus, no one knows what it is anyway. Social Work? So teach it." Faced with the reality of this friend's preceding quote, Pat reconciled his persistent nagging thoughts that, "I'm not dedicated enough to be a good professor," and said to his aunt Jean: "Scholarship and learning is one thing, and like art, a value in itself, but it is not a sufficient motive to teach."

Pat did not wish to work for his father, or anyone else, so he finally decided to become a professor, but explained to his family that he must take some courses in Education in preparation for a teaching position. When asked by his aunt and father, if his professors had taken such courses, he admitted that most had not, and explained: "The lack of Education courses is one reason why some of my professors were not good teachers. They did not know how to teach." So with family reluctant approval he enrolled in a respectable second-tier state university's Education department; signed up for four courses, but dropped all four before the end of one semester and gave this paraphrased reason for doing so: "(1) They were boring and without content; (2) They did not tell me how to teach; (3) Only mediocre students took them. (4) Why should I waste my time?" (On this latter point he had finally seen the light.)

In any event, he "took the plunge," as he put it, and applied for and obtained an assistant professorship in a University of California system university near his hometown area. He conformed and interacted with colleagues in a congenial fashion; worked hard at lecture preparation and delivery; and, read a few papers at professional meetings; and, managed to publish one, 'I think' article per year. The latter did not please him because he said: "These publications do not provide any worthwhile data for my students, colleagues, or anyone else." He knew what required research data were, but just was not interested in doing research himself. Further, though he liked bright students who were in his classes to learn, he had little interest in average students, or those who were just there for a passing grade. And there were too many of both he could not flunk. Some students complained to his department head that he was too hard; expected too much; assigned too much homework; and, that he was not really interested in them. This bothered Pat, and he began to lose sleep over what he told friends was his "precarious situation." His colleagues and the head advised him that such problems were endemic to academia; and, suggested that he not take matters so seriously. He disagreed and could not manufacture a zest for teaching average students, doing research, or publishing in Sociology journals which he did not find very useful. This should not have been a shock, because he had examined these journals along with other sociological data sources as an undergraduate and graduate student. But he expected more now that he was a professional, not just a student. He even began to question the value of sociological theory which he found to be derivative and esoteric rather than insightful and original. Again, this should not have been a surprise because he knew that Sociology was a relatively young discipline that drew extensively from other traditional disciplines like History, Philosophy, Economics, Demography, and Political Science. After more near sleepless nights, long discussions with his friends, family and colleagues, and a painful self analysis, he determined the following reasons for his malaise: (1) he had lost faith and interest in Sociology, but was really interested in the Classics, Art History, Philosophy, and literature; (2) he realized that he had (erroneously) adopted Sociology as a career plan to satisfy his family's pressure to major in, "something that he could use after graduation;" (3) he recalled his original (and correct) hunch that he was not cutout to be a teacher; (4) he was not driven to teach, and did not want to educate average students; (5) he had no desire or intention to do empirical research; and, (6) he really wished to stay home; read, write, and paint; and discuss art history, the classics, and philosophy with a literate.

His dislike of empirical research did not only dismay himself, but also that of peers. Consequently the totality of the foregoing explanations brought him to see himself (he said) as a "Deviant Dilettante;" and, those who knew him capable of doing what he could but would not do agreed with this self definition. One detractor said, "He had to know beforehand that all professors in the California University System have to research and publish; and that all students are not "A" or "B" scholars, but we must teach them." As tenure time drew near, Pat Junior became more anxious, edgy, dissatisfied, and unhappy; and he knew his continued malaise affected relationships with students and colleagues. Therefore he solidified his self definition as a "deviant Dilettante" and resigned. Later, several friends, suggested that he take a position in a second-tier California State University System institution where there was little pressure to research and publish, but they emphasized a caveat that all of his students would not make "A" and "B" grades. He rejected this option and repeated the old adage, "Do not teach unless you cannot conceive of yourself as doing anything else."

Pat took a constructive attitude toward his failure as a professor, and explained in a (paraphrased) diatribe: "I am no effete aesthete. I only want to be a Dilettante like the members of the 18th century society of Dilettanti. You know the society of Dilettanti that was established in England in 1734 by the educated, well to do who were educated and dedicated to the study of ancient Greek and Roman art. The motto of this exclusive club was Serra Ludo, a paradoxical Latin phrase, which means that in their playfulness, Ludo members, also addressed serious matters. Serra membership included nobles, scholarly gentry, artists, poets, historians, diplomats, and arty rakes, who sponsored scholarly publications, plays, grand tours and historical expeditions." The Dilettanti aimed to become Renaissance men (See Redford 2009).

When Pat's father eventually helped him purchase a winery and grape acreage he wanted, he said: "The Livermore Valley is not the ideal intellectual perch for a gentleman scholar, but as Graham Greene might have said, 'It is a fair getaway from somewhere else.' And everywhere is somebody else's nowhere." To top that he might have mentioned that San Francisco and the whole attractive San Francisco Bay Area was nearby.

In summary, Pat Junior appears to be representative of a narcissistic personality disorder type—and a deviant in academia. So-called Dilettanti, in the authors' view are numerous in academia, where most are qualitative scholars who really do not like to teach, but do like to preen, and enjoy a leisurely, respectable life style. What else can they do with a PhD, especially in the liberal arts field? Unlike Pat, most are not gentlemanly scholars, mannerly, erudite or intellectually or monetarily equipped but just distant cousins of the indolent teacher and the prima donnas academia is full of. According to these authors, "Should you wish to be a scholarly gentleman and a Dilettante professor, marry a rich woman!" Usually Dilettanti are deviant by omission rather than commission, nonetheless, most are ineffective professors; do not motivate students; are unwilling and/or unable to collect and analyze new data; frequently lecture from dated, obsolete notes. And most are lazy and not team players who expect to be pampered and lauded for nothing—and they are entitled to nothing. Dilettanti should not be selected by the academy. And those unmasked as trouble makers should be required to undergo psychological treatment after which should they not improve be dismissed.

Though self-centered, spoiled and somewhat rigid and narcissistic, Pat was honest and wise enough to get out of academia. His social background was advantageous though his father did not give him enough of his time. He endured severe situational stress problems while teaching which drove him from academia where he did not belong. It is too bad that so many deviant wannabe Dilettante are not rich enough to get the hell out of the academy. Perhaps Pat should have been a museum curator, say like at the D'Young Gallery in San Francisco or at the Tate Modern in London.

(24) Swindler the Liberal's Pet

Academic administrators are not educated or trained in administration. Generally they began as PhD assistant professors who were appointed by PhD administrators who stumbled on to or climbed the academic ladder in a tedious bureaucracy. Most these authors have known are not scholars and switched (or escaped) from teaching to administrative positions because they found the professorship role too difficult, boring or too slow in providing money, comfort, self-realization, and prestige. Some were remiss or inept at teaching and/or research; and, many changed course to salvage or promote an academic career. One of these authors asked students in one of his classes to take a trip to the administration building, the power tower, and request that official occupants stand in the halls; then tag every third person; and, tell the other two to go home. Those tagged could stay provisionally.

Swindler was removed from office as head of a respectable, southern university's criminal justice department wherein he had once been a professor and department head ostensibly because a professor under his jurisdiction had been convicted of embezzlement of departmental funds by a government court. Though reportedly involved himself in the embezzlement, he managed to avoid criminal charges by secretly turning over states evidence to the prosecution. Swindler was replaced as department head by a professor whom he had hired several years before the scandal occurred, and he was disgruntled and reluctant to accept his replacement's role as head. Contrariwise he attempted to undermine his replacement's effectiveness and authority in all sorts of ways as explained later below.

Swindler was born and reared poor in the rural deep south in an uneducated, but stable, intact family. His parents (both extroverts) were respectable, hardworking field hands, who had not finished high school, and who were born into a cycle of poverty. At age 10, Swindler and his younger sister moved with their parents to a large, northern California city, where mother and father found jobs cleaning hotel rooms. The family lived in slum areas with other minority group members, where Swindler resided throughout his elementary, secondary, college, and graduate-school years. Tall, long-muscled, and slender he was a healthy, energetic, aggressive, extrovert of slightly above average intelligence. Verbal, street glib, athletic, and outgoing, he made friends easily among rowdy, street youths (delinquents, and tough schoolmates and hustling-types) and older street-wise acquaintances. Well disciplined at home in a pious, church-going family, he did not smoke, drink, use drugs or engage in serious street delinquency; and, was never arrested, though, he picked up conning and street smarts and was known as a smooth operator by peers and associates. Smooth, nice looking, sensual, and a good dancer, he was admired by males and females, and lead a promiscuous sex life from puberty, which resulted in courtship and marital relationship problems throughout life (including two failed marriages, and the fatherhood of two illegitimate and two legitimate children). Classmates and professional associates found him to be likable, clever, and fun to be around though some were wary of close social interaction with a known about "city slicker."

Despite his social background, the Swindler was very ambitious and aspired to a white collar, middle class lifestyle. Though only an average student he learned how to play tennis in high school from middle class friends and became a star on his school's team. Tennis prowess was his first ticket to success and at high school graduation he was recruited as a tennis player by a small so-so private liberal arts college where he fitted in, made average grades, and majored in social science. At graduation he was recruited by a Sociology and Criminology department housed in a state university as a preferred minority student. Now in graduate school he studied hard but made only average grades again with the assistance of his liberal, do-gooder professors who had recruited him. Likable and entertaining with a carload of jokes about lowlife and the south, his professors took him on as something like their minority-group pet. Adept at encouraging favoritism and the aid of his so-called liberal promoters, he was on his way. His personal relationships derived from those who had made him their pet enabled him to complete an MA program with marginal grades, and acceptance into a prestigious west coast university that offered a DC (doctor's degree in Criminology), a brand new government sponsored program designed to train minority group students in the fields of Criminology and Penology. Some of his do-gooder mentors were scholars and influential leaders in the field of Criminology, who puffed him up and fueled his career ambitions; and, in doing so not only recommended him for positions (following a special doctoral degree in Criminology) above his performance level, but rescued him from positions he failed in. First they gave him grades he did not earn; then elevated him to graduate school where they helped him grade-wise to graduate; found him his first academic position in a prestigious school, where he was unable to receive tenure; and found him a university position as a director of a Criminal Justice Program where he failed again. Lastly, when he was fired from this last Criminology position for corrupt practices detailed below, they helped him get another administrative position in yet another university. Swindler, following his appointment as Head of a Criminal Justice Department (after his dismissal from his first academic position) no longer had to worry about research and publications, but he had other problems.

Now faced with the challenges of his new administrative position above his capabilities, he recruited Criminology faculty with more experience and knowledge than he in teaching and administrative duties which kept him afloat for a few years. However, his chief problems over time were his dishonesty, inability to write, and his dictatorial management style. He attempted to run the department he headed and its programs as his own private fiefdom. In so doing he depended on his favorite clerical administrative assistants (non professionals) whom he elevated to a status higher than that of professional scholars in Criminology. Consequently, quarrels and turf battles developed between these administrative assistants and the faculty, who taught courses, directed theses, conducted research, and supervised the grant work. Swindler also relied on his conning skills, status and cultivated professorial front to supplement his dearth of research methodology and management skills. However, his faulty micromanagement style did not hold up and he also failed in his academic professional role.

Moreover, along the way he adopted several deviant measures to fulfill his personal ambitions to acquire power, prestige and money, which did him in. Utilizing his conning skills acquired as a youth; for example: (a) he attempted to place blame on others for his wrong doings; mismanaged grants and stole government grant funds; (b) charged other faculty members with misconduct to the administration for errors and thefts he was responsible for; (c) while on forced sabbatical leave off-campus, he attempted to monitor, and control government grants issued to faculty in order to cling to power; (d) mismanaged government contracts by engaging in fraudulent activities in their administration; (e) solicited questionable university personal reimbursements without adhering to procedures; (f) continually undermined his supervisors' professional competence and character to numerous persons, by derogating them on and off campus in an attempt to promote himself; (g) directed and encouraged students to complain to the university administration should they have any problem with his headship replacement; (h) magnified his replacement's disagreements with supervisors; (i) physically threatened faculty and supervisors with whom he had disagreements with bodily harm toward the end of his tenure (before he was fired); (j) attempted to sell electronic equipment in the department to an outsider for personal monetary gain and as a means of revenge against the university authorities for demoting him; (k) in a government research grant's meeting involving a panel of researchers from various university campuses throughout the United States, he openly expressed his intolerance toward various racial categories (For example, he suggested that all white professors now employed on Historically Black College and University campuses be replaced as soon as possible with black professors; that white professors currently on HBCU campuses were only temporary hired help). In brief, he proposed a reversal of white segregation policy. Following his dismissal for the above conduct violations in his last Criminal Justice position an eminent so-called liberal professor found him another administrative position as dean in another university's Minority Students' Affairs Program. (Readers are reminded that the authors knew several non-deviant and efficient minority-group-member administrators throughout their careers.)

In summary, the Swindler was a "short con" man reminiscent of such types one of the authors had studied while a case worker and researcher in prison. He faced stressful structural and situational conditions throughout his career because he was under continual pressure to perform at levels beyond his capabilities. Negative social background factors such as delinquent companions fueled and enhanced his false persona and con-man activities; however, his personality resembled that of an antisocial personality disorder type, and this was his basic problem. People like Swindler tend to be fearless and cool under conditions that would distress and swamp others. His antisocial personality disorder was a two edged sword which permitted him as an ambitious person to engage in deviant behavior for success and simultaneously enabled him to withstand the pressures of defeat. But he was not intelligent and fortunate enough though to con his way through. Short con men usually come up short and their shortsighted caper compensations are not worth the risks involved.

Unfortunately Swindler's liberal sponsors chose the wrong type of person to mentor and promote. Swindler's kind require strict stiff discipline, sanctions, and firm social control at all times. Impulsive and transparently greedy they do not make adequate professional administrators, and are incapable of taking advantage of their breaks. Having been reared in a strict, law-abiding home, probably dissuaded him from "breaking real bad," until the end of his professional career and kept him out of jail. Some called him an affirmative action baby. Finally criminals should not be permitted to remain in academia; and, when detected should be fired.

(25) Judy the Greedy

Judy was born and reared in a poor, large, lower middle class family in a large deep southern city in the United States, where she grew up with two brothers and two sisters; and, all family members were blue collar workers. Religious, extroverted, law abiding parents maintained a morally strict household where relationships were affectionate and harmonious. Above average intelligence she made slightly above average grades in public schools where many of her classmates were middle class products and superior to her in general knowledge, etiquette, and social relationship skills. An aggressive extrovert, and socially and professionally over ambitious, she made up her mind as a teenager to succeed occupationally by hook or crook despite background limitations. She sought out well educated and successful people as acquaintances and friends who taught her much about the middle class world including social networking, correct speech, dress and lifestyle. This knowledge coupled with intelligence and a pleasing, charming, outgoing personality aided her in achieving success as she saw it. Capable and streetwise but not scholarly she struggled her way through high school and college with good grades and conduct reports. Affable, entertaining, verbally glib, and apparently well behaved; she managed to impress her teachers and acquaintances with her industry, charm and ambition. Graduating from a small denominational college where she conformed; made above average grades; she took an AB in Education. One year later she married and later said, "I made the biggest mistake of my life by choosing a pretty boy who dropped out of college and would not work, and expected me to take care of him and our son." She divorced the playboy and thenceforth struggled and conned her way to provide for herself and son, never remarrying because she said: "Men are too unfaithful."

She taught in an elementary school for three years, and then enrolled in a second-tier university where she took a MA and PhD in Education and Social Science after eight years of intermittent schooling and work as a school teacher. Upon graduation and with political pull, she was appointed an assistant professor in a new Criminal Justice Department that offered an MA degree in Criminal Justice, though she had taken only two Criminology courses. She adjusted and met and entertained several noted PhD Criminologists and government officials who were active in the field of Criminology and Penology as well as several big city police chiefs, sheriffs, and prison wardens throughout the United States. She also cultivated acquaintances with several city mayors and politicians who were involved in corrections. Judy was a real social and professional networker. At the time the government issued considerable amounts of grant money to a number of colleges and universities for teaching, training, and researching in the field of Criminology and Penology (especially grant money for criminological research projects). A clever, socially engaging, and attractive professor and hostess Judy learned quickly the steps (technical and political) necessary for grant procurement, and eventually became a grantsman herself; that is, with the aid of research professors in her department and elsewhere who taught Criminology courses and research methods. Within five years she belonged to several government Criminology networks and became a full professor; and, two years later she was associate head of her academic department. By this time she was connected on a first name basis with a number of people inside and outside academia, who were active in Criminology and Penology research projects and grant programs. Judy was known about and praised by many criminologists despite her weak academic background. On the negative side, she was dubiously feared by her underlings, who thought she was a conceited, demanding, dangerous "bitch" (Wurtzel 1998).

Unfortunately and surprisingly to many she eventually began to steal government grant money, and consequently was charged, tried, convicted, fired, and jailed. A summary of criminal charges she was convicted of follows: (a) made and caused to be made and used materially false, fictitious, and fraudulent statements and representations in a matter within the jurisdiction of a government agency; (b) had been an agent of grantee of an organization that received over $10,000 under a Federal Program in any one year; embezzled, stole, obtained, by fraud and otherwise without authority, knowingly converted to the use of persons other than the rightful owner, and intentionally misapplied property that is valued at $5,000 or more, and is owned by and is under the care, custody, and control of such organization, in violation of a government code; (c) devised and intended to devise a scheme to defraud the funding agencies, and to obtain money by means of false and fraudulent pretenses, representations and promises, causing the mails and interstate wire communications to be used in the execution of said scheme and artifice to defraud; (d) defrauded the funding agency by depriving it of its money and property; by depriving it of its right to have its programs funded in whole or in part through government grants administered honestly and fairly in compliance with applicable laws and regulations and free from dishonesty, favoritism, conflicts of interest, self-dealing, and other corrupt practices; by perverting its program goals and purposes; by deceiving its officers and employees assigned to review said programs through trickery, deceit, and by other means which were at least dishonest; and, (e) concealed and covered up the conspiracy and its objects.

In summary, Judy was an overly ambitious, charming, intelligent, glib, sociable, deceptive con artist with a limited professional education. A wannabe, excessively greedy, and dishonest she did not prepare herself academically for a career in Criminal Justice; that is, she took no degree in Criminology, Criminal Justice, Social Work, Psychology or Sociology. Nonetheless, she faked at being a criminologist; stole money for personal reasons; bluffed her way along; and became a criminal. Despite her dishonesty many professional criminologists admired her and found her to be a fountainhead of good jokes, camaraderie, and fun to have around. In the company of authors and several other professors who were castigating (though admiring in one sense) a noted and popular female swindler, she remarked: "Gentlemen say what you will, but you cannot beat good sex." On the negative side she was a seductive con artist with an apparent antisocial personality disorder type. Many intelligent charming rogues, "bitches," con artists, professional criminals, gamblers, white collar criminals, and loaches at times are fun to have around, and frequently make an entertaining party, but they do not wear well and may bite you in the back. "Leave them at the bar," said one sage. Judy's social background was adequate and she did not appear to have structural or situational stress problems. She was too cool for worry and she would have made a charming madam in an upscale house of ill repute or say a courtesan. White collar criminals like Judy should be fired; and, unqualified professors should never be hired.

(26) Taylor the Overreacher:

Taylor and an older brother, Tommy, were born into an upper middle class family located in the urban, upper south. Both parents, his father, a successful dentist, and his mother, an intelligent, loving, optimistic, efficient housewife with a university degree, were stable ambiverts. Conscientious, stable, and politically conservative, they were friendly and accommodating within their restricted social class milieu, but contacts without were minimal and formally polite, as was customary in their social circle. Family relationships were apparently congenial and emotionally satisfying though the caring father, who was admired among his peers and by his two sons, dispensed his affection and love conditionally. In brief, he was a traditional, successful, professional, male. Erroneously the parents supervised and mentored their two boys (who had marked personality differences) in the same fashion; that is, they set the same goals for each, and were openly and equally ambitious for each—socially, educationally and professionally. Tommy, their oldest son was everything they had ever wished for. Mesomorphic in body type, very intelligent, handsome, and gregarious, he was a stable extrovert who made good grades in school where he was admired by teachers and classmates. Somewhat aggressive and formidable he enjoyed athletics and a playground dominated by boys of his type. Very popular with girls, his parents found it necessary to monitor his dating activities, including their control of family cars, and the supervision of his night-time activities with females. They succeeded in these endeavors because Tommy was flexible and basically a conscientious, conforming person like his father. Heterosexual, his sex life was normal for one of his age, place, class, and time. In brief he was moderately sexually active after age 18, but not a macho or a chaser.

Taylor, slim and ectomorphic in body build, was a stable introvert of average intelligence, who was shy and tentative in social interacting; made friends with other male and female introverts who shared his disposition and interests (art, reading, music, and movies). Though he tried hard to play several athletic sports under the guidance of his brother Tommy, he failed, as well as in ordinary, competitive playground activities and gave up all of them. He had been strangely enough moderately successful as a bantam-weight boxer but a broken nose ended that. Though considered nice, he was not sexually attractive to females, who thought him too soft, indolent, sweet and retiring. One girl said, "Taylor is a little teddy bear." Taylor said: "Girls think I am too quiet and peaceful, and they are right." Contrariwise, females did not think him a sissy and to many, as one said, "He is like a brother, not a lover." Male classmates respected him as a quiet, serious minded decent person, but shied away from one with whom they had no common interests.

Most of his spare time was spent with a few friends while studying, doing homework, watching movies, water coloring, storytelling and listening to civilized music (classical). Throughout secondary school he adapted, made a few friends, and was known as a quiet, obedient student by his teachers and classmates. His parents hired tutors for him in foreign languages and math during his junior and senior high school years which enabled him to maintain slightly above average grades. Relations with his brother Tommy remained cordial, but they drifted apart with maturity. Tommy, a lover of physical action, hunted, danced, socialized, and excelled without tutors' aid in school; graduated far ahead of Taylor; went on to a private prestigious university (his father's almamater); graduated with honors; graduated later from law school; and, continued on his merry way to promotion and pay socially and professionally (which pleased his parents to no end).

Taylor's career plans and activities were something else. Neither he, nor his parents, or school counselors were sure of what he should do following high school graduation. Though arty by temperament neither his school counselors nor his significant others considered him gifted enough for a professional career in art. A few of his oils, water colors, landscapes, and genre paintings were plausible and passable, but obviously did not foretell a creative artist. What to do? He finally opted for a university Arts and Crafts degree which along with some education courses would equip him to teach in some large, urban high school where he had heard art courses were occasionally taught. His parents agreed and sent him off to a second-tier university in his state that offered an Arts and Crafts degree for high school teachers, within an Education department where he adapted, studied hard; made a few friends, but was known as a marginal student and artist by his professors, who did admire his industry and obedient conduct. With tutors in math and science he graduated with an AB in five years and stayed on for another year, and took additional courses in Education. A dearth of critical analysis and original thinking was his school problem. With the help of his parents he obtained a junior high school teaching position in his native city where he fitted in and achieved a two-year acceptable teaching record.

Then, negating his parents' and former professors' advice, Taylor applied for enrollment in a Arts and Crafts MA degree program at his almamater which would render him eligible for a junior college teaching position. Obviously Taylor's ambitions exceeded his capability. Nonetheless, following an application turndown, he applied and received acceptance in another second-tier university's MA program in Art History, Musicology, and Education where, again with the help of tutors, he took an MA degree following a two-and-a-half-year struggle, though still seen by professors and classmates as a good industrious person, but a marginal student. His sex life remained void, because he was still a "brother", not a "lover" in the eyes of his female friends.

Unable to find a junior college position because of his poor academic record, he returned again to his native city where he made a marginal teaching adjustment in a senior high school position. He also engaged in a satisfactory sexual relationship with an old girlfriend whom he married shortly thereafter. Two years later he ditched his junior college teaching goal, and sought an even higher aim, a four-year college position. Despite his past marginal academic status and the counsel again of his former professors and parents, he claimed that with a vaunted maturity he was now ready for a PhD program in Art History and Musicology, leading to a college-teaching position (affording him the status he thought he deserved and desired). To his credit he had read up on art history for several years while in and out of school. Noting that his MA almamater was currently offering a new PhD program in Art History, the Fine Arts, Musicology, and Education (housed in an Education department, and actually an Education degree by some other name), he applied for enrollment and was accepted. He was not at ease among several professors and classmates whom he had encountered during his former MA program. Again critical art analysis and criticism was his problem. His knowledge of Art History and the aid of tutors barely got him by, though he was still known as a good fellow, but a drudge.

Five years later Taylor received a D.Ed. and obtained an assistant professorship at a southern college where he taught Art, History, Art and Crafts and some Education courses with a split appointment in an Education and Fine Arts and Crafts department. There he was accepted by his colleagues, and students, who tagged him a kind, so-so professor without enough depth. He knew the history and methods of the old masters and that of some modern painters, but could not render a critical analysis of their paintings on a comparative basis. In brief he had some appreciation of art and its techniques but was unable to pass this on to students in any critical, aesthetic fashion. Art students like to see their professors produce some passable artwork themselves (at least on an amateur level). Barring this they expect art teachers to tell them how to read paintings (See Thompson, 2006). Taylor was remiss in both areas.

Taylor was denied tenure on the faculty basis of the lack of a publication record, but had he been an excellent teacher, or perhaps even a good one, he would probably have received tenure in an institution that was certainly not a research institution. Further, he a had a limited knowledge of the methods in the physical examinations of paintings that indicated provenance and iconography. He experienced the pleasure of mind engrossed in a visual image, and also knew the differences between kitsch and a serious painting, representative vs. abstract art, and something about the visual unity of space, color, tone and shape; but, he could not explain a painting that had no common text or unity. In brief, his painting interpretations were weak. For example, in Edward Manet's masterpiece, "A Bar at the Folliers-Bergere" he understood the nighttime, uninhibited gaiety of Parisians at play, but not the significance of the fully clothed, pensive, self-reflecting mirror image of the Venus figure, the barmaid, the central figure, who was condemned always to be an onlooker, never a participant in the evenings' pleasures. Or for another, in Henri Matisse's painting, "The Joy of Life," he could not explain how Matisse had successfully detached the language of natural color from mimetic representation, and turned it into an entirely synthetic thing, depending on the overall organization of color. Or how this among others of his fauvist paintings led to the musical and rhythmical paintings of the late 1940s, and the original collages he constructed toward the end of his life.

In Taylor's defense, his PhD program housed in an Education department had not prepared him for teaching art at the college or university level. Though "disheartened and rebuffed" as his parents put it, Taylor did not react to tenure failure in a self pitying, destructive way, nor did he become disgruntled, spiteful, or antagonistic toward academia. He had survived failure before; but this time, he finally realized his artistic and academic limitations, and decided not to be an "overreacher" any longer; he continued his interest in art, and found another teaching position in a junior high school where he succeeded at last. Only a stubborn, stable introvert could have endured his struggles as a misguided overreacher; but, from an academic perspective his struggles were unnecessary (and deviant).

In summary, Taylor's parents erred in trying to rear two children with different personalities in the same way; and, Taylor's stubbornness in pursuing a college career beyond his capability were negative insurmountable factors in his adjustments. However, his stubborn personality and inflated ambition enabled him to face and mitigate structural and situational stress problems. Certainly he should have known at several points in his career that he was limited both in capacity and artistic ability, and in his effectiveness as a teacher at the college level. His denial of the obvious and stubbornness resemble that of an obsessive-compulsive personality disorder type, and one with a limited intelligence and artistic insight. Such types should never be hired in academia, or when detected, dismissed.

Taylor's profile illustrates some of academia's shortcomings in dealing with similar cases, and some remedial suggestions regarding curriculum problems and procedures thereto follow:

1. The curricula in graduate school programs leading to the MA and PhD degrees should be plainly spelled out specifying course content and the qualifications of those with each of these two degrees; and, the academic positions graduates thereof are qualified for.

2. Split MA and PhD curricula in two or more disciplinary departments are frequently watered down in the number of courses required in each discipline, in course content, and, in the qualifications of the MA or PhD obtained in such graduate programs. For example, upon graduation one should be either an Art Historian with a PhD earned in an Art History department, or an educator who has earned an Ed. D. degree from an Education department that offered some courses in Art History. Interdisciplinary degrees are sometimes weak and confusing. Who is the graduate? What courses did he or she take? What titles are they entitled to? What profession is he or she qualified in? At what level?

3. (a) Graduate school departments in the various university colleges should detail in writing the specific requirements for admission to specific academic programs; and, carefully screen all applicants in a strict formalized fashion. A social and academic case history, and careful interviewing techniques would screen out applicants like Taylor, who though a sterling character in many respects was not graduate school material. Too frequently graduate school programs make all kinds of exceptions; for all kinds of reasons; and, sometimes accept applicants who do not meet admission criteria. Many administrators know they need students in order to inaugurate their proposed specific graduate school programs in the first place, and how to keep them until graduation once these programs are established. Therefore unqualified

students at times get accepted and graduated. That is, once accepted there is a compulsive or financial need to graduate them.

(b) Unfortunately university departments in the social sciences with the exception of Psychology and Social Work do not usually teach interviewing techniques; nor do many professors in many departments know how to conduct professional interviews. Certainly the departments of Sociology, History, and Political Science (if not others) should teach interviewing as well as the rudiments of social case history construction. Currently most Sociology departments eschew interviewing as an "occupational technique," the concern of Social Work, an occupation but not of Sociology, a science. This has never been the position of the Chicago School of Sociology that educates social psychologists.

4. Once admitted, requirements for remaining in a graduate program, and completing it should be carefully spelled out; and, a system should be devised whereby those who do not meet the criteria for retention or graduation can be easily dismissed from the program. The authors know of many cases where "weak sisters" (males and females) have been erroneously admitted to graduate programs; and, permitted to remain and graduate despite below marginal performance levels; and even then recommended for academic positions they are really not qualified for following questionable, marginal graduations.

5. Departments should issue honest recommendations for all of their graduates that specify the strong and weak points of each.

    The authors have taught in a few departments where this has not been the case, and where subsequent negative reactions have followed a department's faulty and flattering recommendations. False recommendations become known about; degrade a department and university; subject students to unqualified professors; and, keep weak programs in academia going.

6. Professors and administrators in Social Science departments should have studied interviewing and the construction of social case histories; that is, under qualified professors. Those without skills in these two areas need to study them.

(27) Brad the Unqualified Head

Brad was born and reared in a medium sized city in the mid-south, the only child of two public school teachers. His father, a stable, ectomorph and an introvert, taught history in a public high school, where he was known as a well meaning, honest, timid, agreeable, pedant by his peers, and a so-so, dry teacher by his students. His mother, a principal of a public elementary school was a formidable, stable, cooperative, sturdily framed extrovert who was well liked and respected by the teachers and pupils she supervised, and by local community professionals. Both parents were self disciplined, with strong drives to get ahead. His father deferred to the judgment of his wife in the parenting process.

Brad was a muscular, well built, moderately aggressive, extrovert who was firmly parented in a modest, comfortable, caring home dominated benignly by his mother. Of above average intelligence he was an energetic, aggressive, headstrong, somewhat stubborn, moody youth who tried to assume leadership roles among playmates. His mother found it necessary to restrain his exuberance to rule the household; for example, Brad insisted that she buy furniture and other furnishings he thought necessary; decorate and arrange things his way; prepare food he selected according to his tastes, etc. He also insisted that his mother assist him with school homework, and check over assignments several times for any grammatical errors he may have overlooked. The significance of the content was of less importance to him than the form (grammar). Often his homework was turned in late because he labored over form and structure. Further, he insisted on choosing his clothing, and demanded that it be neat and fit for the occasion at hand—his occasion.

Pushy and bossy, he was not admired by many classmates, who found him too fussy, well dressed, and uninterested in sports. Though physically presentable and heterosexual he did not appeal to females who deemed him too stuffy, stiff and aloof. Moreover, they said he was not interested in popular entertainment or anything exciting. Female inattention did not bother Brad who was never much interested in sex, and anyway he found it difficult to express affection for others, but he did date girls occasionally. His emotional affect was weak and flat.

His parents, especially his mother, surrounded him with educational toys from babyhood and instilled in him over ambitious goals, and a strong sense of personal worth. Consequently he was cocky and superior acting among his peers, which turned them off. One classmate said to him: "Brad, you are not the only rooster on the block." He adapted marginally at school where he sometimes disagreed a little too adamantly with his teachers and classmates; although, he was never considered a disciplinary problem, because teachers learned to deal with him firmly. He made above average grades, and studied hard to please his parents who set very high academic standards for him (a problem then and afterwards). Brad, an average student, never developed abstract serious scholarly interests; however, he found it necessary to simulate scholarship on many occasions in order to seek the approval of several audiences throughout his career. And though his natural impulse control was never very strong, he strived at self control. He did not drink, smoke, take undue risks, or use drugs. Known to some as a "health freak," because he maximized strict dieting rules; took special exercises; used super vitamins; and followed strict sleep regimens. He remarked once to male classmates: "My need to keep healthy keeps me away from drinking and chasing girls."

At high school graduation he was unsure about a career, or what university to attend. All he knew for sure was that he wanted to please his parents; become an "important person" of some kind, and, he said, "Live a good comfortable life." Both parents having encouraged a generalized ambition from the jump suggested that he might consider attending their almamater, the state's premier university, noted regionally as offering a strong liberal arts education. There, they pointed out he could prepare himself for a career in "teaching something" in high school, which they had hinted at all long. Neither (correctly) thought him strong enough scholarly for "A more lofty academic career," as they put it to close relatives.

He enrolled with some trepidation at his parents' almamater where he studied moderately, settled down, and made a few friends. Customarily, he spent brief stints in student hangouts, where he felt a little strange and isolated because he did not drink, smoke, emote, or josh around. He avoided coeds and preferred home girls, he said: "Back home simple girls who are not so advanced." He majored in Social Studies, made above average grades, and was known to his classmates as a stuffy, dull, nosey student with too much ambition. At graduation he returned home for a year, where he lolled around and read his mother's college Education textbooks; socialized with a few friends; and then, returned to his almamater and took the extra education courses required for a high school teaching certificate in social studies. He also enrolled in a few Social Work courses he had belatedly become interested in through contacts with one of his professors who had a MSW (Masters Degree in Social Work). Following this two-year period he secured a high school social studies teaching position back home where he taught for two years with moderate success, and was said to be: "A dry, ordinary, adequate teacher." During the second year there, he married a colleague, another social studies teacher. His and her parents funded later the two's graduate school education for two more years at their almamater, which led to an MA in Education and Social Studies for Brad, and an MA in History for his wife.

Brad also took some more Social Work courses during the summers while working on his MA. Both now adjusted in a stable routine marriage obtained instructorships (he in a Sociology and Social Work Department, she in a History Department) in a respectable state university—university in name only, really a former teachers' college that had evolved into a liberal arts college which offered a few MA programs.

Brad's wife, more energetic, intelligent and scholarly than he, eventually earned a PhD in History (by way of summer school courses and a sabbatical). Her superiority rankled, but pleased him at the same time though he said he was proud of her (well, maybe in an economic sense). Initially Brad succeeded but (erroneously) thought his MA in Education and additional courses in Social Work equipped him to teach Social Work and Sociology courses in place without further education. It was not, and even when first hired he was not really academically qualified to teach either Social Work (without a MSW) or Sociology (which he had no degree in). However, after his appointment, student enrollment in the two-winged department increased rapidly, and there were not enough professors with MSWs or PhDs to teach them. Brad was hired for this reason over the objections of some MSW and PhD faculty. Over time the so-called university became a real one; enrollment doubled; the infrastructure expanded and improved; several colleges and additional programs were added; graduate schools offering MAs and PhDs were rapidly developed; admission and graduation standards were raised; and, curriculum were reviewed, revised and upgraded; and, qualifications for teaching in Sociology and Social Work then required PhDs or MSWs. Brad should have foreseen the necessity of further graduate study leading to a MSW or a PhD; and, he should have demonstrated more interest in research and publications. Sadly he did neither, and claimed that his RSW (Registered Social Worker), a dated certificate, and appellation that his state had issued in the past for those with AB degrees who worked in Welfare Departments. Moreover, Brad maintained that Social Work did not require advanced study or knowledge of theory and research. This stance did not sit well in a university department. Some colleagues (behind Brad's back) referred to him as a "Registered. So what."

Nevertheless, he was tenured by the head, a deadwood MSW, who had hired him initially because he liked him personally stepped down and recommended Brad as his temporary replacement pending an outside search for a permanent head. No one else wanted the position because turf battles loomed between PhD Sociologists and MSW Social Workers; and further, no agreement could be reached on an outside candidate (several of whom the Dean of Arts and Sciences had approved). Brad's temporary appointment by default became permanent; and, he muddled through initially; but over time he began to argue vehemently with his colleagues about qualifications and teaching schedules between those who taught either Sociology or Social Work. He also claimed that he was qualified to teach both; and, that professors teaching either should not be compelled to take any further education or do research. Moreover, he passed these flaky defensive views and academic values on to undergraduate and graduate students thereby violating university rules and academic customs and standards. The university faculty handbook and policy manual clearly stated that all professors in the department without PhDs or MSWs must go back to school and attain them within fixed time limits; and, that all new faculty must have either a PhD or MSW when initially hired. Brad also announced to his faculty that he was staying on until retirement; and, only then should anyone even think about a new head. He even refused to introduce the Department's new faculty as Doctor so and so, and called them by their first names on and off campus to all audiences. For example, he would say something like: "John is prepared to teach Criminology. You can read about his credentials in the campus newsletter." Moreover, he favored Social Work professors over Sociology professors with PhDs; and, extended questionable perks to his favorites among this group.

Brad thereby lost administrative effectiveness in an ambiguous hostile environment, precariously aligned with two incongruous departments; Sociology and Social Work. Aggressive, rigid, stubborn, uncooperative, uncompromising, and increasingly moody, disgruntled, and uneasy about his qualifications and academic status, he found departmental structural-functional rifts and rivalries beyond his legitimate control. Consequently, he resorted to further deviant and illegitimate methods to solve his angst, personal and departmental problems, and formed a cabal (he headed) of established "good ole boys" (tenured but non-scholars) by bribing them with various perks (salary increases, etc.); and, with their aid attempted to run the department. Eventually this led to a rebellion, and Brad was forced to step down and resume teaching until retirement—a disgruntled and bitter professor.

In summary Brad represents the case of one with an adequate social background, who was overly ambitious and who tried unsuccessfully to function in an academic position for which he was not qualified by formal education or by personality. Intelligent but not research or intellectually inclined (and academically limited), dishonest, suspicious, envious and spiteful by nature, he probably had an obsessive-compulsive personality disorder and certainly a lazy one. He could not manage structural and situational stress problems that he was partially responsible for, and he was miserable and nearly stressed out most of the time; and, he made others miserable. Brad's chief academic and professional problems were: (a) a stubborn resistance to further education required by his academic position; (b) an envious and spiteful attitude toward those who held the required advanced degrees for their positions which he did not have; (c) overall rigidity; and, (d) dishonesty. Dishonest and obsessive-compulsive professors or administrators are not needed in academia, and those when becoming violators like Brad should be fired.

(28) Brown the Clown

Brown was born in an upper middle class Reform Jewish home located in the mid-south where he grew up with his parents, and a brother and sister. Both parents were conscientious, stable, agreeable, conforming extroverts with undergraduate university degrees, who owned and operated an upscale clothing store, where all family members worked from time to time. Brown's father was known as a successful and honest business man, and his mother as an efficient, affectionate, housewife. They, in an equalitarian manner, mentored and supervised their children in a firm, moderate fashion within a congenial household, where relationships were adequate for all. Brown lived in a Hispano-Moresque styled house replete with reproductions of historical paintings, a library similar to that of Sarai, the princess, furniture of mahogany, teak and rosewood, marquetry and antiques, velvet curtains, brocaded appliquéd coverings, tiled flooring, silverware and porcelain, and luxurious hand-woven silk and wool pictorial tapestry.

Brown's parents applied moderate pressure on all three children to succeed academically and materially, which triggered sibling rivalry in Brown, and a crave for attention. All three were intelligent and gifted, but the two oldest were more intelligent, and talented in particular areas than was Brown, whose aptitudes were spread and less outstanding. Furthermore, Brown's sister and brother in body build were more linear and evenly proportioned than in his. Brown was an endomorph, a roly-poly, who was told by many that he was fat, and therefore should be happy. His sister excelled in music and aspired to be a concert pianist; his brother highly verbal, excelled in English and History, and planned to study law.

Though Brown adapted and conformed at home, his parents and siblings were amused at his exaggerated comical mannerisms (standing on his head for example) and verbal and body language demands for attention. All concluded he was just the baby in the family acting out his immaturity. And it was more than difficult for two superior, lively, extroverts to extend equal attention to a younger less attractive sibling. However, he made friends easily at school and in his community where he was known as a fat and jolly kid who liked to tell jokes and "clown around." A good-all-around student he made above average grades in all subjects none of which he was particularly interested or gifted in.

And though a normal heterosexual he did not appeal to girls sexually because of his rotund physique, silly jokes and apparent immaturity, but he did have some female as well as male friends. His attitude was, as he said: "Sex is not everything, and I'm not a Casanova."

Brown was apparently socially adjusted, yet preoccupied with finding some area where he could excel or match the skills of his siblings. Over time he considered or tried several endeavors: tinkered with a chemistry set, but found it tedious, smelly and boring; played baseball, but could not run fast enough to catch fly balls; tried acting in school and community plays but attained only cameo parts. Thinking of counseling he accompanied a social worker on her chores at a welfare department, and concluded social workers were either "naive dreamers" or "self-righteous do-gooders." He toyed with the idea of medicine but thought he could not stand sick and bleeding patients; attempted to paint but lacked artistic skill or aesthetic perspective. He did attain moderate success at two things: playing pop songs on the piano at parties, and cracking jokes with classmates—learning the first with piano lessons, the second by watching comedians on television and in movies; reading joke books; and, practicing repartee with family members and friends. He finally decided that he had a natural talent for amusing others and self deprecation which he had learned from slapstick, and the Marx brothers pantomime. At age 16 and only 5'5" tall, he went to a party where everyone attended costumed and told jokes on themselves, dressed up in Superman attire (long flowing black cape, mask and all) with large printed red letters on his back spelling *Super Jew,* and recited self depreciating Jewish jokes. He won the prize with high acclaim and thenceforth was known as "Brown the Clown the round one, who gets around." These two assets assuaged his envy to a degree, and his thirst for attention at home and in the community. Upon high school graduation he enrolled in his state's premier state university without knowing what to major in; adapted and earned above average grades in all courses but again excelled in none. In his sophomore year a course entitled the "Sociology of Leisure Time" attracted his interest; and, he reasoned that Sociology might serve as a background source for some of his descriptive joking material. "After all," he said, "Sociology is about funny groups, and a screwed up society, and is generally interesting about everything but not too technical about anything. You know amorphous. I like its ambiguity that somebody said was made for the joker." (He was perceptive.) Brown said he majored in Sociology rather than Anthropology which he too liked, but "Anthropology," he said, "was about dead people and the past rather than funny people alive." He had no interest in sociological theory, methodology, or sociology as a science—"A joke in itself," he said. After receiving an AB and still in a quandary about a career he ploughed on and took a MA and a PhD in Sociology. He claimed later that he had to grind his way through several courses in theory and methodology, all of which he said, "sucked," and he proclaimed that his MA thesis and PhD dissertation were "just long stories about playtime activities that everybody knew about already." Though he made average grades in graduate school, his dissertation was marginal, and he was not considered a dedicated scholar. He said he was, "Just another Sociologist who didn't know what else to take." Further, he had no interest in empirical research and publications (just the minimum that would get him by). And it took him eight years to complete the MA, and PhD. Some said his professors, "passed him on through" because "They grew tired of looking at the clown." This was not the case because he made average grades and met all requirements though in his own time, but he did look funny with a round face, heavy eyebrows, round body, and a silly smile—"just like a clown." He did take timeouts for "clowning around" and playing the piano among friends in student hangouts and at other bars. Moreover, he spent intermittent periods, at home, clerking in the family store where he was known as an amusing and excellent "bait and switch" salesman. His parents called him: "A good boy who likes to have a good time, laugh and 'clown around' but he does not smoke, drink heavy, gamble or chase loose girls." Brown told a friend who insisted that he have another drink, "No, Jews are not supposed to get drunk."

Brown told his friends that there was nothing else to do but teach after taking the PhD in Sociology; but, he said "The idea of teaching does not turn me on." Nevertheless with family pressure he applied for and received a Sociology assistant professorship in a state university. His students liked him and his "funny, stimulating, unorthodox lectures," and claimed they learned a lot from him about the foibles of society, and the ever changing silly leisure-time activities of middle- class people in the United States—"like golf," he said. Moreover, they appreciated his jokes and said: "His jokes tie-in with his *hilarious lectures.*" They also reported he was not a "puffed up stuffed shirt," and that he lectured in ordinary language they could understand. Moreover, he permitted students to exchange jokes in class about topics under discussion which did not seem to disrupt the more formal class proceedings. To students he was a "jolly good fellow" and very entertaining in and out of class. They also found him to be honest and straightforward: "When he didn't know the answer to our questions, he did not stammer around, but admitted he didn't know but would find out," said one. Occasionally he drank beer with some of his students at a local tavern not known as a student hangout, where joking was a bit more ribald, jocular, and exuberant than in the classroom. Now and then he played at a local piano bar, where students joined him in singing in karaoke fashion. Brown spent most of his weekends at home only a few miles away where he joshed around with many friends and family members who laughed at his jokes whether they amused them or not. But all thought he should take his profession and academic life more seriously; and his siblings complained to their parents: "The buffoon must grow up."

Brown's colleagues' attitudes toward him were ambivalent; that is, they liked him as a jolly good fellow, but did not see him as a real professional. For example, they claimed he was not strict enough with students; too easy in grading; too informal in class; presented too clownish a persona to students whom he treated as equals; encouraged students to call him by his first name; did not pay enough attention to research. More seriously, they disapproved of his drinking with students at local bars. They also frowned at his frivolous conduct at professional meetings. For example, occasionally he would approach a prominent Sociologist he had not been introduced to and engage him in brief conversation; and, at leaving present him or her with a blank business card, and say: "I'm pleased to have met you, please take my card for future reference." He carried a pocket full of these blank cards around for this prank. He would also, now and then bump into some noted professor "accidentally on purpose" and say: "Please excuse me, my name is Brown... and by the way would you like me to parrot the voice of one of your close friends"? And then without waiting for an answer, he would render derisive renditions of one of this professor's rival's voice. He was so good at mocking the voices of eminent professors that people would crowd around him and beg for the mockery of one of their favorite preferences. Further he amused many with his risqué tales about the peculiarities and foibles of noted professors (some of which were neither funny nor fictional). For example, he announced once to a group of professors: "Did you know that Dr. So and So's wife is not here? His secretary is."

Brown did not disagree with or challenge any of the above criticisms, when he was denied tenure but maintained that he was a good teacher who did not subscribe to all of the ideas and conduct norms his colleagues desired to impose. He said: "I am different, maybe even a rebel, but I see no compelling need or desire to change course." Though very popular with most students and many faculty members, when denied tenure; he accepted this decision without rancor. He returned home and entered the family business and said: "Success in this country comes in different colors, and I guess I will have to make mine in green."

Academia is not a vehicle for entertainment or for one to clown around in. Perhaps Brown should have gone on the stage or practiced his art as a comic at a cocktail lounge or somewhere on stage. His negative attitudes toward theory, research and publications were unacceptable. More seriously professors should not drink booze and josh around with students in public bars. His type is frequently found in academia though rarely in research institutions; and, his type is not as numerous anywhere as it was in the 1960s. Current academic clowns are more subtle, less flamboyant and arguably more competent.

In summary Brown was a very decent man, in many respects, and he possessed some qualities of a good teacher, but he was not a professional and did not belong in academia. He was a consummate entertainer and a clever buffoon. As a professor he was not equal among students and should have been more of an educational authority figure and leader. Some assistant professors similar to him erroneously think they can enhance their status and popularity by an equalitarian facade, and some actually identify with their students who are in many cases near them in age and world view. Some senior professors assume this position because they want to be students' close friends or (foolishly) surrogate dads. The authors think that social distance must exist between professors and students which is necessary for the teacher-student relationship's purpose, learning. The professors' differential status and teaching function require social distance from students. On the other hand, professors must treat students with respect and provide them with freedom to ask questions and disagree. Professors are not parents, nor are they equals. Secondary group relations rather than primary group relations for the most part should prevail within a hierarchical order in the classroom. Though formal, professors should be kind, considerate and caring.

Brown's sibling rivalry was disadvantageous, and he had some of the qualities of a Peter Pan; and, he certainly suffered from an inferiority complex. Though not pernicious, Brown appeared to have a histrionic personality disorder. His unbecoming physique and sibling envy engendered situational stress problems which he tried to alleviate by clowning around. Being a real scholar, that he could have been, would have proved more effective. Finally, he should have sought psychological counseling early on which he did not. Those with a histrionic personality disorder who slip between the cracks and become problematic professors when unmasked should be required to seek psychological treatment. Retention would depend on the success of treatment.

(29) Bob the Ideologue (coercion of ideas fixes)

Bob was born and reared in a upper middle class family located in a quiet and peaceful suburb of a large northeastern city. The only child of well educated and dutiful parents, he lived in a comfortable well appointed home that provided him with the New York times, a bunch of liberal books and periodicals, a small literary type library, and a private bedroom and bath. His father, a stable, well adjusted, extrovert was employed as an attorney for a well established labor union. His mother, a stable ambivert was an efficient housewife who taught English part-time as an adjunct professor at a local liberal arts college The parents, products of educated middle class backgrounds, had graduated from the same nearby Ivy League university where they met as students, were conscientious in their professional careers and in Bob's parenting (on an equalitarian basis). Parents and son formed a closely knit, congenial family group. Father and mother were active members in the local "leftwing" of the Democrat party wherein they were considered intellectual activists. Bob's mother wrote short stories, some of which were published. To the more conservative members of his community his parents were known as respectable cheese, truffles, and wine liberals who practiced a nominal Protestant, civil religion. When growing up, to Bob they were affectionate, loving, caring parents and household companions—as he played parlor games with friends; played with educational toys; performed domestic chores; did school homework; watched TV and helped entertain house guests

Bob was a physically and mentally healthy, intelligent extrovert, who developed into a wiry, tall, long-muscled, curious, energetic youth who was eager to learn about everything. Though adventurous and sensual, he was basically a scholarly directed, conforming, ambitious youth, anxious to succeed and please his parents (by behaving and getting good grades in school). He avoided risk-taking behavior and risk takers; drank moderately, did not smoke, gamble, or roam the neighborhood, or stay out late at night; chose friends like himself; did not frequent bars or poolrooms; and kept away from rowdies, and promiscuous females or males. He once said to a friend: "The world is made up of winners and more losers. The first rule is to associate with winners" (adopted, he said, from his mother's advice). Throughout life he was closer to his mother than his father, though close to both.

He conformed at home though his parents noted that he searched for what he thought was the right way of doing things and the right way of thinking (like dress, chores, the interpretation of stories, arranging belongings, etc.) and after finding whatever way he defined as right, it remained fixed. When his parents explained there were many acceptable ways of doing things and of thinking, like singing for instance, or interpreting phrases, stories, or history, he would reply something like: "I know, but there has to be the best way to do that, and figure out anything." His friends and relatives noted this single mindedness, and his insistence on doing things and thinking about them in his way, but overlooked the fault. One said: "Bob is a little bossy, and he insists one should do things his way and think his way, but he is honest about it. And, after all, his assets make up for his amusing righteousness." (But not amusing to others later on.) He also adapted in school where he made excellent grades, and was known to teachers and classmates as a pleasing, well behaved, intelligent but very opinionated youth. Most classmates were products of an upper middle class social milieu, and therefore, like him, "well bred," ambitious achievers. He held his own on the playground where he was a fair baseball and basketball player, but he had no real interest in sports of any kind. Most of his spare time was spent on the internet and in public libraries reading up on what he called: "The social and economic history of the United States."

Bob traveled with his parents throughout the United States during summer vacations and observed with keen interest historical sites, particularly those located in the antebellum south connected with slavery, plantation agriculture, and the Civil War (all his chief academic interests). He dated a few female classmates who admired him, now and then, but most females thought him a little bit too one-sided to the left, and a "know it all." Though bookish Bob liked females and was a normal heterosexual who led a discreet, somewhat restricted sex life in keeping with his class, age, place, and time. When he announced to parents and friends his decision to become an economic historian, and a university professor, no one was surprised, and both parents were pleased. One friend commented: "He looks and acts like a professor already, all he needs is black horn-rimmed glasses, a pipe, a brief case, and an elbow patched jacket … and maybe a bicycle."

Having excellent grades throughout his school years and high SAT scores at high school graduation, he enrolled in his parents' almamater, noted among other things, for a strong history department at the undergraduate and graduate levels; and, majored in 19th century United States History, minoring in Economics. After taking a few History courses he became very curious about the economic reasons leading to the Civil War.

Upon graduation with honors, he enrolled in his university's History Department's graduate school where he was initially awarded an assistantship; and, after taking a MA degree, was awarded a TA, while working on his PhD During graduate school he drank a few beers in student hangouts, and dated a few classmates now and then, but spent most of his spare time in study. Professors, classmates, and students, thought him to be a scholar and a good instructor, though too conscientious, preppie, stiff, formal, and cocksure in social interactions. More pertinent, some prescient, professors and graduate students observed his tendency to overstate economic reasons to the neglect of other plausible causes for historical events and outcomes; that is, in keeping with his known about economic determinism; not that he could not fathom multiple causation. He could, but he understated the significance of probable, if not plausible, causes other than economic variables, although, he was not an orthodox socialist or Marxist. Some professors and graduate students called him a neo Marxist which he probably was. His professors chided him about his economic determinism to no avail. According to Bob, there had to be one real major cause in the "historical process" just as there had been one right way of doing things and thinking. He thought he had found the "magical cause" of the historical economic process and social structure. His scholarly heroes were Hegel and Marx, though he was "in denial" of this position.

When Bob received his PhD several nearby Ivy League universities were interested in him, because he had already coauthored two published journal articles with one of his professors. However, he reasoned that he should teach and live in the geographical section of the country where his historical research interests lay, the south. Therefore, he obtained an assistant professorship at a prestigious Ivy-League-type university in the upper south where he taught modern United States History to undergraduates, and one upper division course entitled, "The Economic History of the Antebellum South," his specialty. He was at home in the academic community and things appeared to go well for three and one-half years, and popular with colleagues and most of his students, who found him to be a brilliant, dynamic lecturer, and a friendly, helpful professor during his office hours. Moreover, he attended professional meetings, read research papers, published five articles in scholarly journals, and coauthored one book based on his dissertation.

Negatively, a few professors and a few graduate students reported to the History Department chair that he pushed economic determinism too far and discounted, in a discursive way in class, data supporting other than economic causation. Some labeled his "lecture proclamations," as they put it, "misleading and deviant," and, some few labeled him an "ideological deviant." (Perhaps they had had a course in Sociology.) Three reported examples follow:

1. Bob claimed that the United States could, and should become a social democracy, and a cost efficient welfare state, similar to some Scandinavian countries. That is, without interfering too much in citizens' private affairs, or rising taxes on the middle class. Such a state could be established should the vast gap between the income and assets of the rich and the poor be drastically reduced through and by (among other things) high taxes on the rich and low taxes on the middle class and the poor (for example sales taxes, especially on food). This utopian welfare state would provide all sorts of free or cheap public assistance and services for all: free education at all levels, cheap or free medical treatment; public pensions, social security benefits, and cheap public transportation; maintenance of police protection, prisons, national defense; extend to all free and untaxed unemployment payments, postal services; provide public housing grants and free legal services to the poor, etc.—that is, in the parlance of conservatives: "Take care of everybody from the cradle to the grave regardless of the individual recipients' work ethics, skills, talents, morals

or ambitions" (See Judt, December 17, 2009). The point here, said the complainants: "It's not so much with Bob's factual base, but his failure to discuss the factual base of contrary positions." For example, "What about the claim of some that this free humanitarian pie in the sky talk is a pipe dream?—and their evidence and reasoning."

2. Bob claimed that the United States had no immigration problems but just people problems because we were all immigrants. And he dismissed the problem of the sheer number of aliens amongst us who place great pressures on public services. Further, he said: "Those who rave about too many foreigners are racists. We must be humanitarians and take care of all the people who come in, and keep our doors open for the needy." Some students said he should re-read Thomas Robert Malthus.

3. In lectures on plantation agriculture, slavery, and the causes leading to the Civil War in the United States Bob discounted the well documented evidence of some scholars about the viability, efficiency, profitability and adaptability of the slavery system in the New World; and specifically, that the slavery system (though immoral) had proved more efficient than "free labor," not only in plantation agriculture (tobacco, cotton, sugarcane, coffee, rice, hemp, indigo, etc.) but also in the trades, industry, mining, sugar mills, factories, and row crops well into the 1890s in Cuba and Brazil. He also claimed that slavery would have died out without the Civil War. These claims were absurd to many scholars who had pointed out the absolute necessity of military force in the removal of slavery, an immoral and evil system, though profitable for some as an institution in the Americas. Further, and more importantly for the historian, he understated the crucial force of Anglo-American and northern U.S. abolitionism, representative government, public petitioning, religious sermons, *the rule of law*, common-law traditions, and the ideas of equality and freedom—all *sine qua non* there would have been no American Civil War and immediate emancipation; and, certainly no western hemispheric abolition of slavery in the nineteenth century (see Fogel and Engerman, 1974; Drescher, 2009).

When the chair questioned him about his one-sided ideological lectures, Bob replied with desultory and discursive answers beginning with something like: "You know the economic history of the antebellum south is my specialty. I stress for students the underlying, major economic causes of the Civil War and other happenings, that's my duty. They can get from the literature and the textbook all the trivial humanitarian, abolitionist, and religious undertones of the slavery system prior to the unnecessary Civil War." Bob's answers neither satisfied the chair nor some others on his tenure committees that met at the end of his fourth year. What to do with a brilliant, popular, dynamic teacher who lectured and wrote as an ideologue? Some members said he should be tenured and persuaded to become more objective. Wiser others pointed out that Bob's proclivity for rigid ideological thinking, teaching, and writing surfaced in graduate school if not before; and, that as a "deviant ideologue" he should drop out of academia, and, "perhaps write historical novels and costume dramas." He was known to be a very gifted writer, but what he wrote was as ideological as what he verbalized in class. Bob was not granted tenure, returned northwestward, married and dropped out of academia. Whether he wrote historical novels and costume dramas is unknown.

Bob was probably an obsessive-compulsive personality disorder type, and perhaps only dangerous in academia. His socioeconomic background was advantageous in many ways, however the far left stance of his parents that he had adopted probably impaired his intellectual elasticity and teaching objectivity. He experienced no structural or situational stress problems beyond the normal range. Throughout his life; and, despite objective criticisms and helpful suggestions from caring others he was unwilling or unable to change his rigid way of thinking and behaving. To the end of his academic career he conceived himself to be an honest, competent, insightful professor with a wholesome personality whose interpretations many colleagues refused to accept despite his superior knowledge of economic theory. Those like Bob who lecture and write from an exaggerated biased stance are deviants in academia, and should be unwelcome there.

Bob's personality profile represents the disclosure of an unidentified academic deviant type that is not delineated in the research literature elsewhere. Those charged with biased and faulty ideological thinking and teaching from the extreme left and right have been ubiquitous since Socrates, but current academic ideologues who are professors have been usually viewed as only a part of a flawed academic social structure, rather than as particular kinds of deviant individuals. This view is a copout and leads nowhere because ideologues are people, not sociological nebulous structures that neither eat, nor think nor act. Many deny the concept of an academic ideological deviant, and maintain that so-called ideological thinking and thinkers cannot be separated from ardent scholarly thinking and scholarly writing and teaching. We disagree. Certainly clinical psychologists can, and have identified obsessive compulsive personality types; and we think that perceptive academic administrators with commonsense, as well as some perceptive professors and students, can also identify compulsive ideologues. Ideologues are an anathema to academia, and should not be employed, and if so, dismissed when identified should they not seek psychological therapy and change course. Retention should be conditional depending on the success of therapy. Bob in spite of his brilliance was an "inauthentic" scholar, who muddled the past, present, and future; and, substituted "prattle for *verstehen* and discourse" (Heidegger 1927; Macquarri and Robinson, 1962).

We sympathize with ideologues like Bob but academia is not a rehabilitation center, and there is no unbiased state or point to send them back to, because they have been rigid and compulsive since childhood (and must start afresh with the help of professional psychological treatment). We think there are many ideologues like Bob in the academy, and that they dissuade students from critical thinking. Mistakenly some administrators and professors maintain that a mix of ideological professors from the left and the right would make for intellectual verve and knowledge among students. We disagree because the mixing of the two biased ideologies does not produce anything but more faulty ideologies. Ideologues are as noxious to academia as psychopaths in our opinion, and when detected they should be dealt with as suggested above.

CHAPTER 4

Summary, Conclusion and Recommendations

We found that 27 out of the 29 foregoing social-psychological types herein were deviant; that is, with the exception of Hamlin the Altruistic Guru, and Sarai the Princess, and that 25 of these 27 apparently had one or more personality disorders; though we placed each in a predominant personality category, and noted any secondary features of other personality disorder types. Clinical psychologists and psychiatrists caution that individuals are not "cured" of these disorders, though psychological therapy usually assuages them, helps with one's self-control; and provides useful information to patients' significant others. However, this study is concerned with a typology rather than with causes, clinical treatments, prevalence, and prevention of personality disorders.

Expectedly, we found some common elements among the 27 deviant types: (1) all but one, Fred (#15) held PhDs; (2) all but one, Fred, had been assistant professors at one time or another; (3) all had taught in liberal arts or social science departments; (4) seventeen were southerners; (5) most (twenty-two) taught in the southeast, though many of these had also taught elsewhere; (6) all but one, Fred, were products of the middle class; (7) most (twenty-two) were nominal Protestants; (8) only five attended religious services regularly (one Hindu, one Catholic, and three Protestants—so much for religiosity); (9) most (twenty-four) were males; (10) none were drug addicts, alcoholics, or psychotics (with the possible exception of Luke the Kook, #16) ; (11) only one, Judy the Greedy, was a convicted felon, though several others were said to have committed unreported felony crimes; (12) twenty-five of the twenty-seven deviants manifested personality disorders linked to their deviancy pattern. Examples of deviant forms of behavior committed by faculty and administrators found in this study include; that is, as observed or reported to us follow:

1. Preaching rather than teaching
2. Biased grading in general
3. Arbitrary grading and/or changing grades without justification
4. Grading to punish
5. Extension of special favors including inflated grades to athletes
6. Refusal to undertake research or publising
7. Knowingly publishing false results
8. Knowingly publishing fabricated data
9. Spreading false rumors
10. Justifying irrational or unreasonable methods of punishment
11. Trading grades for sex, service or money
12. Sexually seducing students
13. Consumption of alcohol and drugs on campus
14. Failure to keep office hours and lack of accessibility to students
15. Failing to provide students' feedback
16. Missing classes without notice or legitimate cause
17. Discrimination based on subjective criteria
18. Discounting colleagues' accomplishments
19. Preferential treatment of students and colleagues without justification
20. Discriminatory practices regarding hiring, retention, promotion, firing, pay, tenure; course and time assignments; allocation of funds.
21. Assigning incompetent and/or unqualified teachers to teach specific classes
22. Breaking nepotism rules
23. Disparaging colleagues and students behind their backs
24. Embezzling funds
25. Rumor mongering
26. Padding resumes
27. Eschewing scholarship, research, and publishing
28. Squelching colleagues or those under one's supervision

29. Physical and/or psychological bullying of all types

30. Academic hijacking, e.g., affixing names on unearned publications

31. Pitting colleagues against one another

32. Falsifying budgets

33. Nonparticipation in professional societies

34. Womanizing; "Vamping" (seductive behavior)

35. Refusing to serve on committees and/or cooperate on assigned group projects

36. Help facilitate huge salary differentials between administrators and faculty; between disciplines, between departments, between colleges

37. Dummying down course content

38. Falsifying administrative reports

39. Administrative hush ups and cover-ups of deviant acts

40. NCAA violations

41. Empire building (fiefdom)

42. Being unprepared for teaching specific courses

43. Swindling

44. Character assassination

45. Facilitating coaches' exorbitant salaries and perks

46. Discretionary spending for unrelated expenses

47. Extending special favors to sororities and fraternities

48. Permitting or tolerating hazing, binge drinking, underage drinking, classroom disruption

49. Ideological lecturing and indoctrination in classrooms

50. Administrative decision making based on legal threats

51. Plagiarism

52. Failure to provide due process

53. Bribery

54. Delegating power to unqualified staff and/or assigning tasks to staff beyond their job descriptions

55. Manipulating students' teacher evaluations

56. Verbal intimidation or threats (either overt or implied)

57. Spying and snitching

58. Paper trailing

59. Overpowering/overruling committee decisions

60. Dictatorial administrative practices

61. Noncompliance with accreditation guidelines

62. Misappropriation and misuse of resources and personnel

63. Blame game, condemning the condemners

64. Rummaging through personal office desks, files, computers, and mailboxes of others

65. Giving false recommendations

66. Engaging in discriminatory sanctioning procedures

67. Failing to allow for students' classroom participation

68. Failing to answer students' questions

69. Breaking rules established by the American Association of University Professors (AAUP)

70. A pattern of using expletives in class

71. Permitting the formation and operation of cabals

72. Facilitating a practice of inbreeding

73. Failure to report or help investigate alleged crimes and serious violations

74. Scapegoating and/or hiding behind human shields (by shifting the blame and responsibility for self-acts to others)

75. Rewarding pet students without justification

Significant Findings:

Overall, the most significant finding of the study is the strong linkage between two variables: (a) deviancy pattern, and (b) personality traits. Additionally, as illustrated in the profiles, the more serious a subject's deviancy pattern, the more likely such deviancy is anchored in his or her personality disorder. A subject with personality traits leaning toward an antisocial personality disorder type motivated the more serious deviancy patterns. This type also possessed more negative social background characteristics than other types as illustrated by Ron the Con (profile #6). Overall social background variables (with the exception of those of Fred the ABD, profile #15), were for the most part adequate, though most were overprotected by mothers, and some fathers were too authoritarian or too demanding. Social background characteristics did not appear particularly significant as determinants *per se,* while they were likely to function as corollaries of personality traits, thereby providing an opportunity (via situational and structural stress problems) for manifestation of their deviant behavior. In other words, social background characteristics, and structural and situational stress factors functioned as opportunity variables whereby personality traits triggered deviancy; that is, they transmitted effect via personality traits to deviancy (see chart below).

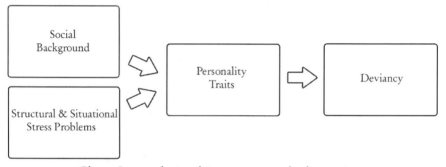

Chart: Inter-relationships among study dimensions

As expected, most deviants of all types did not recognize or admit their personality problems; and, those who did were in partial denial, and claimed they were just a little bit different, in certain ways, from other people. Negatively, they were sensitive and defensive in stance concerning their personality problems which they minimized. Common expressions heard among those targeted as deviant troublemakers, went something like: "Oh no, not me; there is nothing wrong with me; it's you;" "It's somebody else;" "I'm really not like that;" "Forgive me this time, I'll never do it again;" "I don't know what I was thinking at the time;" "I acted out of myself;" "Everybody does it but they just never get caught;" "Well, they got what they deserved for the way they treated me;" "Nobody was harmed;" "I was lead to believe what I was doing was okay;" "I was actually helping them, but they misunderstood me." These reactions blocked attempts by themselves or others from a search for help or treatment. To reiterate, all evidenced long lasting inflexible patterns of behavior that varied from cultural expectations and professional norms which impaired their personal and professional relationships with others. Most frequently changed their minds and decisions about everything: dress style, cars, personas, jobs, girlfriends, boyfriends, wives, doctors, opinions, beliefs, views, work and dwelling locations. Some expressed an exaggerated ethnic and regional pride, and a somewhat rigid communal conformity of thought apart from, but probably anchored in a religious epistemology. (See Cobb, 2005:164-184).

Common Negative Characteristics and Habits of All Deviant Types

Deviants of all types shared a large number of negative characteristics though in differential combinations with the exception of those leaning toward antisocial personality disorder. All were disaffected as youths with the exceptions of Farmer the Foreigner, and Beecher the Incompetent Teacher. Most were unstable, unhappy, disgruntled, temperamental (moody), impulsive, quick tempered, arrogant, self-pitying, hedonistic, anxious, irritable, and untrustworthy of others. They were also a complaining group who had difficulty in making and keeping friends, or in forming close personal relationships. Frequently demanding of others, faulty in judgment, hard to please, impatient, mercurial, and negative in general attitude, they had difficulty in working with colleagues. Ambitious and self-serving, they did not often exemplify empathy when competing with others. Many were superficially glib, conceited, pseudo-intellectual "liberals." A left-wing predilection was usually found in their social science departments that ensured the predominance of pseudo-liberal professors, along with an atmosphere and favorable conditions for liberal ideologues. One of their most negative and persistent characteristics was a tendency to react swiftly with certitude when facing problematic situations, rather than in a reflective measured manner; and, such hasty reactions were regretted later on.

Those with personalities including some antisocial personality disorder type traits were the most disruptive, resistant to therapy and social control measures, the most dangerous, and the hardest to detect. Intelligent, lacking in emotional affect, superficially charming, ruthless, cold, callous, extremely selfish, guiltless, manipulative, aggressive, deceitful, impulsive, cunning, and without empathy for others, they were social predators—especially when occupying administrative positions. They also shared many of the noted negative characteristics in an exaggerated form found among the other deviant types. Obviously, such a group is anathema to academia and if mistakenly selected should be dismissed as soon as feasible; that is, within the guidelines of university policies of termination for cause. Their deviant acts appear to have been committed without immoral intent, but with object thoughtlessness (a self-deceptive, vacuous remoteness from reality) barring the conception of another's viewpoint. Such an interdependence of (a) routine *thought-defying* and (b) wrongdoing (at a much higher level) is described by Hannah Arendt as the *banality of evil* in her analysis of Adolph Eichmann's vicious *legal crimes* in Nazi Germany. Eichmann was neither insane nor monstrous, but a misguided, compulsive, bureaucratic *idealist*, who acted thoughtlessly as a devoted cog in a hideous machine (Arendt, 2003).

Primary Recommendations (based on typological data)

In the foregoing typology we suggest some selection, social control, treatment, and dismissal measures for each of the 27 deviant social psychological types. Here we reiterate and offer some additional and more specific measures that the academy could utilize with these types.

1. <u>Selection</u>: The Academy's purpose is the higher education of citizens; and, it is not a rehabilitation or treatment center for those with personality disorders, nor are most of its institutions equipped to render such services. Therefore, in the best interest of its charges, students, candidates for academic positions (professors and administrators) with personality disorders should not be employed. Therefore, (a) At the departmental level a social case history should be developed on each candidate including data beyond the necessary academic information (schools attended, majors, grades, graduations etc.). Available information on the social background, bio, characteristic behavior, lifestyle and personality of each should be requested and gathered when possible from the following sources: all schools attended, former employers, military records, organizational records; arrest and police records, all institutional records, vital statistics; occupational and work records; reports from relatives, friends, ex-spouses, acquaintances and the web. We realize that laws overtime have restricted access to personal information pertaining to complete case histories, however we must try to obtain as much background information as possible (via telephone calls, correspondence, news reports, technology and electronic sources) beforehand for each candidate's recruitment. (b) The applicant's vita should be closely examined, and particular items should be checked and verified: employment claims, documents related to institutional graduations, publication verifications, listed awards and achievements, student and peer evaluations. Questionable time gaps in educational and employment records must be checked and verified; padding of resume must be explained. (c) In addition to the customary interviews conducted by each department in the selection process, a staff member who is especially good at employment interviewing should interview the applicant. As previously mentioned, interviewing techniques are no longer taught in many departments and many members do not know any more how to interview for anything. (d) The applicant should be required to take a personality test administered by a

clinical psychologist professor in a psychology department and/or by a social psychologist in a sociology department. This tedious but necessary process will help screen out undesirables including those with marked personality disorders. However none of us are perfect and some defects must be allowed for depending on the particular qualifications required by specific institutions.

By way of illustration for the need of such social case histories we note here the case of one who should never have been hired, and would probably not have been had her social case history been available. The recent media headlines of Amy Bishop Anderson, a Biology Professor and shooter at the University of Alabama at Huntsville (UAH), presents a violent case of a deviant faculty member in academia, who in our opinion, was not properly screened for employment. Bishop, a 44-year old female, shot six of twelve colleagues attending a routine biology department faculty meeting in Room 369 on the third floor of the Shelby Center for Science and Technology, UAH, on February 12, 2010 around 4:00 p.m. central standard time. Three of them were found dead on the spot, and three others were wounded and hospitalized. Reportedly, her attempt to kill additional faculty members failed because her gun "either jammed or ran out of ammunition." The 9 mm pistol she used was possessed (illegally) for practice in an indoor shooting range, where she had practiced during the previous week. As a sole suspect in the incident, Bishop was charged with three counts of capital murder and three counts of attempted murder.

Bishop was hired as an assistant professor in 2003; denied tenure; and, was serving the beginning of her last semester at UAH. A native of Braintree, Massachusetts, with a PhD from Harvard University, she had demonstrated violent behavior on at least three previous occasions. First, at the age of 19, in 1986, she killed her 16-year old brother with a shot gun. Three rounds were fired, one in the ceiling, one in the wall, and one in her brother's chest. Following this act she tried to escape; pointed a shotgun at a car dealer, and demanded an escape car with keys, explaining that her husband was trying to kill her, and she had to get away. When police arrived on the scene, she was arrested for carrying a deadly weapon, but after the police questioned her and her mother, the shooting of her brother was deemed an accident; and, charges were dropped (including her armed attempt to hijack a car from the car dealer) without further investigation. Ironically the police report of these crimes was lost and resurfaced only after the instant arrest; however newspaper accounts of her offences were available. Second, she along with her husband, James Anderson, were prime suspects and were questioned in a 1993 pipe-bomb incident directed via mail to Dr. Paul Rosenberg (her then professor and lab supervisor at Children's Hospital in Boston). Bishop was concerned about a negative evaluation from this professor, Dr. Rosenberg, prior to the pipe bomb incident had engaged him in a heated dispute. Subsequently, she resigned from her position at the hospital, thinking that she could not meet Dr. Rosenberg's standards and expectations, and knowing that she was suspected of the pipe bomb crime. Reportedly she had been upset and on the verge of a nervous breakdown, and wanted to "shoot, stab, or strangle Rosenberg" (she had said to a colleague prior to the attempted bombing). However she and her husband, both students, in the pipe bomb crime denied involvement, and denied threatening Dr. Rosenberg. The case was closed without charges being filed because of lack of sufficient evidence.

Third, she was charged with and pleaded guilty to a misdemeanor assault, and disorderly conduct in 2002, for punching and shoving a woman, Michelle Gjika, who had received (and refused to give up) the last booster seat at an International House of Pancakes in Peabody, Massachusetts. For this she received probation, and despite the prosecution's stipulation that she attend anger management classes, she never attended any.

Further, several of her colleagues at UAH noted what they called her "strange, erratic and bizarre behavior" throughout her teaching career there. For example, they said she interrupted meetings abruptly; reacted in inappropriate ways; and, demonstrated her "out of touch with reality." Perhaps she should have been dismissed prior to her tenure turndown (following an investigation).

1. <u>Problematic Situations</u>: Following her tenure denial in March 2009, she appealed but lost her case, and was not expecting the extension of her contract after March 2010. Distressed, she had hired a lawyer to help her overturn the university decision to deny her tenure, but her lawyer kept finding one problem after another in his efforts to overturn the university's decision to deny her tenure. This potentially losing battle may have reduced her confidence in every securing tenure and spurred anger and malice, which in combination with the past untreated (and unpunished) violent behavior may have motivated her resort to the instant shootings. She had exhibited a violent and unstable personality since a teenager.

Amy Bishop is currently held in jail awaiting arraignment and trial, and her lawyer proclaims she is "wacky" and does not remember the shootings and killings. Regardless of the future fanfare and disposition of her case, the point herein is that had a proper social background check been made by the UAH dean and her department head (the hiring authorities) prior to her employment, she would not have been hired in the first place. That is, newspaper accounts, school records, her arrest records, family history, and a few telephone inquiries would have revealed her emotional instability and violent behavioral patterns.

2. <u>Social control measures</u> must be in place for: (a) those who have been

adjudicated chronic trouble makers, misfits and/or persistent minor rule breakers (illegal or not), on or off campus by university "tribunals" (hearing committees, administrative boards, etc.); and, those convicted of misdemeanors by police and courts; (b) those who have been adjudicated "guilty" of serious university rule violations (including illegal acts) by university "tribunals," and/or law courts, for violations on or off campus. We maintain that all illegal charges reported (or known about by university administrators) against professors and administrators (on or off campus) should be investigated by off campus police and officials, as well as by university police and officials. University officials should report to the police all crimes they know about on campus. We have known about many campus date rapes and alcohol related offenses (rape, assault, and substance abuse cases) that were hushed up or covered-up by campus police, administrators, sororities, and fraternities. All those charged with criminal conduct violations on or off campus should be properly and, legally charged and given due process protection.

Throughout this work we have taken the position that professors and administrators who become chronic troublemakers and/or difficult misfits (deviants), and/or who commit serious violations of university rules and procedures should be held accountable for their deeds; and, subject to campus investigation and sanctioning procedures of institutions where they are employed, as well as by courts of law for criminal violation on or off campus. Should an institution decide to keep its sanctioned deviants on the payroll following adjudication with reservations, then we have some suggestions regarding these arrangements: (1) the troublemakers and/or rule breakers must immediately cease his/her troublemaking or rule braking behavior; (2) be placed on institutional probation for a specific period of time; and, be subject to dismissal should he/she indulge in further troublemaking or rule violations; (3) acknowledge his/her responsibility for deviant acts involved; apologize, and make amends to those who may have been maligned or injured in anyway; (4) required to seek psychological therapy from a board certified practicing clinical psychologist with a PhD or a psychiatrist MD on or off campus along with the cooperation of campus counseling services and institutional administration; that is, should he or she appear to have a personality disorder. The confidentiality of a treatment regimen would be assured. On campus counseling could be underwritten by the employer. Off-campus treatment would be at the deviant's expense but could be supplemented by the university employer. Treatment professionals, clinical psychologists and psychiatrists, would be required to submit routine progress reports on the deviants under treatment to the university human resources department. We are aware that some might not have a personality disorder, but this research study shows that almost all do. Those few without a personality disorder could be automatically dismissed or placed on probation depending on the seriousness of violations. (5) Probation violations would include further troublemaking and/or violations of institutional rules in general as well as specific rules pertaining to behaviors proscribed or prescribed by therapists to fit the needs of individual cases (for example, rules pertaining to drinking habits, sexual conduct, associations, mobility, recreational activities, treatment attendance, further rule violations, etc. (6) At the end of the probationary period the deviants could be released from probation and either continued in employment or dismissed (should he/she continue to prove risky). (7) Certainly there would be legal ramifications in this process; for example, rules, decisions, and dismissals would vary from those with or without tenure, different civil and criminal charges, etc. Obviously the above recommendations would entail the extension of bureaucratic services requiring additional committees, boards, and additional responsibilities for offices of legal services and outside agency cooperation. For example law enforcement, probation and parole, psychological and treatment offices, etc., because those on institutional probation would require monitoring on and off campus. Decisions concerning retention or dismissal of personnel would not be based solely on internal bureaucratic discretion, but at times on the views of outside agencies and the law. The supervision, rulemaking, sanctioning, treatment and guidance of deviant professors and administrators must strike equitable balance between the need and well being of individual deviants and the values and interests of university campuses—and at times community and the law.

We think that our typology would prove valuable in the maintenance of a healthier environment on college and university campuses and to researchers and scholars in constructing typologies. We certainly hope so.

Secondary Recommendations (based on general impressions)

1. Reduce the number of administrators on college and university campuses by one-third to one-half depending on the purposes, size, functions, and complexity of each institution (number of student body, number of separate units, departments, schools, colleges, faculty and staff, building complexes, research facilities, etc.). There are too many administrators and assistant administrators, most holding PhDs and/or EdDs—assistant deans and vice presidents of "this and that." The authors throughout the years have asked their students questions like: "What are the functions of a dean, assistant/associate dean and a vice president"? Obviously baffled they answered when pressured: "I don't know," "They run things," "They manage the school," "They throw their weight around," "They don't do much that I can see," "They discipline those who get in trouble." Further, PhDs

are scholars who by definition and education are teachers, researchers, and theorists; and, the scholarly role does not complement or mesh too well with that of administrative roles. Administrators are practical managers of people who prepare schedules, make appointments, pore over records, prepare and monitor budgets, arrange meetings, and deal with practical and mundane things like ordinary adjustments and personnel management.

Perhaps academia needs fewer PhD and EdD administrators and more managerial types with business degrees who can be assistants to this or that superior official or bureaucrat. Certainly they will cost less than PhDs and fit in better with paper pushers.

2. The differential in salaries between administrators and professors is obscene, though the latter do most of the important work (teach, research, and advise) but are paid much less. A cogent analogy and comparison here is the work role and pay of the MD in a hospital who practices his profession there, whereas the hospital administrator (with a business degree) administrates. Only a very few MDs actually administrate. And of course the salary and power of the two actors is reversed in relationship to the pay and power of administrators and professors in academia. The gap between professors and administrators should be reduced in favor of professors.

3. Intercollegiate sports, particularly football and basketball, intramural sports; and, other nonacademic activities should be severely de-emphasized. Further the athletic department and/or athletic departments inclusive of varsity sports teams, intramural and intercollegiate (baseball, softball, golf, hockey, tennis, swimming, tract) on the campuses where we taught had more coaches and staff, twice the size of the combined staff of several arts and sciences departments (and plusher quarters to boot, plus higher salaries). All of these extracurricular programs and activities should be drastically reduced or eliminated. Campuses should not devolve into (as some have) recreational and amusement parks. The purpose of higher education is education and not the production of super athletes and glorious and winning teams. Excellent colleges and universities do not have winning football or basketball teams, if any teams at all. Nor do the Europeans in their universities. Intercollegiate sports' teams in the United States serve as minor leagues for professional teams. Moreover most athletes as a rule are neither good scholars nor good boys. In many cases, they are rowdy poor students, who are always looking for handouts and entitlements they demand. We have witnessed a dearth of academic excellence in some southeastern institutions of higher learning that is facilitated by the tremendous overemphasis (and resources) placed on winning football teams—including the highly inflated money allocated to football coaches. Funds from sports' ticket sales are ploughed back into athletic programs.

4. Another campus array of tangential but very expensive nonacademic activities and services should be reduced in size and operations, and perhaps some of these should be eliminated: the students' affairs office; overall student recreational facilities; for example, poolroom and board game tables, Hollywood type theaters, sports areas, students union buildings, etc.; employment counseling services; various and sundry health clinics to treat this and that (substance abuse, eating disorders, broken hearts, birth control); fund raising and alumni affairs, chapel services. In brief a youth community center to meet the needs of pampered adolescents, rather than a serious formal setting for academic learning (see Rohde 2007; Office of Public Affairs 2007).

5. Colleges and universities should not be burdened with providing uninterested students with remedial courses (usually freshman English and mathematics). Such courses if provided should be the responsibility of public high schools. They require costs including professional teaching resources that most colleges and universities can ill afford; and, the type of students who are referred to these courses are not college material in the first place, and should never have been enrolled.

6. Students entrance requirements to colleges and universities should be appreciably strengthened; that is, enrollees should be high school graduates with at least average grade point records and SAT scores. Otherwise freshman classes must be dummied down. Students when flunking classes should be flunked and professors should not be punished for flunking them as is frequently the case. The authors think that there are too many students in academia who do not belong there because they are unprepared, and lack interest in higher education, or lack the ability (for whatever reason) to perform at the college level—and additionally there are too many of these erroneously passed along and graduated with gentlemen Cs; that is, should they be star athletes, or just athletes.

Higher education is a very expensive enterprise in a time of limited resources, and an increase in expense occurs every year. Perhaps we should take another look at how European universities avoid problems entailed in our open door policy of student enrollments. However, our screaming pseudo-liberals would scotch any ideas along these lines before they were fully born. For in their kind of democracy, every mother's son and daughter would have the privilege (and right) to enroll and graduate from the college or university of their choice—preferably an Ivy League school costing their family from $75,000 to $100,000 per year; and, should this family pretend not to have the money, some government entity could be found to absorb the cost (See Hacker 2007). We have seen this happen.

7. All fraternity and sorority houses, facilities, and functions should be

removed from the campus (and excluded thenceforth) and subject to public jurisdiction and oversight, rather than college or university jurisdiction. Such action would relieve academic institutions from a plethora of thorny and unnecessary problems (for example, ubiquitous date rape and alcohol related deviant acts). Of course, campus officials should be informed about any illegal or serious violations that occur in these private institutions.

Currently two-thirds of American College age youth actually start in four-year schools or two-year school programs. Perhaps the most exigent problem is that according to the US Department of Education, 25 percent of teenagers do not finish high school; and, many who do graduate are unprepared for basic college work (Hacker 2009). We strongly recommend that those who are not at least average high school students (grades, SAT scores) should never be enrolled in institutions of higher learning. Many of our colleagues with whom we interacted agree and share the same sentiment we expressed in foregoing recommendations; however, for some reason or the other they do not want to go on the record.

In summary, we have constructed a typology wherein different types of deviant professors and administrators have been identified. In our campus observations over a long period of time we think that students who engage in serious violations (like date rape, theft, vandalism, assault, violent acts, class disruptions, and binge drinking) are more likely to be those with personality disorders than those not so encumbered. Frequently we have found these deviants to be athletes and "fraternity boys." We postulate that by implementing the preceding six recommendations, campus deviancy could be curtailed or reduced.

References

American Psychiatric Association (2000). *Diagnostic and Statistical Manual of Mental Disorders,* Fourth Edition, Text Revision (DSM-IV-TR). Washington, D.C.

Appiah, K. A. (2009). *Experiments in Ethics,* Boston, MA: Harvard University Press.

Arendt, H. (1951). *The Origins of Totalitarianism.* New York: Hartcourt.

Arendt, H. (2003). *The Portable Hannah Arendt* edited by Peter Baehr. New York: Penguin Books, pp. 313-408.

Barchies, A. (1998). *The Poet and The Prince.* Berkeley, CA: University of California Press.

Becker, H. S. (2003). Moral entrepreneurs: The creation and enforcement of deviant categories. In D. H. Kelley & E. J. Clarke, *Deviant behavior: A text-reader in the sociology of deviance* (pp. 33-40). New York: Worth.

Barlow, D. H. and V. M. Durand (2009). *Abnormal Psychology: An Integrated Approach.* 5th ed., Belmont, CA: Wadsworth.

Bartol, C. R. (2002). *Crime and Behavior: A Psychosocial Approach.* Upper Saddle River, NJ: Prentice Hall.

Benedict, H. (1992). *Virgin or Vamp: How the Press Covers Sex Crimes.* Oxford: Oxford University Press.

Blais, M. and D. Norman (1997). "A psychometric evaluation of the DSM-IV personality disorder criteria." *Journal of Personality Disorders.* 11:168–176.

Braxton, J. M. and A.E. Bayer (1999). *Faculty misconduct in college teaching.* Baltimore, MD: The Johns Hopkins University Press.

Briggs, W. A. (1941). *Great Poems of English Language: An Anthology.* New York: Tuder Publishing Company.

Brown, L. M. and C. Gillian (1992). *Meeting at the Cross Roads: Women's Psychology and Girls' Development*. New York: Valentine Books.

Casanova, G. (2007). *History of My Life*. Translated from the French by William R. Trask. Baltimore, MD: Johns Hopkins University Press.

Cash, W. J. (1941). *The Mind of The South*. New York: Alfred Knopf.

Cleckley, H. M. (1982). *The Mask of Sanity, 6th Edition*. St. Louis, MO: Mosby.

Cobb, J. C. (2005). *Away Down South: A History of Southern Identity*. New York, NY: Oxford University Press.

Decoo, W. (2002). *Crisis on Campus: Confronting Academic Misconduct*. Cambridge, MA: MIT Press.

Delbanco, A. (March 10, 2005). "Colleges: An Endangered Species," *NewYork Review of Books* 52:18-25.

Denzin, N. K. (1978). *The research act: A theoretical introduction to sociological methods*. New York: McGraw-Hill.

Dotter, D. L., & Roebuck, J. B. (1988). The Labeling Approach Re-examined: Interactionism and the Components of Deviance. *Deviant Behavior, 9,* 19-32.

Drescher, D. (2009). *Abolition : a history of slavery and antislavery*. New York : Cambridge University Press.

Erikson, K. (2000). On the sociology of deviance. In L. M. Salinger, ed., *Deviant behavior 00-01* (pp. 8-9). Gauilford, CT: McGraw-Hill.

Ermann, M. D., & Lundman, R. J. (2002). *Corporate and governmental deviance: Problems of organizational behavior in contemporary society*. 6th ed. New York: Oxford University Press.

Eysenck, H. J. (1964). *Crime and Personality*, Boston, MA: Houghton-Mifflin Co.

Eysenck, H. J. (1967). *The Biological Basis of Personality*. Springfield, IL: Charles C. Thomas.

Eysenck, H. J. (1982). *Personality, Genetics and Behavior: Selected Papers*. Publisher unknown.

Eysenck, H. J. (1990). "Biological dimensions of personality". In: L.A. Pervin (Ed.) *Handbook of personality: theory and research*, Guilford, New York, pp. 244–276.

Eysenck, H. J. (1992). "Four ways five factors are not basics," *Personality and Individual Differences* 13: 667–673.

Eysenck, H. J. and G. H. Gudjonsson (1989). *The Causes and Cures of Criminality.* New York, NY: Plenum.

Eysenck, H. J. and S. B. G. Eysenck (1995). *Manual for the Eysenck Personality Questionnaire.* London: Hodder and Stoughton.

Eysenck, H. J. and S. B. G. Eysenck (2008). *The Social Consequences of Modern Psychology.* Edison, NJ: Transaction.

Fogel, R. W. and S. L. Engerman (1974). Time on the Cross: The Economics of American Negro Slavery. Boston, MA: Little Brown.

Forman, D. (1994). *A Night of the Opera: An Irreverent Guide to the Plot, the Singers, the Composers, the Recording.* New York: The Modern Library.

Gibbons, D. (1977). *Society, Crime, and Criminals: An Introduction to Criminology*, Englewood Cliffs, NJ: Prentice Hall.

Gibbons, D. (1988). "Some Critical Observations on Criminal Types and Criminal Careers," *Criminal Justice and Behavior*, 15, 8-23.

Gibbons, D. (1994). *Society, Crime, and Criminal Behavior*, 6th Edition, Englewood Cliffs, NJ: Prentice Hall.

Goffman, E. (1959). *The Presentation of Self in Everyday Life.* Garden City, NY: Doubleday Anchor.

Goffman, E. (1963). *Stigma: Notes on the management of spoiled identity.* Englewood Cliffs, NJ: Prentice-Hall

Goffman, E. (1971). *Relations in public: Microstudies of the public order.* New York: Harper.

Golderg L. (1993). "The structure of phenotypic personality traits," *American Psychologist* 48:26-34.

Goode, E. (2007). *Deviant behavior.* 8th ed. Upper Saddle River, NJ: Prentice Hall.

Hacker, A. (2007). "They'd Much Rather Be Rich," *The New York Review of Books, LIV* (November 15): 31-34.

Hacker, A. (2009). "Can we make America smarter?" *The New York Review of Books, LVI* (April 30): 37-40.

Heidegger, M. (1927). *Sein und Zeit*, Gesamtausgabe Volume 2. Translated by John Macquarrie and Edward Robinson, *Being and Time*. London: SCM Press.

Hickson, M. and J. Roebuck (2009). *Deviance and Crime in Colleges and Universities*. Springfield, IL: Charles C. Thomas.

James, H. Jr. (2004). *The Portrait of a Lady*. New York: Bares and Noble Classic Series.

Judt, T. (2009). "What is Living and What is Dead in Social Democracy," *the New York Review of Books, LVI* (December 17): 86-96.

Kerr, C. (2001). *The uses of the university*. 5th ed. Cambridge, MA: Harvard University Press.

Kimbell, R.; B. Day, M. Kreuger, and E. Davis (2010). *The Complete Lyrics of Johnny Mercer*. (eds.) New York: Knopf.

Lepadatu (July 4, 2010). "The Stranger in Academe," *The Chronicle of Higher Education*.

Liazos, A. (1972). "The Poverty of the Sociology of Deviance: Nuts, Sluts, and Perverts," *Social Problems* 20 (summer): 103-120.

Macquarrie, J. and E. Robinson (1962). *Being and Time*. London: SCM Press.

Marcus, G. (1989). *Lipstick Traces: A Secret History of the Twentieth Century*. Cambridge, MA: Harvard University Press.

May, A. (2007). *Pilate's Wife*. New York: Harper.

Murphy, B. (1996). "Henry James Jr. 1843-1916.\," In: *Benet's Readers Encyclopedia*, 4th ed., Pp. 519-521. New York: Harper Collins.

Office of Public Affairs (2007). *The Williams Directory, 2006-07*, Williams College, Williamstown, Mass.

Paglia, C. (1994). *Vamps and Tramps: New Essays.* New York: Vintage Books.

Pinker, S. (2002). *The Blank Slate, The Modern Denial of Human Nature.* New York, NY: Viking.

Redford, B. (2009). *Dilettante: The Antic and the Antique in Eighteenth-Century England.* J. Paul Getty Museum, Getty Research Institute.

Rohde, D. L. (2007). *In Pursuit of Knowledge: Scholars, Stars and American Culture,* Stanford University Press.

Roebuck, J. B. (1967). *Criminal Typology: The Legalistic, Physical-Constitutional-Hereditary, Psychological-Psychiatric and Sociological Approaches.* Springfield, IL: Charles C. Thomas.

Roebuck, J. B. and W. Frese (1976). *The Rendezvous: A Case Study of An After-Hours Club,* New York: The Free Press.

Roebuck, J. B. and M. Hickson (1984). *The Southern Redneck: A Phenomenological Study of Social Class. 2nd ed.* New York, NY: Praeger.

Roebuck, J. B. and K. S. Murty (1996). *The Southern Subculture of Drinking and Driving: A Generality of Deviance Model of Southern White Males.* New York: Garland Publishing.

Robin, R. (2005). "The Myth of Academic Deviance," *George Mason University's History News Network* [http://hnn.us/articles/ 9562.html (accessed on 12/24/2009)].

Schmidt, P. (June 8, 2010). "Workplace Mediators Seek a Role in Taming Faculty Bullies," *The Chronicle of Higher Education.* [http://chronicle.com/article/Workplace-Mediators-Seek-a/65815/ (accessed on July 28, 2010)].

Sheldon, H. (1940). *Varieties of Human Physique.* New York: Harper.

Sheldon, H. (1942). *Varieties of Temperament.* New York: Harper.

Simmel, G. (1908). "The Stranger." In: Donald N. Levine (Ed.) *Georg Simmel on Individuality and Social Forms.* Chicago, IL: The University of Chicago Press, 1971.

Strelau, J., and H. J. Eysenck (1987). *Personality Dimensions and Arousal.* New York, NY: Plenum.

Thompson, J. (2006). *How to Read a Modern Painting: Lessons from the Modern Master*, New York: Harry N. Abrams.

Waldron, J. (November 15, 2009). "Right and Wrong: Psychologists vs. Philosophers." In: *The New York Review of Books*, Vol. LVI:39-41.

Westen, D., J. Shedler and J. Harnden (Dec.1997). "A Q-sort method for assessing personality structure, pathology, and change," Paper presented at the annual convention of the North American Society for Psychotherapy Research, Tucson.

Westen, D. and J. Shedler. (1999a). "Revising and Assessing Axis II:I. Developing a clinically and empirically valid assessment method," *American Journal of Psychiatry*, 156: 258-272.

Westen, D. and J. Shedler. (1999b). "Revising and Assessing Axis II:II. Toward an empirically based and clinically useful classification of personality disorders," *American Journal of Psychiatry*, 156: 273-285.

Widom, C. S. (1977). "A Methodology for Studying Noninstitutionalized Psychopaths," *Journal of Consulting and Clinical Psychology* 45:674-683.

Wolff, K. H. (1950). *The Sociology of Georg Simmel*, New York: Free Press.

Wurtzel, E. (1998). *Bitch: In Praise of Difficult Women*. New York: Doubleday, A Division of Random Houuse.

About Authors

Julian B. Roebuck, native of Eastern North Carolina, is a social psychologist: AB Atlantic Christian College, MA Duke University, PhD University of Maryland. First president of the Mid-South Sociological Association; Classification Officer and Researcher in the US Bureau of Prisons and the District of Columbia Department of Corrections. University teaching experience in the Mid-Atlantic, West Coast, Southwest, Southeastern regions and Puerto Rico, Europe, and Africa.

Komanduri S. Murty, currently Professor and Coordinator of Sociology at Fort Valley State University, Georgia, is a recipient of numerical recognitions including 2005 Aldridge McMillan Award for Outstanding Performance in Overall Achievement at Clark Atlanta University; author and coauthor of several books, book chapters and journal articles; principal investigator and program director of a jail diversion project for first-time offenders for 25 years; and, a counselor of Cuban halfway house, among other activities and accomplishments.

Although elite deviance is studied for quite some time, specific focus on college campus deviance started gaining attention only recently; and, much less has been focused on deviance among faculty and administrators in higher education. However, the increasing frequency of reports in *The Chronicle of Higher Education* and elsewhere about deviant acts such as alcohol use, date rapes, grade manipulations, sexual harassment, false reports, bullying, illegal hiring practices, etc. on college and university campuses, including the recent faculty shootings at the University of Alabama in Huntsville make this book on *Poison Ivy: A Social Psychological Typology of Deviant Professors and Administrators in Higher Education* both timely and necessary. Instead of simply relying on mere quantitative information like frequencies and percentages of various deviants acts, Roebuck and Murty, for the first time, delve into life-histories of a group of deviant professors and administrators on various campuses to provide a link between social background, structural and situational factors on one hand and on the other, personality disorder types as classified by DSM-IV-TR and Big-V personality inventory modals. This thoroughly researched comprehensive work is a must read for everyone engaged in higher education—lest they be researchers, teachers, practitioners, staff, or administrators.

CLIFTON D. BRYANT
Emeritus Professor of Sociology
Virginia Polytechnic Institute and State University